Force *of* Nature

Force *of* Nature

THE UNLIKELY STORY OF
WAL-MART'S GREEN REVOLUTION

Edward Humes

HARPER
BUSINESS

An Imprint of HarperCollins*Publishers*
www.harpercollins.com

The world can certainly save itself, but only if we pause from our relentless competition. . . . The barriers are in our limited capacity to cooperate, not in our stars.

—JEFFREY D. SACHS, *Common Wealth*

Capital isn't scarce. Vision is.

—SAM WALTON

HarperCollins books may be purchased for educational, business, or sales promotional use. For information, please write: Special Markets Department, Harper-Collins Publishers, 10 East 53rd Street, New York, NY 10022.

FIRST EDITION

Designed by Renato Stanisic

Library of Congress Cataloging-in-Publication Data

Humes, Edward.
    Force of nature : the unlikely story of Wal-Mart's green revolution / Edward Humes.—First edition.
        p.   cm.
Includes bibliographical references.
    ISBN: 978-0-06-169049-5 (hardback)
    1. Wal-Mart (Firm) 2. Sustainable development. 3. Wal-Mart (Firm) I. Title.
HC79.E5.H86   2011
    338.9'27—dc22

                                                                    2010052578

11 12 13 14 15   OV/RRD   10 9 8 7 6 5 4 3 2 1

Contents

Prologue: The Confluence

Stanislaus County, California

The three rafts glide into the green waters of Meral's Pool, gathering speed in the strong, silt-free flow of the lower Tuolumne, one of the most pristine and best protected river runs in the world. Cold enough to burn from Sierra snowmelt even in June, the Tuolumne River flows for the next eighteen miles through a green, steep-walled gorge. There are no roads in sight, no traffic noise, no wires, signs, or towers—just a few crumbling prospectors' shacks, their gray boards sprung and gapped like bad teeth, and the rock and mortar remnants of a century-old mining trail planted in the bony incline by Chinese laborers.

Bundled in the bright armor of wetsuits, helmets, and bulky orange life vests, the rafters brace themselves as the quiet of the pool gives way to the hissing, slapping roar of water striking thickets of boulders. The first set of rapids, Rock Garden, is a mere tenth of a mile from the put-in, a quick baptism for the passengers perched on the tubular sides of the inflatable rafts and leaning tentatively out over their paddles. The river guides bark commands—left, right, back, stop—and the paddlers struggle to react before the next directive is shouted out. Most have never run any sort of white water before, much less such a treacherous

Level IV cascade. These rapids demand that every paddler in the boat act in concert or risk being tossed into the foam and rocks.

One by one, the rafts enter Rock Garden, spray flying, gouts of water sluicing over the sides to soak the riders, who hoot and gasp and laugh like lunatics at the mixed sensations of speed, roller coaster dips, and chilly water. When the rafts pop into the clear and no thrown riders are seen bobbing in the water, the crews raise their paddles and make clattering high fives. Then the guides tell them to prepare for the next run, Nemesis, just a half mile off and coming up fast. By the time they reach it, nearly every paddle is beating through the water in an easy, matching rhythm.

The guides will tell you there's a kind of magic to this. Jib Ellison has built a career around it. The river guide turned corporate consultant turned sustainability guru uses the churning white water and the teamwork it fosters to make adversaries into unlikely allies. For this three-day event in the summer of 2009, he has drawn leaders of some of America's most powerful and influential companies to the rafts or the follow-up conference in Berkeley: Nike, Sony, Barclays, Hewlett-Packard, Microsoft, Waste Management (the nation's biggest garbage collector), and Dairy Management, Inc. (i.e., most of America's milk cows). More than half of them had hired Ellison to help them go green. There's also the Patagonia clothing company on board, small compared to the others but esteemed as a green business leader ("The Coolest Company on the Planet," according to *Fortune* magazine). Then there's the big draw, Ellison's marquee client: Wal-Mart, the world's largest corporation, mover of markets and monument to consumption, whose buying decisions can make or break businesses and shift the course of whole industries—a company so big that when it unplugs the lights inside its employee break room vending machines to lower carbon emissions, it saves $1.5 million in electricity a year. The leaders at Patagonia once swore they'd never do business with the Wal-Mart behemoth, but now here they are, on the river together, contemplating a partnership of a most unusual sort.

Finally, there is a select group of environmentalists, academics, and activists on board whom the corporate executives would have studiously avoided in years past. But after they row together all day, then crack beers around the campfire that night, they are in a position to find more common ground than they imagined, which is a good thing, given the daunting purpose behind this trip. They have assembled to plot what could be the next industrial revolution—the one in which the pursuit of profit and the protection of planet stop being mutually exclusive and start being one and the same.

This has been Jib Ellison's mantra for years: businesses should brave such waters not simply because greening the factory or the supply chain is good for the image or because reducing waste, carbon emissions, and the use of toxic materials and fuels is the "right" thing to do. Rather, he says, businesses should strive to become sustainable because it will bolster their bottom lines. The most sustainable business, the cleanest, most energy-efficient, least wasteful company, will have the competitive advantage—not just in a distant, utopian future but now. And if you accept that proposition, the key question of our age is not *if* business will obey the laws of nature but *when* and *how*—and on whose terms. Will you innovate and lead? Or will you wait for the competition—or the courts or Congress—to compel you to follow someone else's vision? As with so many other business imperatives, Ellison argues, the first movers will win. They will be in the best position to define what a sustainable business looks and acts like.

This idea is enticing enough (or scary enough) to get some of the busiest corporate executives to disappear with a bunch of environmentalists on a river in northern California for three days. No assistants, no conference rooms, no BlackBerrys, no PowerPoint decks—just a wild river as backdrop and prod. They represent huge global brands with huge global footprints, billions of dollars in revenues, hundreds of millions of customers, countless tons of waste generated and fuel consumed. Here, for a few precious days, they will do what river guides do year-round as they chase the rafting season from hemisphere to hemisphere and expedition to expedition, living off the grid and in the moment—living the dream, the guides call it. Or, in this case, allowing themselves to dream of a new way of doing business.

The companies represented here have all accepted, more or less, the proposition that there is a business case for sustainability—that making greener products, and even greening whole companies, can enhance opportunity and profit. This combination river trip and high-level meeting, which Ellison's company, Blu Skye Sustainability Consulting, has dubbed the "Confluence," is about what comes next. Can whole supply chains, whole industries, and whole business sectors become sustainable—not because of some onerous regulatory pressure but because it's just better business? And can competitors figure out a way to cooperate, to share data and discoveries, in order to accomplish such a transformation?

Driving these questions, to the surprise of many of those in the rafts, is one of the world's most traditionally secretive, go-it-alone companies: Wal-Mart.

Since 2005, Wal-Mart has become an object of fascination for business leaders trying to figure out exactly what sustainability means and for environmentalists who know what it is but can't get anyone to listen. Wal-Mart of late has embraced sustainability in such a big and fundamental way that it has surprised its critics, its admirers, its partners, its investors, and its own leadership. Renewable energy, zero waste, support for climate legislation, reduced packaging, and partnerships with environmental groups—these are the sorts of things Wal-Mart has been focusing on. Wal-Mart's CEO has declared that becoming greener is now a core business proposition for the company and, by extension, for its 100,000 suppliers. He got started in this direction for one reason: Jib Ellison persuaded him to do it.

This is why the rafts are full, the rowers drawn not so much by Ellison's big idea as by the fact that the senior vice president of sustainability for all of Wal-Mart's global operations is here, with advance word on the company's next big green announcement. His fellow rafters want to talk to him, plot with him, get tips and hints from him. It doesn't hurt that Matt Kistler is the biggest person in the rafts by far, a good six feet, six inches, broad-shouldered, impossible to miss. He's no eco-warrior—he's an MBA, a product guy, formerly of General Mills, Oscar Meyer, and Kraft Foods. Yet there he is talking about world population closing in on nine billion people in the next four decades, of nations with virtually no consumer culture a few years ago now witnessing the evolution of burgeoning, big-spending middle classes. There is a rapidly accelerating worldwide demand for the same energy-intensive, carbon-spewing creature comforts Americans have so long enjoyed, and it cannot be sustained, Kistler says, not in its current form. The world simply lacks the raw materials, energy, fuel, water, and breathable air to stay the course of business as usual. Wal-Mart, as much as any company, unthinkingly set this scenario into motion decades ago with its outsourced, low-price, buy-more imperative. Now it sees the consumer tsunami cresting through the vantage point of its rapidly expanding stores in China, India, Brazil, and a dozen other countries—a grim truth most industry leaders don't want to talk about or think about, much less plan for and act on. Growing foreign markets are among the few economic bright spots for megacompanies such as Wal-Mart. But here on the Tuolumne River, a Wal-Mart senior vice president is delivering the environmentalists' most dire lines: Business as we know it cannot be sustained. Something has to change. Somehow consumption must become more sustainable, or we all lose.

Wal-Mart's upcoming announcement, Kistler suggests, is aimed squarely at this realization, a project the company has dubbed "The Index." Wal-Mart's startling goal is to measure the sustainability of itself, its suppliers, and the products that the chain store sells, all half million of them—their carbon footprint, their water use, the working conditions in suppliers' factories, the products' health effects, toxic substances, energy use, waste, and what happens to them once they are used up and thrown away. The Index will initially be used inside the business to inform buying decisions about suppliers, raw materials, and products to stock. But the ultimate goal is to put this information into customers' hands.

This task is Herculean even for the world's biggest company. Wal-Mart needs help—not only to create The Index but to figure out exactly what standards should be used and what measurements should be made. Other businesses, even competitors, are being invited to join the effort, so that The Index might become an independent and ubiquitous standard rather than a Wal-Mart thing. The rafters are getting a preview—and a chance to take part, to influence what could be the biggest driver of environmental good in a generation: transparency.

Wal-Mart is proposing to go public with product information that has always been kept secret or that hasn't existed at all. Few really know where the stuff inside their toothpaste tubes or frying pans or hard drives comes from or how they are made—at least until some sort of contamination or sweatshop scandal erupts, long after the harm to the public and the bottom line is done. So many things on the shelf and in the home are black holes, from what happens to the plastic tops on your shampoo bottles (nothing—most are nonrecyclable) to the key ingredients in leading brands of perfume, mentioned only as trade-secret "fragrance" on labels (but containing hormone disrupters, allergens, asthma triggers, and chemicals linked to headaches, infertility, and cancer). Because finding this out requires extensive investigation, few people notice the lack of truly useful information about products filling their homes. And this blindness is not just on the consumer end of business. Not even the companies that make these things like to trace the origins of the parts and chemicals and raw materials they use—they fear the information and just how bad it would reveal so many products and companies to be. And when they do have it, they hide it.

The Index is Wal-Mart's attempt to fill in at least some of those blanks, to provide a kind of origin story for products, revealing where all the stuff we buy, sell, burn, and eat comes from, how it is made, what goes into it, what it does to our air, water, climate, and soil, as well as to our diets, children, bodies, workers, and quality of life, and finally where it ends up. The nature of commerce and the workings of markets would be radically altered by such an index, for it would make the true but hidden cost of things visible. Transparency would become a market force.

Almost every member of the group assembled by Blu Skye for the Confluence trip has been working on a piece of this transparency puzzle: Tensie Whelan of the Rainforest Alliance has been documenting sustainable tree harvests and illegal logging. Green architect William McDonough, who designed a 10-acre "living roof" for Ford's Rouge River assembly plant, created (with chemist Michael Braungart) new ways to examine the safety or toxicity of common chemical ingredients and materials. Berkeley professor Dara O'Rourke has launched a young but promising Web-based "GoodGuide" rating of products. Nike and Patagonia have led the fashion industry by setting the standard on organic fabrics, recyclable products, and nontoxic, sustainable dyes. Wal-Mart has already tried out the origins story concept by tracing jewelry (no one sells more) from mine shaft to monocle and putting the results, good and bad, on its Web site and labeling.

What would happen, the rafters ask one another, if such transparency existed for everything Americans buy and sell? All things being equal—price, quality, availability—wouldn't consumers choose the good and green over the dirty and unhealthful every time, the $9.99 T-shirt made without sweatshops, toxins, or excessive carbon emissions over the $9.99 shirt that's an unknown quantity or worse? Wouldn't people buy the shampoo made without chemicals linked to cancer in children instead of shampoo containing carcinogens? What if the cost of being dirty, made visible by The Index, were borne by those who make and sell and consume such products? Wouldn't making and selling green, sustainable products become the most profitable business model there could be?

Informing this discussion, though unspoken, lies a more sobering

question: Could even the forward-thinking companies afford such risk—
the risk of committing to transparency, then failing to measure up?

"Imagine you're sitting around this campfire with your grandchildren twenty years from now," Ellison suggests to his fellow rafters.
"They want to know what you did about these questions and what you
did to make the world—their world—better. What will you be able to
tell them? What will you be most proud of?"

The next day, in small, intense huddles during lunch, on river-
side hiking trails, and in the rafts during the quiet stretches between
rapids, the conversations continue between the men and women on the
river, between the CEO of Walmart.com and the creator of the Good-
Guide, between the vice president from Nike and her counterpart at
Patagonia, between Wal-Mart's sustainability head and the Rainforest
Alliance. And soon the deal making begins. There is talk of partnerships, of collaboration, of new standards, of sharing data once kept
secret, of a coalition of apparel makers led by little Patagonia and giant
Wal-Mart. The ideas taking shape on this river trip are not so much
about the greening of their individual products or companies as about
transforming whole industries.

Shooting the rapids of the Tuolumne River, this group begins to
see itself as a catalyst for a second Industrial Revolution—a genera-
tional opportunity to mend our ways and our planet. And as odd and
counterintuitive as it seems, Wal-Mart, the big box, the big evil, so
long in the crosshairs of environmentalists, is urging them on.

THE IDEA OF A green Wal-Mart would have been inconceivable a
few years ago. Laughable. Yet now the likes of Jeffrey Hollender, a
cofounder of the green home products company Seventh Generation,
for years a vocal Wal-Mart critic, is saying, "Wal-Mart has become
a legitimate sustainability leader . . . Wal-Mart's enormous size and
influence holds the potential to create the tipping point the corporate
responsibility movement has been waiting for."

Can a company such as Wal-Mart really be green? Or are the two mutually exclusive? Or is the reality somewhere in between, a journey rather than a destination—a way to buy the world more time by putting profit and planet onto the same ledger, and proving that the two can be aligned rather than in opposition?

Make no mistake: Wal-Mart's commitment to sustainability is not grounded in philanthropy or activism or conscience. It is based on a belief that sustainability can be good for the business, good for competitiveness, good for the bottom line. It's one thing for a small company to go green, to make a line of earth-friendly clothing or laundry soap, and to carve out a small market for its premium products. Fortune 500 leaders can dismiss such businesses as niche players and write off sustainability as a risky, do-gooder constraint their huge scale and slim margins cannot support. But it's another thing entirely when Wal-Mart embraces the business case for green. Other companies follow Wal-Mart's lead. They can't afford not to—partners, suppliers, and competitors alike. That's why this project launched by one CEO and his river guide is bigger than Wal-Mart and why Hollender senses in it a tipping point: First it drove other companies, and then whole industries, to sign up. Now even Wall Street is rethinking the way corporations are valued, examining ways in which sustainability can increase the worth of a company or a stock—or its absence can drive that value down. That, in turn, expands the range of sustainability projects in which investment generates a return—so that green is slowly becoming something that even the most miserly, profit-driven companies can embrace.

All this is happening because one of the most unsustainable businesses on the planet, with its sprawling supercenter stores and goods shipped from halfway around the world, decided to go green. Its size and dominance, so often linked to negatives—the death of local businesses, declines in wages, declines in quality, the outsourcing of U.S. industry—is now also being used to drive sustainability and environmental protection. The stakes could not be higher or more worthy:

survival of nature, survival of business, survival of a standard of living far more precarious than most Americans will admit.

For Wal-Mart, there is another, less obvious impetus, something the company is quietly, anxiously focused upon: history. No leading retailer has ever maintained its dominance beyond a single generation. None. Wal-Mart's leaders believe their best hope to break this pattern and cheat history is to embrace that which the next generation of customers cares about most: clean air, clean energy, the environment, nature.

Sustainability and empire have become inextricably linked in an unexpected and unprecedented way. Love it or hate it, Wal-Mart, compelled by its own business needs, is trying to become a force of nature.

PART I

The Nudge

History teaches us that men and nations behave wisely once they have exhausted all other alternatives.

—ABBA EBAN[1]

CHAPTER ONE

Exposure

Bentonville, Arkansas
Spring 2004

The biggest company in the world had a problem.

The problem wasn't lack of business: the company had at that time 176 million customers—a week. It wasn't an inability to find talent: only the People's Liberation Army of China, the United Kingdom's National Health Service, and the massive Indian Railways employed more people. And it certainly wasn't money: with annual revenue that year of $285 billion, it was not only the biggest company in the world; if it were a country, it would rank ninth among nations, just behind China and ahead of Russia, Korea, Australia, and Saudi Arabia.

The problem was the company had become a big, fat, and not particularly well-liked target, attracting more lawsuits than any other corporation in the world. The year was 2004, and there were endless bad press, protests, political opposition, investigations, labor problems, health insurance problems, zoning problems, and, more than ever, environmental problems.

That year Wal-Mart—with its 12,000-mile, computer-controlled supply chain feeding 7,022 stores, its immense fleet of 7,200 trucks in constant, diesel-belching motion, its continual bulldozing and construction, and its voracious demand that suppliers cut costs at any cost—had become a poster child for global warming, mass extinction, smog, and urban sprawl. Many observers believed the bad rep to be deserved. The CEO, H. Lee Scott, was sick of it—and the threat it posed to the company's bottom line. And he knew that, despite Wal-Mart's unmatched wealth and power, the threat was real, one that could not be dismissed by the usual tactic of attacking the critics as snobbish elites who had no sympathy for customers trying to save a few hard-earned bucks. An internally commissioned study, eventually leaked to the press (much to Scott's irritation), showed that as much as 8 percent of Wal-Mart's customer base had stopped shopping there because of the company's increasingly bad reputation. On Wal-Mart's scale, 8 percent represented millions of customers and hundreds of millions in revenue—the margin between a successful fiscal year and a disaster.

Scott cast about for a solution to a straightforward question, the gist of which summarizes how just about every U.S. CEO thought about environmentalists' complaints at the time: What do I have to do to get these guys off my back?

Scott adopted what he would later describe as a defensive mindset. Attacked—unfairly, he felt—he wanted to hit back at the critics wherever they could be depicted as unreasonable or incorrect. He also thought it prudent to shield the company from further criticism by identifying some positive green gestures Wal-Mart might undertake to placate environmentalists and heal the PR wounds—or, at the very least, to limit the company's "exposure." That was the term Scott used, *exposure*, and it was a telling word choice, a common corporate term used to describe business behavior that, if publicized, might threaten the company's bottom line or a CEO's job security. The term had been appropriated years before from the legal community, where it was used to quantify the risk of being sued or prosecuted, and the lawyers had in turn lifted the concept from the military, where its true meaning remained refreshingly clear: the opposite of "cover." Limiting exposure, whether in the military, legal, or corporate sense, has nothing to do with reform or change or "going green" and everything to do with staying out of the line of fire. Scott's goal, then, was to take cover and get past this distracting image problem so the company could continue with business as usual: selling more stuff at lower prices to more customers than anyone else in the world.

Toward that end, Scott was willing to embrace some reasonable environmental philanthropy, even if he felt coerced. That would enable Wal-Mart to point proudly at the ecological aspects of its program of "corporate social responsibility"—a purposely vague term for "good works" on which a company spends time and money even though the activities do little or nothing to increase shareholder value. Although this can sometimes accomplish great things—the considerable relief efforts Wal-Mart would soon undertake in the wake of Hurricane Katrina in 2005 would be rightly celebrated as the epitome of meaningful corporate social responsibility in action—"CSR" is sometimes a derogatory term in the corporate world, a source of as much resentment as pride. Wal-Mart's leadership had always asserted that the greatest social good the company could do was to offer products that people use every day at the lowest price possible, saving real and needed cash for its customers. Many of its customers, after all, live paycheck to paycheck; one out of five gets by without a checking account. That was Wal-Mart's founding mission and its competitive edge. By that definition, Wal-Mart asserted, it already did enormous good in the world by helping the working family stretch its dollars. The added burden of spending on corporate social responsibility ran counter to Wal-Mart's goal of reducing prices as much as possible. It was a moral and social good, sure. But it didn't help Wal-Mart serve its customers. And it didn't help Wal-Mart compete.

It never occurred to Scott, or to anyone else in the company's leadership, that the answer to Wal-Mart's environmental woes might lie not in defending the core business of Wal-Mart but in *changing* that core—and that doing so could make Wal-Mart *more* competitive rather than less.

And, really, why would he think such a thing? Wal-Mart ranked among the most successful enterprises on the planet, having grown from the randomly stocked, pile-it-high-and-sell-it-cheap department store Sam Walton opened in 1962 in Rogers, Arkansas, to a company that could decide one day to enter the grocery business, as it did in 1990, and within the decade become the leading seller of groceries in the country. Wal-Mart soon had more grocery sales than its two nearest competitors combined, Safeway and the former market leader, Kroger, which had been in the grocery store business for more than a century. Wal-Mart's core business model had taken it from zero to grocery market leader in less than ten years, so awash with cash that it could open seventeen supercenter stores (average size: 200,000 square feet) every month, sell the same salmon and celery and canned soup as its competitors for 15 percent less, and drive twenty-nine supermarket chains into bankruptcy in the process. In a good year, the floor space of its newly constructed supercenters would be enough to pave over the world's most visited urban oasis, Central Park in New York City.

The idea that there might be something wrong with this core business model and that it had to be fixed—not just for the good of the planet but for the good of the company—would have seemed absurd to Lee Scott if anyone had articulated such a seemingly far-fetched idea. But that was about to change.

THE ROOTS OF THE change are varied, but its earliest moments can be traced to a conversation in early 2004 between Jib Ellison and his friend and mentor Peter Seligmann, founder, chairman, and CEO of the environmental organization Conservation International. Seligmann's nonprofit had become a major force in the battle against habitat destruction and deforestation, and Seligmann had garnered the support of an impressive list of tycoons and celebrities, from the actor Harrison Ford to the founder of Intel, Gordon Moore, to S. Robson

"Rob" Walton, the chairman of the board of Wal-Mart, eldest son of the company's founder, and tenth richest man in the world at the time.

Seligmann, a legendary environmental rainmaker, routinely brings in a hundred million dollars or more a year for Conservation International from people like Moore and Walton. Ellison had almost gone to work for Conservation International years earlier, but his wife had not wanted to move from California to the East Coast, where Seligmann is based. Ellison had instead partnered with three other young corporate consultants to start up a boutique business strategy firm in the San Francisco Bay Area, a successful venture named The Trium Group, that had taken him in a different direction from the concerns of Conservation International. Now the former river guide was on sabbatical from Trium, giving himself twelve months to test whether he could make a living advancing his long-simmering ideas about a new sort of corporate environmentalism. He had flown to Washington to the Conservation International headquarters to ask for Seligmann's help.

"Your board of directors is filled with the captains of industry. I know they're giving you millions of dollars a year to do what you do so well," Ellison said. "But back home it's another story. Their organizations are doing nothing."

Ellison's argument: These same corporate scions should—and could—be convinced to go beyond the sort of philanthropy that supported Conservation International. Their next step, a potentially world-changing one, should be to remake their businesses into environmentally sound powerhouses. What if doing good for the environment didn't cost the company but made more money for it? In Ellison's view, businesses could seek out competitive advantage over other brands by pursuing energy efficiency, leaner packaging, cleaner plants, conservation, and systemwide transparency and sustainability. They could, in short, boost their profits, their image, and their market position through the elimination of waste—because waste is not only bad for the planet, it costs money. Yet every day, U.S. companies that prided themselves on penny-pinching and efficient operations were squandering billions of dollars because they were riddled with waste without realizing it. Ellison was convinced that if waste elimination and sustainability were made a core strategy, not viewed as a pilot project or as a bit of good citizenship but baked into the culture and mission of a company, it would provide a winning business model. He had made a study of it, he told Seligmann, and had documented a small number of businesses that were succeeding with this approach of serving both profit and planet—Patagonia, for one, had made it a core purpose of its business and developed a loyal customer base; Nike had reversed its reputation for sweatshops and environmental disregard and gained market share in the process. The solutions were all there, he said, just waiting, hidden in plain sight.

"Give me five minutes with any of them," Ellison begged Seligmann. "That's all I ask. A CEO-level conversation."

Asking Seligmann to take advantage of his coveted access to busy and wealthy chief executive officers, whose time and meetings are scripted months in advance, was no small favor. Ellison's notions about sustainable private enterprise weren't just outside the mainstream in 2004—they ran counter to the knowledge and experience of most American CEOs. By and large, they heard the word "environment" and thought: regulations, bureaucracy, lawsuits, obstacles, delays, added costs, bad press. They did not think: business opportunity. Ellison's consultancy partners back in San Francisco thought he was, at best, too ambitious. Ellison was blunter: "They think I'm crazy," he admitted. But Seligmann did not think Ellison was crazy. Intrigued, he promised to think about how he might help. It turned out that Seligmann had already engaged some corporate leaders in just the kind of conversation Ellison had in mind. The timing couldn't have been better.

Three months later, without prelude, a bland e-mail materialized on Ellison's home computer in Healdsburg in northern California wine country. Seligman had shot him one short line: "Rob Walton will call you."

The name seemed familiar, but Ellison couldn't quite place it and he had to look up Walton on the Internet. The first words that popped up in the Google search were " . . . officially took over as Wal-Mart's Chairman two days after his father's death," and Ellison realized the opportunity he had sought from his friend at Conservation International had arrived, bigger, better, and more fraught with possibilities than he had imagined.

Seligmann, he would learn, had just begun a series of eco-expeditions with Walton and his sons—to Costa Rica, Madagascar, Brazil, the Galápagos Islands. This relationship, and the knowledge of endangered species and landscapes it was giving Walton, led the magnate to donate $21 million to Conservation International through the Walton Family Foundation to support ocean habitat protection. On one of their trips, Seligmann had pitched the idea Ellison had championed: that the Wal-Mart juggernaut itself could be a far more powerful force for environmental reform than any donation, no matter how generous. Walton seemed interested in hearing more but pointed out that as chairman of the board he was removed from day-to-day operations at the company. Such ideas would be more appropriately discussed with the chief executive officer. What Walton could do, however, was make such a discussion possible—he would arrange for Ellison to get his wish, a CEO-level meeting. And so, a few weeks later, with Seligmann and Walton in attendance, Ellison sat down at Wal-Mart's famously modest redbrick, tin-roofed headquarters in Bentonville, Arkansas, with Lee Scott, the leader of the biggest company in the world.

The meeting felt like an audition to Ellison, and with good reason. Scott already had met with several prominent environmentalists and green consultants, among them Amory Lovins, the head of the famed Rocky Mountain Institute and the recipient of a MacArthur Foundation "genius grant." Now the CEO looked over the thin, casually dressed Ellison with a wary smile. Lovins was a rock star, but Scott had never heard of this guy "Jib" or his fledgling Blu Skye

Sustainability Consulting. He would never have taken the meeting but for the intervention of Rob Walton.

Just the third chief executive since Wal-Mart's founding almost a half century earlier, Scott was the only top executive at the company to have gotten his start managing the trucking division rather than a retail line, and he would be the last CEO to be groomed by company founder Sam Walton. He was a practical man, a workaholic CEO, and he was not sure how he felt about this river guy in blue jeans. Ellison had spent a third of his adult life sleeping in a tent next to rivers around the world and rarely set foot inside a Wal-Mart, unless it was to scrounge supplies during river trips. The gulf between the two seemed to expand as Ellison, in introducing himself, excitedly described his family's current lifestyle: "Now we live on eighty-five acres off the grid in northern California and—"

"Whoa, whoa, whoa," Scott interjected, staring at Ellison. "You live where?"

"In northern California," Ellison repeated.

"No, what did you say before that?" Scott asked. "Off the grid? What exactly does that mean?"

Ellison's smile didn't falter, even as he silently berated himself for potentially blowing the whole deal by revealing a bit too much about himself in this first encounter. "Off the grid" might sound enviable in true-green San Francisco, where there were more Toyota Priuses per capita than anywhere else on the planet and the mayors in surrounding towns competed like prizefighters for the title of "greenest city." But in Bentonville, Arkansas, it just sounded weird. Ellison kept a poker face and explained that it meant his home did not tap into the electrical grid, that the family generated its own electricity with solar panels, and that he was practicing what he preached—living sustainably. To his relief, Scott nodded at this last point. Wal-Mart, it turned out, had a company tradition that encouraged similar put-your-money-where-your-mouth-is behavior, urging executives to experience the consequences of their decisions out in the real world, a process they called

"Eat what you cook." This was more likely to involve visiting a store and talking to staff and customers about some new product or practice than stringing solar panels on one's roof, but still, Ellison's departure from the grid didn't seem quite so far out in this context.

Next Ellison recounted how he had parlayed his background as a river guide and expedition leader into starting a nonprofit that had run international rafting trips and student exchanges between the Soviet Union and the United States. This was during the height of the Cold War, when rapprochement between the superpowers seemed unattainable. The challenging journeys down Siberian rivers and through California wilderness had helped the rafters find unanticipated common ground as they pulled together through dangerous waters, which Ellison considered a perfect metaphor for the times.

Wal-Mart needed to navigate different but no less treacherous waters, Ellison told Scott, with the world's future, as well as the economic future of the company and the country, once again at stake. Wal-Mart needed to enter a new kind of détente, this time between the demands of business and the limits of the natural world.

"We're getting hammered in the press," Scott agreed. "I know we don't know anything about our environmental impact. Could you do some research and tell me where we might be exposed?"

Ellison considered. Scott's question was just another way of asking how they might solve Wal-Mart's "green problem," which he knew was a very logical question for Scott to ask. It's the question many CEOs were asking at the time, how to limit exposure and get on with business as usual. But Ellison also wanted to make clear that he felt that this was the *wrong* question to ask.

"Sure," he finally said, "we could do the research. But if you really want to cut to the chase, given your size and if you include your supply chain, you're exposed in everything that matters to everybody. There. I just saved you ten million dollars and two years."

Lee Scott is not, by reputation, easy to catch off guard. In 1996, when he was just one of the company's numerous vice presidents, he was asked to be the voice and face of Wal-Mart during one of its worst public relations debacles to date: the revelation that the company's Kathie Lee Gifford line of wholesome celebrity-endorsed clothing was produced in sweatshops. He had never been at a loss for words in steering Wal-Mart through that crisis—and himself into the CEO's chair. But Ellison surprised him that day. So Scott said nothing and waited, his interest piqued by this most endangered species of all, a consultant uninterested in being paid millions of dollars to do a study.

"Lee, the thing you have to remember is that all this stuff that people don't want you to put into the environment is waste," Ellison continued. "And you're paying for it!"

It takes a different sort of perception, a different lens on the world, to see it, but the truth was, Ellison argued, that inefficiency and waste were omnipresent, even in a notoriously stingy company like Wal-Mart, with the waste not only damaging the environment but damaging the company's bottom line as well. Waste in packaging. Waste in shipping. Waste in the supply chain—in the fisheries, forests, canneries, and textile mills. Waste in how energy and fuel were being used. Consider the humble bottle of liquid laundry detergent. The industry standard always came in a 120-ounce container close to the size and weight of a gallon milk jug, but it was also made in an ultraconcentrated version—same brand, same soap, just concentrated so it fit into a container the size of a large ketchup bottle. Both versions wash the same amount of clothing with the same effectiveness, and both sell for the same price—but the ketchup bottle uses one-fourth the packaging, weighs one-fourth as much, costs one-fourth to ship, and takes up one-fourth the space on ships, trucks, and shelves. The larger bottle had one ingredient in greater supply in comparison to the smaller bottle: extra water. That's all. The ketchup bottle version is better for the bottom line, more convenient for the customer, more profitable to sell, and way better for the environment. Yet, when Ellison and Scott spoke that day in 2004, most of the one billion bottles of laundry soap sold each year in the United States—one out of four of them at

Wal-Mart—were the big ones. So why would a smart, cost-conscious retailer like Wal-Mart even carry the big bottles instead of the small ones? If you thought about it, it was completely insane, even without the obvious environmental impact. But nobody thought about it. The waste—the habit—was so ingrained it was invisible. And the craziest part was that businesses, from CEOs on down, had been trained for a century or better to think of environmentalism and sustainability as extra costs, rather than what they truly could be: imperatives to eliminate waste and the costs that go with it.

"If you really want to know something cool about this whole environmental and social side of the equation, here it is: It's a massive business opportunity. The best business opportunity of our time."

The CEO hired the river guide that day. Wal-Mart became Blu Skye's first client, and the greening of Wal-Mart had begun.

BY 2008, EVERY WAL-MART store in the country stocked only the bottles of concentrated detergent. Over a three-year period, that meant 95 million pounds of petroleum-based plastic resin would not be used. Four hundred million gallons of water—used to bulk up those big jugs of detergent—would be conserved. About 125 million pounds of cardboard used to box and ship that detergent would not be used. And more than a half-million gallons of diesel truck fuel would not be burned hauling those heavier soap bottles around the country—meaning that 11 million pounds of CO_2 emissions were not released into the atmosphere.[1]

All that arose from seeing the waste—and the opportunity—in a single product.

What happens when the world's largest company starts looking for that same opportunity in every item in the store and in every branch and operation of the business? And what happens next, when that same company realizes that such thinking is just a first step? That is the river Jib Ellison persuaded Wal-Mart to navigate, and though the reach of its impact and the sustainability of its commitment won't be known for years, perhaps decades, the greening of Wal-Mart became, in a matter of months, one of the most influential environmental initiatives in history. Wal-Mart's move shook corporate America as nothing else could, and other companies—Wal-Mart's suppliers and competitors alike—began to reconsider their own environmental stances, if for no other reason than they knew the retail chain would never go green unless it made sense for the company's bottom line. Some of them went to Blu Skye to seek help with their own green problems, drawn by the Wal-Mart aura, new clients who also had the ability to change the course of whole industries: Staples. Purina. Microsoft. Sony Pictures Studios. The U.S. dairy industry. The city of Cleveland. The state of California. The reach and influence of Jib Ellison's little company was unprecedented. It was bewildering to many, this sea change among such bedrock conservative companies and their cadres of executives, who began competing with one another to see who could find the next sustainability triumph, something that could trump little detergent bottles. In Bentonville, a few insiders among the growing cadre of people engaged in Wal-Mart's environmental initiatives began referring to Ellison as "the CEO whisperer."

Blu Skye had one employee at the time Ellison met with Lee Scott: Ellison himself.

"I guess," he told his wife after the meeting, "I better hire some more people."

CHAPTER TWO

The Soul of a Discounter

When H. Lee Scott took over as CEO of Wal-Mart early in 2000, the environment was the last thing on his mind. And the notion that one of his close advisers would one day be a river guide who lived "off the grid" and hailed from the San Francisco Bay Area—where Wal-Mart stores were most unwelcome—would have sounded ridiculous.

Wal-Mart's single most important priority at the time could be summed up by its long-standing motto: "Always the low price. *Always.*" Variations of that slogan had been in place since the company's birth, and it formed the one commitment Wal-Mart aimed never to bend or break. Lee Scott knew, as had his two predecessors, that Wal-Mart's success arose from a single-minded focus on achieving low prices for consumers by any means necessary. If that meant finding the cheapest DVD player or T-shirt or pair of sneakers on the planet at a manufacturing plant in China that turned a nearby river black, so be it. As long as it was legal, no problem—Wal-Mart was serving its customers, saving them money, and empowering them to buy ever more stuff. It's not as if Lee Scott or anyone else at the company made that actual mental calculation, lower prices for higher pollution. It was an unintended consequence, invisible to the stalwarts back in Bentonville, if not to the people in and around the Chinese factory. This is not to

excuse it; indeed, the CEO in later years would wonder at how blind
he and his staff had been—blind to the damage inflicted, blind to the
opportunities missed. The truth was, Scott and his executive staff were
too consumed by more familiar concerns back in 2000: expanding the
Wal-Mart brand in the United States and abroad, consolidating the
company's wild success in the grocery business, turning back a push
by labor unions to gain a foothold in the determinedly antiunion Wal-
Mart, and fending off the increasing tide of negative media stories
about the impact of Wal-Mart on the world. The last rankled Scott
from the outset of his CEO tenure.

"Not every day was as pleasurable as you would want if you were
the CEO of Wal-Mart," he would say many years later. "There were a
lot of people . . . wondering when we were going to wake up to the fact
that we needed to do something different. . . . We needed to change."

It would take him quite a while to realize it, but he eventually came
to see that the first thing at Wal-Mart that needed to change was Scott
himself.

LEE SCOTT WAS BORN in Joplin, Missouri, and grew up fifteen miles
away in Baxter Springs, Kansas, a city of four thousand in the southeast
corner of the state where the struggling economy trumped all other
concerns. Baxter Springs' heyday as a major cattle-drive town was a
century in its past. In Scott's youth, it was the traffic that still hummed
along the Mother Road, Route 66, that helped keep the town's businesses going. He spent his high school years working at one of them—
the Phillips 66 gas station his father ran.

After high school, Scott worked his way through college at Pittsburg State University, a small regional campus a half hour's drive
from his parents' home. While attending classes full-time, Scott
worked a full-time night-shift job, too, making molds at a local tire
company for $1.95 an hour, commuting between school and work in

his aged Ford Falcon. He set aside the time between midnight and two in the morning to study.

Scott was twenty-two, married with a young son, and renting a cramped and drafty home in the Pittsburg, Kansas, Lone Star Trailer Court when he earned his business administration degree in 1971. He took an entry-level job with a midwestern trucking company, Yellow Freight, which moved him to Springdale, Arkansas, where he rose from driver to terminal manager. And it was there, in 1979, that Scott had his first contact with Wal-Mart.

For the future CEO, it was not love at first sight.

Wal-Mart at that time was not a high-tech global behemoth but a fifteen-year-old regional retail chain, having expanded from its Arkansas roots into ten states in the Midwest and South. It had just over two hundred stores and annual sales of about half a billion dollars—big and growing, but nowhere near dominating the retail sector. Wal-Mart had not yet begun to carry what would become its signature, high-profit items—the celebrity-branded fashions, groceries, prescription drugs, auto service, jewelry. Founder Sam Walton was in charge in that era, combining his unique brand of folksy and paternal management, traditional conservative values, and legendary cheapness (executives were expected to share hotel rooms on business trips and steal the pens from the rooms, per Walton's orders) with a ruthless drive to undercut competitors' prices and a virulent stance against unions, labor laws, the minimum wage, and overtime. Wal-Mart was just beginning a period of explosive growth then, but few outside—or inside—the company imagined that the chain Sam Walton had launched with a single dime store would become the biggest and most powerful company in the world.

Scott had gone to Wal-Mart headquarters to complain in person about an overdue bill for $7,000 owed to Yellow Freight. He ended up in the office of David Glass, the head of distribution and finance for Wal-Mart (who would go on to succeed "Mr. Sam," as Walton was known companywide, as the old man's handpicked successor as CEO). Glass disputed the accuracy of the bill and refused to pay, but Scott impressed him. Glass asked if he'd be interested in a job at Wal-Mart managing a distribution center, but Scott told him to forget it. "I may not be the smartest person who ever walked into your office, but I am not going to leave the fastest growing trucking company in America and go and work for a guy who cannot even pay a seven thousand dollar bill."[1]

Far from being put off by the wise-guy exit line, Glass—who shared Scott's small-town, midwestern roots—told the younger man to think about it. Scott didn't know it at the time, but Glass's reaction stemmed from his own less-than-impressive first contact with Wal-Mart back in 1964. Glass had decided to gauge the job prospects at the then-new retail chain by visiting the small Ozark mountain town of Harrison to check out the grand opening of Wal-Mart store number two. The opening proved to be not so grand. Sam Walton had set up a donkey ride for kids in the parking lot next to several truckloads of discount watermelons. The melons burst in the hundred-plus-degree heat, mixing with the donkey droppings to produce a stinking, mucky mess that customers tracked all over the new store. Glass had left the reeking scene certain that he would never work for a company that could create such a bad first impression. "Sam was a nice fellow, but I wrote him off," Glass recalled in *The Watermelon Story*, an account of the event enshrined in Wal-Mart's official history. "It was just terrible." After observing Wal-Mart's success in subsequent years, Glass revised his opinion and would go on to become Mr. Sam's protégé in the mid-1970s and his successor in the 1990s.

Scott ended up following the same pattern, accepting the job offer from Glass later that year. (Wal-Mart never did pay the $7,000 to Yellow Freight.) Promised the position of head of the transportation department—the former truck driver now in charge of the retail chain's rapidly expanding truck fleet—Scott arrived for his first day to find his predecessor still in place, the corporate musical chairs that would free up Scott's position not yet complete. He did not react with the same sort of hotheaded performance he had given with the disputed invoice but took the second-in-command position without complaint for the few months it took to shift the executive ranks. That impressed his bosses. "Taking one for the company" rather than displaying towering ego or pique—even when pique would be justified—showed Scott could be a good fit with what Mr. Sam liked to call "Wal-Mart Culture."

Sam Walton spoke passionately and often about Wal-Mart Culture. Under his leadership, it amounted to a kind of retail rules to live by that he spread like a merchant gospel. He expected his managers to embrace it as true believers. Although Scott passed his first Wal-Mart Culture test with his unexpected job description downgrade, it wouldn't always be so easy for him to swallow. Scott was part of the company's up-and-coming generation of college-educated baby boomers who would later dominate the executive ranks—but who, during Mr. Sam's tenure, sometimes chafed against the old man's notions. Despite his miserly approach to paying others (he patronized the same five-dollar-a-haircut barber most of his adult life—and never tipped), Walton had distinct ideas about the need for treating workers in ways he believed engendered teamwork and loyalty. They were never to be called "employees," for one thing, but "associates," the personnel department was rebranded the "People Department," and long after becoming one of the richest men in the world, Walton insisted that the Wal-Mart CEO ensconced in his modest office in the Bentonville headquarters had to have an "open door" to any associate with a gripe, insight, or problem. This sort of access is mostly unheard of elsewhere in the corporate world, where CEOs of large companies can be as guarded and inaccessible as heads of state. But at the home office in Bentonville, a truck driver or cashier could walk in at almost any time without an appointment and without fear of reprisal. That was the way it was when there were a handful of Wal-Mart stores in a few rural towns, and that's the way it was when there were hundreds of stores with billions of dollars in revenue.

Early in his tenure at Wal-Mart, Scott resisted this management style, paying for it when Mr. Sam called him out for being too high-handed with employees. As head of the trucking fleet, Scott had cracked down, sometimes harshly, on drivers who broke regulations or resisted his ideas about logistics and efficiency. The drivers bristled at his authoritarian approach. Several of them, some of whom had been with Mr. Sam since the retail chain's early days of donkey rides and bake sales, marched through Walton's open door to let their patron know they were unhappy. To Scott's surprise, Walton chastised his new executive, then ordered him to apologize to each of the drivers, shake their hands, and thank them for taking advantage of the open-door policy—a humiliating expression of gratitude to subordinates who had ratted him out to the boss. Walton capped off the episode by rehiring a driver Scott had fired. Scott had no choice but to follow orders, the lesson made clear: to succeed at Wal-Mart, he would have to work within the company culture, not outside it.

At least, that was the intended lesson. The real lesson was subtly, crucially different: he realized that Wal-Mart Culture was too power-ful to fight. The trick was to find ways to use that culture to achieve his own goals.

Scott ended up firing the same driver again—five times. Mr. Sam hired him back four times, before Scott found the right reasons and the right way to get what he wanted, the Wal-Mart way. Scott would use this lesson again and again—to change Wal-Mart's old practices on logistics, to re-form its supply chain, to help persuade the computer-phobic Walton to embrace automation, even to change the historically inept way Wal-Mart dealt with the press and with critics.

Every time Scott changed course on some long-standing company practice or devised a decidedly un-Wal-Mart-ish plan of action, he would spin it as being in service of Wal-Mart Culture. That was the key. That was the best way, the only way really, to get the Titanic to turn, and turn fast. Lee Scott had figured out the one characteristic that could distinguish a caretaker CEO from a transformative one.

. . . .

TRANSFORMATION WAS NOT REALLY something Wal-Mart did. The company's model has always been to transform others—its competitors, its suppliers, its markets. But Wal-Mart itself has remained consistent throughout its long years of growth. Though Sam Walton left the CEO position in 1988, his presence and the culture he expounded still permeated the corporation. Wal-Mart's next generation worked hard to cultivate his mystique (and to claim a connection to it). The company still instructs its employees on the commerce-centric, libertarian-flavored traditional values that the company's genteel, tightfisted founder espoused. The old pickup truck Mr. Sam drove to work—even after he became the richest man in the world as calculated by *Fortune* magazine's annual list—is on display in the Wal-Mart Museum near the home office in Bentonville. Nearby, inside one of the company's 120 mammoth regional distribution centers, where twelve miles of automated conveyor belts and a laser bar code–scanning system send streams of canned soup, laundry soap, and Nintendo Wiis on high-speed journeys from dock to warehouse to trucks, stands a replica of Walton's original five-and-dime storefront. Team-spirit sessions and staff meetings are held on a stage in front of the fifties-era mockup. And every day, in executive meetings and in Wal-Marts across the nation and around the world, the company cheer, which Walton copied in 1977 from a Korean tennis ball factory he toured, is still shouted and danced out, from the lowest-ranking staffer to the highest:

Give me a **W**!
Give me an **A**!
Give me an **L**!
Give me a **squiggly**!
Give me an **M**!
Give me an **A**!

Give me an **R**!
Give me a **T**!
What's that spell?
Wal-Mart!
Whose Wal-Mart is it?
It's my Wal-Mart!
Who's number one?
The customer! Always!

It's been said that no leader has been quoted posthumously more than Mr. Sam, except perhaps for Chairman Mao. At major company meetings, Lee Scott and the other top executives customarily retold some personal anecdote about Walton. These usually involved an emblematic bit of wisdom passed on by the founder, even a gentle scolding from the old man, retold with the self-effacing manner that Wal-Mart Culture demands of its executives—thereby maintaining the Walton connection and legend. A Wal-Mart corporate meeting is truly unlike any other: part revival, part rally, part cult ritual, part homage to a singular business vision.

As Walton laid it out, Wal-Mart's culture revolved around three basic values: "service to the customers," "striving for excellence," and "respect for the individual." To make those values concrete in the business of storekeeping, Walton created a web of folksy techniques for his associates to pledge to enforce. One was his "ten-foot attitude," which required store workers, whenever they came within ten feet of a customer, to look him or her in the eye, issue a warm greeting, and ask if the customer needed help. Walton claimed to have first used the ten-foot rule to meet people while earning a business degree at the University of Missouri, engaging strangers walking the campus (students, professors, secretaries, and janitors alike) so thoroughly that he got himself elected senior class president and was nicknamed "Hustler Walton" by his fraternity. He figured a similar personable, interested approach would work well in a store, and to this day Wal-Mart employs greeters to welcome customers. He also wanted his early Wal-Marts to replicate the feel of a hometown store (the sort he was putting out of business as his chain rapidly grew): there were bake sales, local scholarships, support for community charities chosen by the staff, and carnival gimmicks such as the now-notorious donkey ride. "Each Wal-Mart store should reflect the values of its customers," he said after launching his first store in the chain, "and support the vision they hold for their community."

Even after the stores numbered in the hundreds, Mr. Sam visited them constantly. He learned to fly and bought a small private plane that he piloted himself, bumping to a stop on little rural airfields so he could visit his increasingly far-flung stores, maintain a personal connection with his workforce, and ask floor workers and clerks and cashiers how things were going. He told them they were smart and motivated and that he was blessed to have such marvelous associates. And then, like all great motivational speakers, he listened to their opinions and ideas, implementing the good suggestions and giving credit to the workers who spoke up—honoring and respecting them even as he paid them fifty cents an hour. Sometimes he'd show up in his old pickup truck with his hunting dogs along for the ride. He remembered names. He'd bum money from employees for a cup of coffee. He'd join the staff morning meetings, tell jokes, relate an inspirational anecdote, and lead the Wal-Mart cheer, squatting down, shaking his hips, and shouting "Give me a squiggly!" Years later in his autobiography, he offered up his ten rules for succeeding in business; six of them had to do with how to treat people. Showing interest and bestowing praise on employees, and treating them like valued partners, were high on the list. After all, Walton wrote, such tactics produced great results. Just as important, they cost nothing. Sam Walton had the folksy and sincere charisma needed to sell the approach—there's no other way to explain his enduring popularity as leader of a company notorious for its mediocre pay and benefits. Beneath the affability was the heart and soul of a discounter, a class of merchant he by no means invented, though he arguably perfected it.

More than two decades after he left the CEO chair, the small-town, bake-sale facade is slipping away from the multinational enterprise that is the modern Wal-Mart, yet Mr. Sam's three core beliefs are still offered up by the company as the corporate equivalent of the stone tablets. These three values, though seemingly distinct, were spun to serve the company's one overriding principle: EDLP—Every Day Low Prices. As Walton explained it, low prices were the best of all possible customer services, the best way to respect an individual (and his hard-earned cash), and the best way to demonstrate excellence. EDLP was also Wal-Mart's great pathway to profits. Walton had proved this part of the formula in his first store. He knocked down prices on ladies' underwear to beat all the competition. Instead of losing money, the lower prices led to many more sales. The increased volume more than made up for any profits he lost on price cuts. Customers flocked to get the best deal, some driving far out of their way to get those cheap panties, the psychology of discounting so powerful that it didn't matter if they ended up spending more on the gas to get there than they saved on their purchases. They wanted the deal. They wanted to feel that they weren't being cheated and overcharged. And when the panties sold out, Walton placed an even larger order with the supplier while demanding (and getting) an even greater volume discount—which is when he discovered the magic of the discount feedback loop, something Wal-Mart has exploited ever since. Sell cheaper, sell more, then lower the price even more: that was the deceptively simple formula for success Walton used to make Wal-Mart king, carried out with relentless, ruthless obsession. Competitors too much in love with their markups failed to match him back when Wal-Mart was smaller and still wrestling for market share; later, when the company was huge, it could bully suppliers into discounts no other retailer had the power to demand. A Wal-Mart product order—or a decision not to reorder—could make or break a business as nothing else could.

Walton figured this out early, not long after he returned from service in World War II, borrowed $20,000 from his father-in-law, and opened a Ben Franklin five-and-dime variety store in tiny Newport, Arkansas. Such a rural location was considered a death sentence by all the major variety and department store chains at the time, but Walton had little choice. His wife hated cities and did not want to move away from rural Arkansas. It was a fortuitous limitation, however, as Walton discovered that rural areas could support a successful retail business, after all. Such areas were underserved. Rural America, it turned out, presented a vast and untapped market opportunity. It didn't hurt that Walton worked seven days a week and hawked his new operation like a carnival barker, drawing in bargain-hunting customers from throughout the region. Soon he opened a second store and a third, and several more elsewhere in Arkansas and Kansas, all in rural and semirural areas, mostly in the Ozarks, and all part of the Ben Franklin five-and-dime franchise chain. He prospered throughout the fifties, a rising dime-store magnate.

But the five-and-dime store format of dry goods, craft supplies, novelties, and household items that had endured since the beginning of the twentieth century—when everything sold there really did cost a nickel or a dime—had its limitations (and would finally drop its signature five-and-dime name to become the modern "dollar store"). Walton's ideas about volume sales, discounts, and low pricing were bigger in scope. There was a world of merchandise out there he wanted to sell that was outside the dime-store inventory. His ideas came to a head in 1962, when he partnered with his brother to open a different kind of variety store, twice the size of a regular Ben Franklin, with a broader range of merchandise, frequent discounts, and a fully self-service style of operation, with barrels, shelves, and racks piled with merchandise and crowding the aisles. Although it was still a Ben Franklin franchise, the new store bore a sign declaring it the "Walton Family Center." It quickly became Walton's most profitable enterprise—and one of the top-grossing Ben Franklin franchises in the nation.

Walton knew he was onto something, and he opened two more successful branches just like it, forerunners of what would become

Wal-Mart. Then he approached two major department-store chains, looking for a partner to help him take his concept national—a discount chain for rural America. They turned him down flat. His idea was too risky, too at odds with conventional wisdom. Why cannibalize a successful dime-store business model? Why put "big boxes" in small towns instead of big cities? They did everything but call Walton, by then in his forties, a rube and a whippersnapper. Forced to give up or go it alone, Walton borrowed, mortgaged, and leveraged his existing stores, and the first full-fledged Wal-Mart opened in Rogers, Arkansas, in the summer of 1962. Two leading retail chains had turned down the chance to become 50 percent owners of what would evolve into the biggest, richest company in the world. Walton had begun his march toward the Fortune 500 list, his chain of stores growing with astonishing speed, spreading through the South and the Midwest, then nationwide. And the companies that waved off Walton's idea as folly? They no longer exist.

By 1967, there were 24 Wal-Marts in Arkansas generating more than $12 million in sales. Eight years later, there were 125 stores in eight states with $340 million in sales. By 1979, the store count had more than doubled again, to 276 locations and $1.2 billion in sales. In 1982, two decades after the first Wal-Mart opened its doors, *Forbes* published its first list of the richest Americans. A man many Americans had never heard of, Sam Walton, appeared at the number seventeen spot on the list of four hundred. Three years later, Walton reached the top of the *Forbes* list with a personal fortune of nearly $3 billion. "I could kick your butt for ever running that list," Walton complained to the magazine (which printed his remark). He disliked anything that detracted from his image as spokesman for the blue-collar buyer. The humble and traditional values he espoused did not mesh well with the "billionaire" label, no matter how broken down his pickup truck might be.

When press coverage focused less on his fabulous wealth and made him out as folksy and plain, Walton was incensed again, accusing reporters of creating a buffoonish image of a cheapskate recluse who behaved like a hillbilly and slept with his dogs. Never mind that Walton contributed to that part of his image by his often outlandish stunts, such as the time in 1984 when he donned a grass skirt and flower leis over his business suit and danced the hula on Wall Street. His thin-skinned antipathy toward the national media (and the East Coast corporate and political elites in general), the sense that he and his discount chain never got a fair shake or the respect they deserved, became one of the most enduring, if never officially stated, parts of Wal-Mart Culture.

THIS TOUCHY, DEFENSIVE ATTITUDE was part of a broader aspect of the Bentonville corporate culture, a kind of willful blindness to the downsides of a business model so focused on ever-lower prices. Discounting is, at its root, a race to the bottom, which requires cutting the costs of doing business to the bare minimum. Throughout his tenure as CEO, Walton often spoke about the need to keep the overhead costs of doing business down, and he identified the largest bit of overhead as people. He loved to make his employees feel good with rousing speeches and open-door policies—as he said, such niceties had the virtue of being both effective and cost-free—but when it came to actually spending money on his people, Wal-Mart revealed its dark side. Low wages, skimpy benefits, and medical insurance many employees couldn't afford became the inevitable consequences of Walton's discount philosophy.

Early in Wal-Mart's history, the federal government had to sue the company because Walton refused to pay the $1.15-an-hour minimum wage guaranteed retail workers by an act of Congress in 1965. Wages were less than half that for some workers. The furious Walton had to be ordered by the courts to meet the minimum wage and to cut checks for back pay. Little changed over the next forty-three years: the average full-time Wal-Mart associate (working thirty-four hours a week at $10.84 an hour) earned $19,155 a year in 2008—below the federal poverty line for a family of four. Half the workers could not afford the company health plan. Forty-six percent of employees' children were uninsured and could obtain medical care only through public assistance—according to Wal-Mart's own internal study.[2]

Pressure on store and district managers to keep payroll costs down led to chronic—and well-documented—abuses of workers. Hundreds of thousands of Wal-Mart employees were forced to work "off the clock" without getting paid, compelled to punch out and work many hours of overtime for free, or risk being fired. Workers have reported being denied breaks for meals, forced to work the lunch hour without pay.[3] One successful lawsuit revealed that a cook-waitress on duty by herself at an in-store restaurant had no relief for entire shifts and could not take even a bathroom break. She soiled herself several times rather than risk being fired for leaving her position unattended.[4] Night-shift workers have been locked in the building overnight, unable to leave, even for injuries or emergencies, as no one was present with a key. The lock-ins, intended to deter employee pilfering, persisted for more than a decade before a *New York Times* article and a congressional hearing exposed the practice in 2004, after which Wal-Mart promised to have a manager with a key present whenever night-shift workers were locked in.[5] The extent and long duration of such problems became clear in December 2008, when Wal-Mart settled sixty-three class-action lawsuits over wage and hour violations in forty-two states, authorizing payments totaling up to $640 million to hundreds of thousands of workers. Combined with earlier settlements, Wal-Mart has had to agree to pay more than a billion dollars to employees cheated and pressured out of wages they had earned.[6] As mammoth as those settlement costs have been, they are a relative bargain given the potential exposure the company faced; without a settlement, fines in Minnesota alone could have topped $2 billion after the company was tagged for *two million* separate wage and hour violations involving 100,000 Minnesota Wal-Mart employees.[7]

Wal-Mart's top leadership has steadfastly denied any companywide

policy to mistreat employees or cheat them out of wages and overtime, blaming any violations on a few "rogue" managers who broke
the rules. But the judge who ruled against Wal-Mart in Minnesota
was unmoved, saying such labor practices were well known within the
company. Of the top leadership in Bentonville, the judge said, "They
put their heads in the sand."[8]

With this history of worker mistreatment, Wal-Mart has long been
an inviting target for labor unions, which have expended millions of
dollars in trying to unionize the world's biggest employer over the
past forty years. They have failed at every store, club, and distribution center in the United States. Sam Walton was rabidly antiunion,
and he built a fervent opposition to labor organizations into Wal-Mart
Culture: managers have received antiunion manuals instructing them
how to spot potential troublemakers, employees have been ordered to
watch antiunion movies, and suspected union sympathizers have been
demoted, moved, or fired.[9]

The first attempt to unionize a Wal-Mart came in 1970, when the
now-defunct Retail Clerks International Union tried to organize workers at a new store in Mexico, Missouri. Walton hired one of the nation's top union-busting attorneys at the time, John E. Tate of Omaha,
who crushed the union effort so impressively that Walton appointed
him to the board of directors and the company's executive committee.
But Tate also suggested future battles would be easier if Walton found
a way to show rank-and-file employees how valued they were—advice
echoed by Walton's wife, Helen.[10] Walton began his open-door policy
then, and he stepped up his visits and gab sessions with store employees. Most significantly, he created a profit-sharing plan that started
the next year, in 1971, the most generous worker benefit Wal-Mart has
ever offered. The plan allowed even the lowest-paid hourly worker to
accumulate stock at a 15 percent discount. For those who worked there
long enough—and in the old days, under Mr. Sam, there were plenty
who did—the profit sharing could be a lucrative deal in the long run,
thanks to Wal-Mart's rapid growth. Walton took the company public

in 1970 with an initial public offering that set the stock price at $16.50 a share. Twenty years later, a single share of that initial Wal-Mart stock had split 512 times for a total value of $32,000. Stories of cashiers retiring with a million dollars or more in the bank (a mere $500 investment in 1970 would have gotten you there) were highlighted by Wal-Mart's press office.

Profit sharing also served another purpose: it was a potent weapon, Walton's best hedge against union organizers, because it was always possible that profit sharing could be stripped away from any workers who unionized. When a distribution center in Searcy, Arkansas, mustered enough votes in 1978 to hold a Teamsters union election, Walton visited with the workers, threatening to shutter the plant and kill their profit sharing if the union won.[11] The Teamsters lost by a wide margin, and no unionization attempt at a U.S. Wal-Mart has come that close again. (The profit-sharing threat, which loomed large then, stopped being such a factor once stock prices leveled off and the average employee's stay with the company started being measured in months instead of years. Annual turnover has been around 50 percent or more at Wal-Mart in recent years, far greater than at better-paying competitors such as Costco and Home Depot. Profit sharing means little to workers who stay eight or fifteen months.)

Gender discrimination has also been an ongoing problem at Wal-Mart since its founding, although it took many years for publicity and lawsuits to catch up with Walton's good-old-boy ways. When the company finally began to take heat for paying women less for doing the same work as men and for putting few women in leadership positions, Walton made a bold gesture: he picked up the phone and called a woman who was then a leading attorney in his home state of Arkansas. "They tell me I have to have a woman on the board," he said. "Do you want to be her?" Hillary Clinton, the wife of Arkansas governor (and future president) Bill Clinton, said yes, and the future U.S. senator served for six years as the first woman on the board and in Walton's all-male, all-southern conservative inner circle. However, little else was done for the next decade to correct what critics and some former employees call a long-standing practice of paying women less than men for the same work and promoting far more men to management positions despite women workers' overall superior performance reviews. The company still faces a mammoth class-action lawsuit on behalf of up to 1.6 million female workers—the largest civil rights lawsuit in U.S. history.[12]

Clinton's tenure on the Wal-Mart board of directors marked a short-lived, small-scale environmental awakening at Wal-Mart when she asked to be appointed to the board's then-ineffectual environmental advisory committee. She focused on policies to increase recycling, pushing suppliers to use greener packaging and building more energy efficiency into new store architecture. At her behest, Wal-Mart came up with a test case: it would instruct deodorant makers to change their packaging. In that era, every can or bottle of deodorant was sold inside a cardboard box, which added cost, took up additional shelf space, and made the product more expensive to make and ship. But why? Why put an essentially unbreakable plastic bottle or a metal can inside a flimsy paperboard box? No one had a good answer. And because it was Wal-Mart asking, and given that Wal-Mart sold more deodorant than any other retailer, the manufacturers killed the box. Not just for Wal-Mart but industrywide. Deodorants have come without the redundant packaging ever since. Millions of dollars, water, energy, and whole forests have been saved as a result. The change wasn't only green; it allowed Wal-Mart to do what it does best: lower prices and sell more deodorant. Twelve years before Jib Ellison met Lee Scott, Wal-Mart had a perfect demonstration of how environmentalism and the bottom line could mesh.

But it led nowhere. Clinton left the board in advance of her husband's successful run for president in 1992, and the opportunity faded; no one else seemed interested in taking up her environmental cause or in building on the obvious business case for green. That was not the Wal-Mart way, not then. Instead, the deodorant box became just another example of Wal-Mart putting the squeeze on its suppliers to do its bidding and cut costs.

WHEN SAM WALTON GAVE up his CEO spot in 1988 and turned the company over to his second in command, David Glass, Wal-Mart had $16 billion in annual revenues. The company's greatest growth lay ahead—as did its greatest image problems. The Mr. Sam era ended when Walton died in 1992 at age seventy-four, a month after receiving the Presidential Medal of Freedom from George H. W. Bush.

Glass and his protégé, Lee Scott, were not the natural-born merchants and motivators that Mr. Sam had been. They were not evangelists who could deliver a fervent Wal-Mart cheer without the least bit of embarrassment. Their attention was drawn to the back office—to logistics, inventory control, data centers, and the largest private satellite communications system in the world. This technology, it turned out, was what Wal-Mart needed to take it to the next level of retail dominance. During Glass's twelve years as CEO, revenues rose by an order of magnitude, from $16 billion when Walton left to $165 billion in Glass's final year, while Wal-Mart's stock price rose by 1,100 percent (which meant that stock bought at the start of Glass's tenure and sold the day he left would have generated an average return of 30 percent a year). The number of Wal-Mart stores worldwide topped three thousand on Glass's watch as the supercenter model emerged, combining supermarket, department store, auto shop, hardware store, and electronics warehouse under one gargantuan roof. Glass was celebrated as a leading CEO of his era, the first retailer in history to make after-tax profits in excess of $1 billion.

On one front, however, he proved to be a disaster for Wal-Mart: public relations. Glass's tenure saw Wal-Mart take its first serious hit to its image—one from which it never fully recovered, because it forever replaced the friendly, folksy image of Mr. Sam with what seemed to be a profound corporate callousness. The story broke in December 1992, just a few months after Walton's death, when the NBC-TV news show *Dateline NBC* reported finding foreign-made goods being sold at Wal-Mart stores on racks labeled "Made in the USA." A *Dateline NBC* crew posing as American buyers filmed a clothing factory in Bangladesh where apparel was being made for Wal-Mart in what appeared to be sweatshop conditions, with children doing the work for a nickel to eight cents an hour. The news program accused Wal-Mart of promoting its image of supporting American businesses and delivering domestic goods to customers even while pursuing the lowest price possible by importing from overseas factories with abhorrent working conditions.

"What we saw were three floors full of children . . . some as young as nine and ten . . . making clothes for Wal-Mart," *Dateline NBC* reporter Brian Ross told viewers. On-screen, viewers could see children making men's shirts for a Wal-Mart brand called "Jeans Wear." Ross reported that the children claimed to have been abused, forced to work past midnight, and paid only twelve to twenty dollars a month. One twelve-year-old girl, out of earshot of factory supervisors, begged a Bangladesh human rights worker who accompanied the film crew to come back the following day and rescue her.[13]

Walton had come up with a "Buy American" program to appeal to customers' patriotism. It had been one of the company's most successful marketing campaigns, but the slogan was losing meaning as Wal-Mart's low-price mission made outsourcing inevitable. Wal-Mart, as much as any company and more than most, drove American jobs and dollars overseas, where goods were far cheaper, wages a fraction of those in the United States, and environmental and health standards essentially nil. Still, the "Buy American" campaign remained in place, an inviting target for a journalistic exposé.

Dateline contrasted its child labor and sweatshop footage with film of a North Carolina sweater factory that had been touted in a Wal-Mart "Buy American" ad campaign but that went out of business a year after the ad in the face of cheap overseas competition. Footage secretly filmed at a dozen Wal-Mart stores depicted racks of foreign-made clothing hung beneath "Made in the USA" signs (although the actual clothing labels correctly indicated the apparel's true overseas origins).

Shown video from the Bangladesh factory during an interview with Ross, Glass appeared unprepared for the onslaught of damaging information. According to Ross, the factory that Wal-Mart had chosen as a supplier in Bangladesh was notorious even by that country's weak standards. It had recently been hit by a fire that had killed twenty-five workers, many of them children, who could not escape because they had been locked in. When he finally responded, Glass sought to dismiss the footage as irrelevant. "There are tragic things that happen all over the world," he observed. Ross, who seemed surprised by this cold response, asked, "That's all you have to say about it?"

"I don't know what else I would say about it." At that point, Glass's public relations handler stopped the interview and the CEO walked out.[14]

Two weeks later, with ample time to prepare, Glass invited *Dateline NBC* back to resume the interview—and only compounded his earlier gaffe by saying that the images of child laborers "mean nothing to me." He then asserted that he had dispatched an employee to Bangladesh to visit the same factory and could find no evidence of child labor there. When Ross expressed skepticism, Glass added, "You and I might perhaps define children differently."[15]

Wal-Mart stock prices fell even before the show aired. Company spokesmen—not Glass—picked up the PR ball at that point, attacking the *Dateline NBC* report as sensational, misleading, and overblown, since most of the goods sold at Wal-Mart at that time were still American-made. But Wal-Mart didn't dispute the key points made in the *Dateline NBC* report, namely that the "Made in the USA" signs had been inaccurate, for which Wal-Mart apologized. Wal-Mart also conceded that the company's imports were on the rise (within a decade, more than 60 percent of Wal-Mart's products would come from China alone).

The similar Kathie Lee Gifford sweatshop scandal created an even greater uproar in 1996, when morning show TV host Gifford's line of Wal-Mart clothing was exposed as being produced in part by child laborers in Honduras making thirty-one cents an hour.[16] Other Gifford clothing came from an illegal New York sweatshop. Wal-Mart again claimed it had no knowledge of any abuses, but this time the company did not downplay the allegations or accuse investigators of sensationalism. Instead, it promised to address the problems and expressed concern for mistreated workers and children. No one tried to parse the definition of "child." Wal-Mart also knew better to than to put Glass out there again. This time, it was a vice president of merchandising who dealt with the public relations crisis, and Lee Scott handled his first crack at national exposure far better than his boss. Positioning the company as the victim of unscrupulous suppliers, Scott vowed to step up Wal-Mart's in-house inspections of foreign manufacturers to avoid sweatshops and child labor abuses.

"If there's child labor, we immediately terminate doing business with those people," Lee Scott promised. And his personal stock at Wal-Mart rose right along with the stock price.

Like Glass, Scott was a technology guy at heart. He had become a star at Wal-Mart by revolutionizing the company's trucking and logistics operation. He rebuilt the company's inventory management system, creating computer links with manufacturers that fed them constant sales updates, enabling them to fulfill small, frequent orders. With this new technology, Wal-Mart could keep its inventories lean and efficient and avoid paying for excess goods just to sit in warehouses. Scott's new approach squeezed out $2 billion in inventory savings in two years' time, creating efficiencies that other major companies had been trying to achieve for more than a decade. It became, in effect, the suppliers' job to make sure there were enough toothpaste and detergent and garden shears headed to the retail giant's shelves, a classic Wal-Mart triumph of giving manufacturers more to do while paying them less.

But while Glass could stay out of the public eye for much of his tenure and spend most of his energy growing the business—except for his ill-fated turn on *Dateline NBC*—Scott did not have that luxury. Beginning shortly after he took over as CEO in 2000, what had been a trickle of damaging stories and missteps that undermined Wal-Mart's public image grew into a tidal wave of negativity that threatened the company's well-being. The transgressions of his predecessors had caught up with the company, and a drumbeat of bad news forced Scott to spend far more time on damage control than either of them ever had.

Pharmaceutical and food companies filed predatory pricing lawsuits against Wal-Mart. The state of Wisconsin sued the retailer, accusing it of trying to gain a monopoly on the state's huge dairy industry. Mexico and Germany also launched investigations of Wal-Mart's pricing practices, with the German courts actually ordering Wal-Mart to raise supermarket prices. After several appeals, Wal-Mart ended up selling its German stores, which was probably for the best, as Wal-Mart Culture had never gone over very well in Deutschland. It was common for German employees to hide in the bathrooms to avoid performing the Wal-Mart cheer.

Shortly after taking over as CEO, Scott was embarrassed by revelations of Wal-Mart's scorched-earth litigation tactics, in which the corporation routinely abused the legal "discovery" process by hiding evidence and refusing to comply with court orders.[17] This legal misbehavior had led judges to sanction Wal-Mart on sixty different occasions between 1997 and 2000. One case involved a woman who was raped in a Wal-Mart parking lot and whose suit sought to show that the company had been aware of parking lot dangers but had done nothing; Wal-Mart lawyers failed to turn over an internal report that seemed to support her point, as it showed that 80 percent of crime at Wal-Mart, aside from shoplifting, occurred in parking lots. A state judge in Beaumont, Texas, threatened to fine the company $18 million for a "corporate policy of deliberately obstructing and thwarting the legitimate ends of the discovery process." Wal-Mart's lawyer made a public apology, while Scott promised reforms. "I don't think we should allow the public to think we would ever have done something that wasn't honest or true."[18]

At Wal-Mart's 2003 annual shareholder meeting, when Scott wanted to discuss his groundbreaking meetings with the president of China, by then Wal-Mart's most important trading partner, he instead had to respond to more bad publicity over labor practices. A flurry of new lawsuits had been filed alleging discrimination, unpaid overtime, and other illegal employment practices. Wal-Mart spokesmen had at first denied the allegations. But then Scott announced the creation of a Wal-Mart office of diversity, a plan to protect gay workers from workplace discrimination, and a pledge to promote women in the same proportions in which they apply for management jobs (along with weeding out old-guard types who opposed reform).

The bad-news onslaught just kept coming. In October 2003, federal agents raided sixty-one Wal-Mart stores in twenty-one states in a crackdown on illegal immigrant workers. Two hundred fifty undocumented night-shift workers were rounded up, and although the workers were employed by contractors rather than directly by Wal-Mart, a federal grand jury also received evidence about Wal-Mart executives.[19] Twelve janitorial firms were convicted of employing undocumented workers as Wal-Mart janitors. Prosecutors filed no charges against Wal-Mart after the company cooperated with investigators, instituted new hiring practices, and agreed to an $11 million settlement—a record amount, four times the previous highest payment in an illegal employment case.[20] Although Wal-Mart executives admitted no wrongdoing, the publicity inflicted yet more damage on the company. Critics began making unfavorable comparisons between Wal-Mart and its big-box competitor Costco, which had a thriving business while offering superior wages and benefits to its workers as well as coexisting with labor unions. More than 80 percent of Costco employees were covered by the company health plan, compared to less than half of Wal-Mart workers. Turnover at Wal-Mart was three times the rate at Costco. But the kicker was that, despite better wages and benefits, Costco made more profit per employee than Wal-Mart's Costco competitor, Sam's Club: $13,677 versus $11,039 in 2004.[21]

Scott responded by announcing improved health benefits for Wal-Mart workers and threw his support behind legislation to raise the minimum wage—a reversal of Mr. Sam's long-standing hostility to wage laws. But an internal memo leaked to the press soon undermined Scott's moves: the revelation that 46 percent of the children of company workers either lacked health insurance or received medical care from state welfare programs.[22] Wal-Mart's low prices, in other words, were costing taxpayers. Welfare costs rose measurably when Wal-Mart came to town.

The memo also showed that the improvements to Wal-Mart's health care plan could be illusory for many workers. Though it was true that some would pay less per month for benefits, the savings were offset by large deductibles that many workers couldn't afford. The Wal-Mart memo seemed particularly callous for its suggestion that the company could cut its health care costs further by weeding out overweight or physically unfit workers in sedentary positions, such as cashiers, by assigning them some sort of additional, physically demanding tasks.

Wal-Mart and Scott also took heat for an epic grocery store strike that crippled Southern California's three major supermarket chains from October 2003 to February 2004. The region's 70,000 supermarket union workers walked out to protest cuts in wages and benefits that the supermarket chains imposed in anticipation of competition from Wal-Mart, which had announced plans to open forty new Southern California supercenters. After five months of picketing, the union caved and accepted a two-tiered system in which new hires got lower wages and benefits than workers hired before the strike. The Public Policy Institute of California quantified this effect with a research paper suggesting that the presence of Wal-Mart stores tended to depress wages in a region by 5 percent.[23]

Environmental groups, meanwhile, attacked Wal-Mart for its

sprawling stores, for building in sensitive habitats, and for its air and water pollution. Stores were constructed on Native American burial grounds in California and Tennessee and next to one of the great archaeological treasures of Mexico, the pyramids at Teotihuacán, leading to massive protests. In 2004, officials fined the company $3.1 million for illegal pollution at twenty-four construction sites in nine states where it had failed to install runoff controls or obtain proper permits. It had settled a similar case brought by the U.S. Environmental Protection Agency in 2001 for $5.5 million. Again in 2004, the company settled another case for $400,000 for air pollution violations in eleven states. Wal-Mart was branded a "serious statewide polluter" and "an environmental law breaker" by the Connecticut attorney general, who charged eleven of the state's sixteen stores with water pollution violations that threatened sensitive wetlands and drinking water supplies.

With each new allegation and revelation of poor labor and environmental practices, Wal-Mart's response grew more defensive. The company tended either to ignore the substance of the latest allegations or to attack the messenger. In Connecticut, it sent videos to home owners suggesting that Wal-Mart stores were protecting sensitive wetlands rather than polluting them, damaging the company's credibility in the affected communities. This pattern escalated when two watchdog groups with slick Web sites and support from labor and environmental organizations—Wal-Mart Watch (www.walmartwatch. com) and WakeUpWalMart.com—became hubs of less-than-flattering information on the company, infuriating Wal-Mart's leaders. The sites provided regular fodder for mainstream media reports by aggregating information on Wal-Mart lawsuits, testimony, audits, and internal documents. WakeUpWalMart.com instigated a teachers' union boycott of back-to-school sales at Wal-Mart; Wal-Mart Watch used automated calls to reach 10,000 Arkansas households in search of Bentonville whistle-blowers.

The negative press reached a crescendo in the spring of 2004, when the Los Angeles City Council blocked construction of a new Wal-Mart supercenter. These 200,000-square-foot behemoths can, with parking, occupy up to 30 acres of land, enough to accommodate a modern professional football stadium. Wal-Mart, which felt it could not allow such a slap-in-the-face precedent to stand, turned to the economically depressed city of Inglewood, a municipal island in the midst of L.A. The company sponsored a ballot initiative asking Inglewood residents to approve the supercenter directly, without seeking City Council approval. The company spent nearly $1 million to promote the referendum, arguing that a supercenter would bring jobs, tax revenue, and low prices to where they were needed most. A coalition of community leaders, small-business owners, ministers, and labor unions took a much dimmer view, warning residents that Wal-Mart would drive local merchants out of business, depress wages, and snarl traffic. Wal-Mart lost by a wide margin, with 60 percent of voters saying no to a Wal-Mart supercenter.

At first, Scott's reaction was dismissive, brushing off the vote as insignificant to the Wal-Mart juggernaut: "It's a single store." He spoke at a Los Angeles Town Hall forum after the election and sounded defiant, accusing critics—principally unions and "our high priced competitors"—of trying to confuse the public in a way intended to undermine "the future of American capitalism."[24]

This was in keeping with his earlier, sometimes derisive observations about Wal-Mart opponents: "You have someone who says, 'My vision of the world does not include a large retail store—it is small shops with lots of trees out front and little parking spaces and individual owners.' That may be a nice dream," Scott said. "Unfortunately, the most efficient form of retailing is in fact the supercenter where the cost is driven out of the process. If you are a working person—if you are one of the twenty percent of Wal-Mart's U.S. customers who don't even have a checking account and you live paycheck to paycheck—that vision of the world [of small shops] may not be one that you can afford. If you are a working person and you need to save money, Wal-Mart is a great thing for you."[25]

But then, with other communities emboldened to repeat Inglewood's stand—Chicago and New York also said no to Wal-Mart—Scott sometimes sounded more contrite, less defensive, and even apologetic for trying to sidestep the City Council in Inglewood. "In doing that, we came across as a bully who would get their way regardless."[26] This humbling admission from Scott was probably the most effective response to negative press he had made in a long time. And it presaged a change in Wal-Mart's approach, a transformation that came in two parts.

The first was the realization by Scott and the rest of the Wal-Mart leadership that they had done a poor job of telling Wal-Mart's story. So Scott hired the international public relations firm Edelman Worldwide to create a political campaign–style war room to provide rapid responses to all criticism and media stories on the company. Running the war room were two Washington heavy hitters, Leslie Dach, a veteran Democratic strategist, environmental lobbyist, and one of Bill Clinton's advisers during the Republican campaign to impeach him (Dach would go on to become Wal-Mart executive vice president for corporate affairs and government relations, overseeing and expanding the company's sustainability efforts), and former Ronald Reagan adviser Michael K. Deaver, the mastermind behind Reagan's "Teflon" image. They set up shop in an old conference room at the home office and the area was dubbed "action alley," the name normally given the main walking aisle that rings every Wal-Mart store. The war room's first assignment was to prepare for the late-2005 debut of a documentary from the filmmaker Robert Greenwald, *Wal-Mart: The High Cost of Low Price*. Heavily promoted on the Internet, the scathing indictment of Wal-Mart's business practices had gotten under the skin of Lee Scott and the Wal-Mart leadership as nothing else ever had. The new war room put out a ten-page press release debunking the alleged errors in the *trailer* for the documentary.

Wal-Mart had never employed such political spinners to safeguard its image. Mr. Sam would have thrown a fit at the cost. But those were desperate times. The damage had gone way beyond mere reputation:

Wal-Mart's stock price had fallen by 27 percent between 2000, when Scott took over, and 2005.

Meanwhile, worrisome customer survey figures on Wal-Mart's image assembled by McKinsey & Company management consultants in an August 2004 memo had shaken Scott badly:

- 54 percent of consumers believe that Wal-Mart's business practices are "too aggressive."
- 82 percent of Wal-Mart customers expect the company to "act like a role model for other businesses."
- 2 to 8 percent of Wal-Mart customers had stopped shopping at Wal-Mart because of "negative press they have heard." That represented as many as 14 million shoppers who had turned to competitors every week because they were upset by Wal-Mart's reputation.[27]

The memo drove part two of Wal-Mart's and Lee Scott's response to the image issue—and that part was far more revolutionary than hiring spin doctors. McKinsey had argued with surprising vigor that its survey suggested that, to protect its reputation, its brand, and its customer base, Wal-Mart needed to do more than just good PR. It had to do good, period. The consultants told the world's biggest retailer to "take public leadership on broader societal issues" through its enormous clout and resources: "Take a proactive stance: shape the external debate by becoming a role model on a significant societal issue."

It was, in a way, an old-fashioned idea, one that evoked one of Mr. Sam's old saws: if only everyone at Wal-Mart lived by the Golden Rule, there'd never be anything negative said about the company. McKinsey was reminding Wal-Mart that the best way to have a good reputation is to do something really good. Something big. Something that was about more than selling a DVD player for nine bucks less than the closest competitor.

Was it a selfish motive, rather than altruism, that drove what happened next, a desire for the bad press to end and the stock prices to stop tumbling? Was it just a defensive move to quiet the critics? Maybe so, at least at first. Even Scott admits it—he says he was in a defensive mode at the time, feeling besieged. Scott had paid good money for the McKinsey recommendations, and the consultants had offered up a strong case that strengthening the business required Wal-Mart to take on a major project for the public good. It could have been health care. It could have been education. It could have been a great many things.

As luck would have it, that was when Lee Scott met Jib Ellison, a river guide with impeccable timing.

CHAPTER THREE

The CEO Whisperer

Whipcord thin, disdainful of suits and ties, and a born campfire storyteller (but for his fondness for philosophical digression), Jib Ellison has a desire, a need really, to be outdoors for significant parts of his life. Too much desk time, too many business meetings, and his mind and muscles rebel. The button-down execs tolerate his casual look, that of a nicely outfitted backpacker who just stumbled off the trail and into the boardroom. It fits their stereotype of the tree-hugger crowd. But any smugness fades when it becomes clear Ellison speaks the language of CEOs, too, and even knows a thing or two about their businesses that they don't, like the awful gas mileage their fleets of trucks get or the money wasted on oversized packaging that not only is bad for the environment but chews up seven figures that otherwise would fall into the profit column every month.

One time a Wal-Mart electronics buyer, encouraged by Ellison, visited a computer assembly plant in Taiwan. There were two separate lines of laptops rolling out of the plant, one bound for Europe, the other for the United States and Wal-Mart's shelves. The sleek portable computers were identical in performance and appearance, differing only in one significant way: the European laptops, thanks to strict EU regulations, had been made without toxins, heavy metals, and other potentially harmful substances. The U.S.-bound laptops were far less green, comparatively stuffed with toxic chemicals—which is why disposal of old computers, cell phones, and other electronics was for years a far greater environmental problem in the United States than in Europe.

The rationale for weaker U.S. regulations has always been cost: stricter regulations would make the laptops more expensive, and American companies would suffer. But the rationale was a sham, Ellison later observed; the cost of the two laptops was the same. The Wal-Mart buyer had never visited the plant before, had never revisited the commonsense idea he had taken as cold, hard fact: that the Europeans were jacking up costs with all their environmental regulations and controls and that the only sensible business decision was to buy the unregulated models. Finally, he pointed at the European laptops, the nontoxic ones. "Can we get those instead?" he asked.

The plant manager said sure. And not only that, but because of the inherent efficiencies of consolidating two lines into one, the cost of the laptops for everyone would come down a bit. Retailers would make more money and could offer the laptops at a lower price. Environmental good and Wal-Mart's low-price mission were, here at least, aligned. Blu Skye Sustainability Consulting had a convert within the Wal-Mart rank and file.

WHATEVER UNIQUE INSIGHTS BLU Skye and its consultants offer corporate America, they begin not with stock market wizardry, bean-counting aplomb, marketing magic, or cost-cutting regimes—the more typical purview of corporate consultants—but with Ellison's personal affinity for nature and his experiences on the wild rivers of the world. That's where such concepts as "waste stream" and "carbon footprint" cease being abstractions. They become starkly visible in the plastic debris washed up on sandy banks, the retreating snows that barely dust once icebound peaks, the fish that vanish from once-pristine streams because of rising water temperatures that allow diseases and parasites to flourish. For Ellison, the science of climate change and the grim news it has brought to light in this new century have provided less a revelation and more a confirmation of what his senses have long told him.

Ellison grew up in the 1970s in Mill Valley, California, just over the Golden Gate Bridge from San Francisco, a former mill town surrounded by state, federal, and local parkland and near the edge of the redwoods of Muir Woods, living monuments to Sierra Club founder John Muir. The town had a rich environmentalist, artistic, and countercultural history, with such celebrated figures as John Lennon, Jerry Garcia, Janis Joplin, Bonnie Raitt, Jack London, and Jack Kerouac calling it home at one time or another. The lawsuit that opened Little League Baseball to girls was won in 1974 on behalf of nine-year-old Jenny Fuller of Mill Valley. Mill Valley's Tamalpais High School (where portions of the coming-of-age film *American Graffiti* were shot) considered itself a bastion of activism in Ellison's time there, though it was not the groundbreaking ecology center that garnered national headlines but its first-in-the-nation condom distribution program. If ever a town encouraged thinking outside the box, Mill Valley, circa the 1970s, was it.

In the summer of 1978, the seventeen-year-old Ellison started working summers for a nearby river outfitter, Whitewater Voyages. By his early twenties, he had become a top river guide, leading expeditions throughout the state, nation, and world, pursuing the whitewater equivalent of the surfer's endless summer. With his friend and fellow guide Mike Grant, now principal and ranch manager for the Walker Creek Ranch Outdoor School in Marin County north of San Francisco, Ellison followed the rafting season from one hemisphere to the next, hopping from the Colorado and Kern Rivers in the American West to the Zambezi River in the southern African nation of Zambia. They had as much work as they cared to do, traveling with everything they needed or wanted stuffed inside a couple of waterproof bags. They were living the dream.

Contentment with this lifestyle did not, however, reflect a lack of larger ambitions. Ellison continued his studies when he wasn't on the river, pursuing an advanced degree through Oregon's Reed College in disciplines that fit an era in which the Cold War seemed eternal: philosophy and nuclear deterrence theory. Even then, he imagined using the strange power of a river trip to bond strangers for some higher purpose.

"Imagine putting Reagan and Gorbachev together in the same raft," he said to Grant one evening while camped on the Zambezi. "Imagine if we could bring them down the Grand Canyon together. Everything would change."

Grant nodded and smiled, thinking that putting the presidents of the United States and the Soviet Union in a raft together would be cool—and impossible. But Ellison could not let the idea go. What about rafting trips in the Soviet Union and in America that would throw the leaders of tomorrow—students—together on white water? That would be the way to start.

And so the nonprofit Russians and Americans For Teamwork was born—Project RAFT. The simple idea called for sponsoring a combined American-Soviet rafting trip through Siberia that would mix students and young adults from both countries. The river adventure would help build understanding and friendship between the superpower adversaries. The rafters would be "citizen diplomats," a term that evolved in an era when professional diplomats seemed at a loss as to how to bring feuding nations back from the brink.

He soon found that obtaining permission for a relatively simple rafting expedition—something that, in the twenty-first century, would be arranged with a single call to a Moscow travel agent—was fraught with difficulties in that Cold War moment of Minuteman missiles and Backfire bombers. After months of fruitless phone calls and requests to U.S. and Soviet bureaucracies, Ellison forged a connection with a California teacher and filmmaker who had studied and taught in Russia, Cynthia Lazaroff. She had launched a first-of-its kind youth exchange program in which participants climbed mountains together in Siberia, and she put Ellison in touch with her contacts in the Soviet bureaucracy.

Not long after, a terse telex arrived from Moscow confirming that Ellison and fifteen other rafters had been invited to an expedition on the Katun River in Siberia, and that $1,000 per rafter had to be deposited in a Moscow bank immediately. The red tape had been brushed aside through the power of personal connections. Mike Grant still remembers how stunned he was when his friend walked up to him and waved the teletyped message as he said, "Hey, remember that idea about changing the world with river trips? Well, check this out."

Grant agreed to help lead the project, and he and Ellison, with no money, credit, or collateral of their own, began making fund-raising rounds to their rafting friends and clients, which by then included some major corporate figures. It went better than they expected. Ellison's vision seemed to have come at a propitious moment. The ice was breaking. Soviet President Mikhail Gorbachev, with his *perestroika* and *glasnost* ("restructuring" and "openness") reforms of the hidebound Communist system, was getting the sort of press in the West normally reserved for movie idols and sports champions. He was having fireside chats with Ronald Reagan less than four years after the U.S. president branded the Soviet Union the "evil empire," and the countries were engaged in promising and unprecedented talks of nuclear disarmament. After decades of distrust, doomsday clocks, and proxy wars, there suddenly appeared to be a defrosting of the Cold War in favor of diplomacy and cooperation—an opening for peace. Why not sail through that opening in a raft?

The group set out for Siberia in July 1987, with an interpreter and twelve fellow guides of diverse backgrounds and personalities. Uncertain of what they would find, they trusted that the river would work its magic. To Ellison's great surprise, the Russians turned out to be fearless experts at rafting treacherous rivers, and they did it with equipment unlike any he had ever seen. Their rafts used entirely hand-stitched fabrics and bladders. The Soviet life vests, if worn at all, were homemade. Paddles were made out of old street signs. The creativity with scraps and discards that would be considered trash back home blew him away. In America, rafting was commercialized; the gear was professionally manufactured, available in stores across the country, along with guides and packaged vacations—an entire economy revolving around the growing sport. Ellison realized that it was the supposedly regimented and bland Communist country that had produced rafts that were statements of individuality, ingenuity, and sustainability, while the American equipment displayed the brilliant, functional sameness of mass production.

Amid welcoming toasts of the ever-present and all-occasion glasses of vodka, the two groups plunged onto the frigid, turbulent river, mixing up crews and rafts, sharing the experience, sharing stories as they traversed a wilderness that was not at all the wasteland Americans expect when they hear the word "Siberia." No foreigners in living memory had been permitted to make a river trip through this stunning landscape of mountains, glaciers, and steppe. Both groups of rafters had spent a lifetime hearing all manner of propaganda about the other. But on the river the differences seemed insignificant, matters of politics and geography but not of the heart and soul, as they shared snapshots of family members and told stories of their homes and their river adventures. Several times they were welcomed into small rural villages to meet the elders. Once a grizzled World War II veteran emerged to greet them with food and vodka and to say he had met Americans before, near the end of a conflict in which no country suffered greater loss of life than the Soviet Union. "I always knew we'd be allies again," he proclaimed as he toasted the visitors.

By the end of the week, the rafters from both countries embraced the idea of a series of youth exchanges alternating between Siberia and the United States. They would bring the young leaders of tomorrow to work together on the river, then send them back home to spread the word, in the belief that the only real cure for national enmity is individual friendship and understanding. All they needed was permission.

Ellison tried to go through channels again, but when that failed, he resorted to crashing a reception in San Francisco for Alex Khokhlov, the head of a major Soviet youth group, where he dropped the name of a mutual friend and then made his pitch.

"We don't do this in Russia," Khokhlov told him after listening to Ellison's Project RAFT spiel. "But I like the light in your eyes. We will do it."

The following year, Ellison returned home from the first student exchange rafting trip to unexpectedly intense media interest in the project, as well as a deluge of applications for the next expedition. "What we're doing is not an abstraction," Ellison told the *Los Angeles Times*.[1] "We're not some foundation that sits around and writes a paper about teamwork. This *is* teamwork."

The *Times* article's enthusiastic coverage of Project RAFT suggested that Ellison had succeeded in part because so many people considered it an inspired idea, even though it was scoffed at initially as a dreamer's impractical idealism. But the reporter also noted the other key element of Project RAFT's success: Ellison's "almost unbelievably lucky timing." It would not be the last time such an observation would be made about Ellison's ideas, their unexpected impact—or their fortuitous timing.

PROJECT RAFT CONTINUED FOR six years, expanding its mission after the Berlin Wall came down in 1989 to include more than thirty countries, including expeditions and exchanges with Japan, Germany, Costa Rica, Turkey, and Zimbabwe. By then the cross-cultural river discussions had moved beyond Cold War divisions and arms control to include the global concerns of poverty, hunger, dwindling water supplies, and threats to the environment. Huge multinational river rallies were held in Russia and surrounding countries, sister-city partnerships were forged between East and West, and Project RAFT crews made ten "first descents" of wild rivers that had never been rafted before.

By the time Ellison reached age thirty, he had achieved a reputation as one of the top river rafters in the world, a "paddler of the century" in the view of the sport's main journal, *Paddler* magazine.[2] He had also built a network of current and former corporate chiefs who had supported Project RAFT with donations and who had sought him out for their own river expeditions. Among them were Doug Tompkins, the cofounder and CEO of Esprit, the fashion powerhouse of the 1980s, and Peter Buckley, CEO of Esprit-Europe, who had made one of the first substantial donations to Project RAFT. They had hired Ellison to lead company-sponsored rafting trips, and they continued the relationship even after each man had sold his interests in Esprit and turned his fortunes toward environmental activism and philanthropy. Tompkins, who would end up buying and preserving more South American rain forest than anyone else on the planet, was part of an informal and somewhat wild group of ageless outdoorsmen and environmentalists who called themselves the "Do Boys," and he convinced Ellison to join them on an expedition to see Siberian tigers that morphed into a wild river float through the vast Bikin River watershed in the Russian Far East. The group's numbers included former NBC anchorman Tom Brokaw; the founder of Patagonia, Yvon Chouinard; and the mountain climber and filmmaker Rick Ridgeway, who filmed a Project RAFT expedition for ABC and would later become Patagonia's vice president of environmental initiatives.[3] They reached the Bikin only after one of the Do Boys bribed an Aeroflot helicopter crew to fly four hours off their approved flight plan, then drop them in the wilderness. They soon encountered a group of tribesmen who fed them a stew pot of moose liver and steak in exchange for Brokaw's fifth of Scotch before sending them onward in the right direction.

Project RAFT by then had grown to six employees and had opened an office in northern California's East Bay, but its founders sensed that it was time to move on. In part, this was because the river guides were older and were thinking about families, mortgages, and "real jobs" that offered a bit more security than the beans-and-rice existence of Project RAFT. But also there was a sense that they needed a new mission. "We ended the Cold War," Grant and Ellison liked to joke, but they came to see that their efforts to build bridges between nations had included some naive assumptions. The nuclear arms race and the constant state of confrontation between the Soviets and the West that had dominated the last half of the twentieth century had been swept aside with a rapidity that could scarcely be believed, yet the former combatants had not turned any of their billion-dollars-a-day defense budgets toward solving the world's environmental and social problems, as the young Ellison had once confidently predicted. On the contrary, less was being done than ever to address these global crises, and the problems were worsening. Ellison had come to believe that engaging visionary business leaders and problem solvers such as Tompkins and Buckley could offer a better response to this inertia. But he was not sure how to proceed, beyond getting corporate leaders away from their offices and spreadsheets and out into nature—where they could see in person the impact that their businesses were having.

Ellison eventually went to work for Tompkins in Chile, using his paddling skills to penetrate remote areas of the Patagonian rain forest, where he would negotiate real estate deals with small landowners and squatters on behalf of Tompkins's park and wildlife refuge projects. He also had the chance to reconnect after many years with a former Esprit employee who had gone to work for the Tompkinses as an interior designer for their building projects. Ellison jokes that it took thirteen years to get a second date with her, but he and Marci fell in love and decided to marry, and they returned to the United States.

Back in the San Francisco Bay Area, Ellison parlayed two of his skills—handling corporate titans and leading expeditions—into a job with a corporate leadership development consultancy, Human Factors. The company specialized in teaching executives how to change corporate culture to foster innovation, teamwork, and communication. After several years, Ellison and three colleagues struck out on their own in 1998 to create a different sort of consultancy, which they called The Trium Group. They sought to combine traditional strategy consulting, aimed at helping businesses solve problems and manage crises, with the sort of leadership training and team building they had been doing at Human Factors. The new partners sensed a market opportunity because few if any consultancies at the time provided both services at once, although the two disciplines were a natural fit. They had come to believe that a flawed assumption was at work in the strategy business, that success would flow from a thoughtful set of goals and a plan to achieve them. Yet they had seen through their work at Human Factors that, at least half the time, companies failed to execute even the most brilliant plans. To the upstarts at Trium, the explanation seemed clear: new strategies take aim at symptoms, but they don't address the core failures of leadership, teamwork, and communication that get businesses into trouble in the first place. So why not do both?

Trium—the name was a made-up word that referred to the three principles they wanted to emphasize in their consultancy: strategy, leadership, and culture—billed itself as a small "boutique" firm. The San Francisco–based consultants began with a big breakthrough, however, when they landed the global cell phone giant Nokia as their first client. This opened the door to other, similarly prestigious accounts: Cisco, Oracle, eBay, Barclays Global Investors, Virgin Atlantic, and the World Bank. The four partners soon had twenty-five employees, and that total would eventually double.

In 2000, Home Depot hired Trium, and Ellison took charge of the account, as it was the firm's sole client with an environmentally themed agenda. The company needed help creating a program for obtaining and marketing wood certified as harvested in an environmentally responsible manner. This was a tall order but a huge opportunity for Trium: Home Depot had remade the hardware and home improvement business in the same way Wal-Mart had changed the retail landscape.

And, like Wal-Mart, Home Depot faced mounting pressure to address its enormous environmental footprint. As the world's largest retailer of wood products, Home Depot profited from the worldwide unsustainable timber harvests that had contributed to the loss of 50 percent of all rain forests since the end of World War II.[4] As the link between deforestation, climate change, and mass extinctions became clear, the pressure on Home Depot to change its ways had mounted.

Home Depot had first turned to an international environmental group known for its work on sustainability, The Natural Step, then hired Trium to turn the group's ecological ideas into a business strategy. Ellison's first task was to organize a series of meetings and planning sessions with Home Depot's top executives and the experts assembled by The Natural Step, bringing the two very different groups together to find common ground and get the company's leadership engaged and excited by a "green" project they might otherwise have seen as a boondoggle. He succeeded initially, all the way up to Home Depot cofounder and CEO Arthur Blank, who agreed with Ellison that the project could bring Home Depot new business and market opportunities as well as making it a much greener company.

The initiative was announced publicly as a breakthrough program for the home improvement chain. But Blank retired a short time later, and his successor, Robert Nardelli, whose controversial tenure would eventually lead to his being named one of the "Worst American CEOs of All Time" by the CNBC business network,[5] dropped the project in 2001 and with it Trium. (Nardelli, a former top executive at General Electric with no retail experience, would come under fire for, among other things, refusing to cut his enormous CEO stock package even as Home Depot's market share plummeted during his reign. He left in 2007 for a brief tenure at the helm of Chrysler, which turned down a $750 million emergency government loan for the ailing automaker because it would have required an executive pay cut; the company went bankrupt a short time later.)[6]

Despite being short-circuited by the change of CEOs, his Home

Depot experience proved a turning point for Ellison. It had cemented his belief in the principles of The Natural Step, an obscure Swedish environmental organization and philosophy that changed the river guide's thinking about business and the environment.

THE NATURAL STEP HAD grown out of a Swedish cancer expert's research on the environmental causes of cancer but expanded into a nationwide program endorsed by the king of Sweden to make the country more sustainable. The key idea was that communities, companies, and whole countries need to live and work more within natural limits, extracting only those resources that nature can replenish and limiting harmful waste to amounts that nature can safely absorb.[7]

Out of curiosity, Ellison had sat in on a Natural Step lecture at Berkeley months before the Home Depot project began, and he was captivated. The lecture had ostensibly been about living sustainable, healthy lives by limiting pollution, waste, and resource exhaustion. But what Ellison heard beneath the rhetoric was a set of core principles that could just as well be applied to the worlds of commerce and industry—principles that zeroed in on factors that could harm profits just as much as they did nature: waste and inefficiency. It had never occurred to Ellison in all his years of corporate strategizing, but now it seemed clear: if you align your business with the principles of The Natural Step, eliminating waste, operating cleanly and efficiently, conserving rather than blindly consuming, your business will win. If you do it better, cheaper, faster, and cleaner, whether you're raising dairy cows, selling lumber, or building supercomputers, all other things being equal, you will win. Ellison calls this his "epiphany." It led him to volunteer as an adviser to The Natural Step, which in turn led to the Home Depot project.

As he saw it, The Natural Step was a more accurate way of seeing the world. Ellison started thinking of it as his "lens of sustainability" that, once you peer through it, changes your view permanently.

Through it you can see the business argument in favor of going green that had been staring everyone in the face since the dawn of the Industrial Revolution, an opportunity that almost no business leader was seizing.

Ellison was by no means the first to reach this conclusion. No less than the influential "father" of modern corporate strategy theory and consulting, Harvard University's Michael E. Porter, had written in 1991 of the "false dichotomy" between environmental protection and business competitiveness that long had prevented companies from seeing the economic advantages of going green.[8] The following year, the Swiss businessman Stephan Schmidheiny, founder of the World Business Council for Sustainable Development, coined the term "eco-efficiency" in his book *Changing Course: A Global Business Perspective on Development and the Environment* to describe how businesses can innovate, profit, and beat competitors by reducing pollution, substituting safe materials for hazardous ones, using energy wisely, and recycling materials.

The economic case behind these ideas was unassailable; logically, green practices that could add millions to any company's bottom line should have become the norm decades ago. Yet these ideas of the early 1990s failed to capture the imaginations of corporate titans or even medium-sized businesses. There were too many institutional and cultural barriers, too many ingrained false assumptions. Environmentalism and sustainability, business executives felt, meant complying with onerous regulations, not blazing new trails voluntarily. Timing undoubtedly played a role, too. When these ideas surfaced, the housing market was just getting pumped, the dot-com bust was still a bubble, gasoline was $1.13 a gallon, and a 1999 best-selling business book entitled *Dow 36,000* ludicrously (and, for many amateur investors, tragically) predicted that the Dow Jones Industrial Average would hit 36,000 in a few short years. Nobody outside the small circle of green niche businesses, the Patagonias and Seventh Generations of the world, was interested in talking about eco-efficiency.

But Jib Ellison understood timing, and the post-9/11 era of high oil prices, climate concerns, and struggling businesses seemed better suited for the logic of sustainability as a business strategy. With the right push, the right argument, the right company, and the right CEO, he believed the idea could catch fire. Had there been no leadership change, Home Depot might have launched a green revolution, Ellison believed. It didn't need articles or books or academic inquiries. It needed a champion, not outside looking in but at the top of a major corporation—the kind of corporation that hired Trium.

The next question for Ellison was what to do about it. Trium and its boutique business had been very good to him—he had never been so prosperous in his life. He had a family, a solid income, eighty-five beautiful acres near Healdsburg, California, in the rolling wine country of Sonoma County. He had a job that brought him into contact with bright and creative entrepreneurs and business leaders and sent him all over the world. And helping businesses succeed was a good in itself, a way of helping large numbers of people find prosperity, new jobs, new opportunities. But ultimately Ellison felt the lack of any socially uplifting or moral component in his work at Trium. The consultants would take on any client that needed their services and would just as soon work for an arms manufacturer as the Sierra Club. His work with Home Depot had reminded him that the component he cared so much about, environmental and social justice, was missing from his everyday work.

In 2003, he began trying to convince his partners that Trium should shift gears and start telling its clients that a sustainable business strategy could be the greatest business opportunity of the century. The consultants would do their leadership training and their business strategy as always, but the strategy they preached would focus on sustainability. Change is coming, Ellison argued—most of the world is in a state of denial, but the pressures of climate, peak oil, and rising energy costs will make fundamental change inevitable. For most businesses, that paradigm shift will be sudden, painful, surprising, and even catastrophic. That has always been the case with denial. World War II was almost lost because of it; President Franklin D. Roosevelt persuaded a reluctant Congress to maintain the military draft in the years before the war by only a single, crucial vote. A similarly epic turning point faces the business world today: those willing to embrace a "sustainability revolution" now will gain an enormous advantage in the future. "We can lead the way on this," Ellison told his Trium partners.

His partners were impressed. But they were not persuaded. They believed Ellison, like the apostles of eco-efficiency in the 1990s, was too far ahead of his time, too ambitious, and, perhaps, too idealistic. The type of high-flying corporations capable of paying the Trium Group seven-figure fees were not seeking green makeovers. The one big environmental job they had, Home Depot, had flopped. And there was little reason to believe in 2003, with a bad economy and a probusiness, antiregulation, antigreen administration in the White House, that this was going to change anytime soon. Switching gears from Trium's successful business model to one filled with uncertainties just didn't make sense to the partners. They told him, "Great passion, Jib. Noble idea. But too risky. Not our mission. Not our business."

Ellison's decision to part with Trium was complicated by the fact that he had a daughter and a mortgage and creature comforts to consider. Gone were the days of living the dream, when he could fit most everything he cared about in the back of his car. He had no idea if he could make a living as a sustainable business strategist. But then he figured the risk of backing down on the idea would be even greater. He would be taking this new course for his daughter, for the future she would inhabit, which he felt certain would not be a very pretty one if humanity's path did not soon change.

So Ellison took the plunge and left Trium. His colleagues wouldn't say it to his face, but Ellison knew they thought he was crazy. Maybe they were right. Or maybe, just maybe, he was onto something.

And then he got his meeting with H. Lee Scott, the CEO of

Wal-Mart, and he was in, against all odds and expectations. His old partners at Trium were astonished. They were happy for Ellison but stunned. They felt Ellison had been an effective consultant, insightful and inspiring to clients and coworkers alike, but he had never been Trium's rainmaker. It had been the other partners, for the most part, who had landed the big accounts. Yet Blu Skye's very first client was the biggest company in the world, capable of initiating a paradigm shift all on its own. And the company's CEO had just hired Jib Ellison to show him the way.

"Breathtaking," one of his Trium partners, Tom Miller, would later say. Miller had hired Ellison for that first consulting job years before at Human Factors, and would eventually work for him at Blu Skye. At that moment, though, all he could do was shake his head in wonder. "Really, we couldn't believe it. Before any of us, Jib saw that the time was right."

PART II

Bursting the Bubble

People, wake up! You've got a company that, if it were a country, it would be the twentieth biggest in the world, pledging to be the world's largest organic retailer, and to be carbon neutral. This is the fall of the Berlin Wall in sustainability. This is a complete sea change.

—HUNTER LOVINS[1]

CHAPTER FOUR

Doing the Math

Five years after Ellison's first meeting in Bentonville, Chris Anderson, the curator of the Technology, Entertainment, Design (TED) conference, would introduce Ellison's packed session in India with an admiring take on Blu Skye's work and impact: "If you want to change the world, take something powerful and nudge it."

Back in June 2004, however, more traditional and less optimistic strictures about nudging large and powerful things came to mind for Wal-Mart's newest consultant: *Let sleeping dogs lie. Don't poke the bear. What do you feed a nine-hundred-pound gorilla?* It was, Ellison thought, the ultimate be-careful-what-you-wish-for moment. He had landed the ultimate rainmaker of a client, a company that could literally redefine the retail industry (again) while at the same time putting the then-unknown Blu Skye on the map.

He knew he was going to have to feed that nine-hundred-pound gorilla something very tasty, very quickly, or his business would be finished before it got started. He had one shot to prove that all this happy talk about profit and planet could lead the company to the sweet spot where environmental commitment and rising stock prices go hand in hand. He needed to find the "low-hanging fruit," as he called it: simple, inexpensive, easily identified moves that would reduce waste and save money. Quick, clear victories would be the key to persuading skittish, risk-averse senior executives.

He found his first piece of low-hanging fruit in the form of a child's toy—or, rather, in the box the toy came in.

Like most major retailers, Wal-Mart hires manufacturers to produce a wealth of different products to be labeled with one of several house brands, which serve as cheaper alternatives to big, national, heavily advertised brands. Wal-Mart's line of toys bears the Kid Connection brand. One such toy was a car and truck set for three-year-olds that came from China in a red corrugated cardboard display box—that was several inches bigger than it really needed to be to hold the product. Nobody noticed until Ellison arrived and put out the word that he was looking for just this sort of packaging waste. Shrinking the boxes would not harm the product, detract from its display appeal, or affect the customer's experience. Indeed, the change would be imperceptible, unless you put the old and new boxes next to each other.

But when Wal-Mart did the math, the company found that the savings from this reduced package would be dramatic. The minor size reduction would allow a much greater number of toys to be boxed and loaded inside a single shipping container. The same number of toys could be shipped using 497 fewer shipping containers—the trailer-sized metal boxes used to haul goods around the globe. These changes led to $2.4 million in annual savings for shipping those toy trucks, which was significant for a low-margin retailer like Wal-Mart. The company would have had to sell $60 million worth of that toy to earn the same $2.4 million in profits. The smaller packaging would also mean that some four thousand fewer trees would have to be cut down for cardboard and about a million barrels of fuel oil would be saved due to the reduced shipping volume.

One toy, one minor adjustment, seemed inconsequential—but on Wal-Mart's scale, the collective impact was stunning.

"That got everyone's attention in a hurry," Ellison told Scott. "They were amazed. And the best part is, they kept asking: 'Why didn't we do this years ago?'"

That, more than anything else, was the question Ellison wanted to hear. The same people who were willing to fight in court against environmental groups and government regulation—who had come of age in a Wal-Mart run by a man who thought the minimum wage was a Communist plot—were looking at a voluntary restriction on their own product's packaging and wishing they had done it sooner. Then they started asking an even more important question: Where else can we do this?

ELLISON BELIEVED SUCH QUICK, simple wins would shift the retail giant's long-standing "race to the bottom," which focused on lowering prices by any means, to a "race to the top," in which the value of sustainable practices to shareholders and customers would improve not only Wal-Mart but whole industries. And this race-to-the-top idea, Ellison suggested to Scott, could be applied to all sorts of social issues bedeviling the company and the nation.

"If you really want to take on sustainability with a capital 'S,' it's not just the environment. It's health care, it's wages, it's ethical sourcing, it's globalization. Everything. A sustainable economy, a sustainable society."

"Yes," Scott said warily, "but let's start with the environment." Scott knew it was too late to limit Wal-Mart's "exposure" on the sorts of social issues Ellison suggested. The company already faced big lawsuits on labor practices and alleged discrimination; Scott was spending up to an hour a day with the lawyers. But environmental complaints and attacks had not reached such a crescendo in 2004, and Scott sensed more room to maneuver on green issues—to try something innovative and perhaps reduce the company's future risk.

Ellison's charge, then, was figuring out what sustainability could mean for Wal-Mart. What would happen if Wal-Mart went beyond greenwash and threw its manpower, resources, and intellectual capital into the effort? What would that look like? In effect, Ellison had license to use the biggest company in the world as a research lab and a test bed for sustainability on a global scale, the ultimate green initiative. But there were limits: he would have to make a business case for sustainability, rather than an environmental or philanthropic appeal, for every single move. The focus always had to be on how such a commitment would help Wal-Mart improve its bottom line in the present—and manage risk and uncertainty in the future. Wal-Mart wasn't going to adopt a new purpose, as Seventh Generation, a privately owned business with no shareholders to worry about, did when it defined its corporate mission: "To inspire a more conscious and sustainable world by being an authentic force for positive change." That meant that Seventh Generation could choose without hesitation sustainable materials over more profitable but less environmentally friendly alternatives and there would be no shareholders to carp when the company donated 10 percent of its profits every year to "organizations that work for positive change."

Wal-Mart, on the other hand, had shareholders and a board of directors to answer to, as well as a mission that demanded growth of the business and its stock price above all else. When Wal-Mart spent money on anything, it was all about ROI—return on investment—and sustainability would be no exception. So the company might experiment with solar panels or wind energy for a few stores, but as long as renewable energy could not compete on price with dirtier conventional options, Wal-Mart would never make a significant switch to green power, no matter how great the environmental benefits. "Even if they wanted to do everything right, they can't. They won't," Ellison would later observe. "The CEO would get thrown out on his haunches, and rightly so, because that's the way the rules of the game work right now."

Those rules set a formidable barrier for his sustainability ideas at Wal-Mart, but Ellison had a few things going for him that were out of the ordinary for other Wal-Mart contractors and consultants. First, his entrée into the home office was Rob Walton, the son of the

Wal-Mart founder, chairman of the board, and, not inconsequentially, the single largest Wal-Mart stockholder. When joined by other Walton family stockholders, he could control more than half the stock of the company. It was Walton who had been traipsing around the world's environmental hotspots with Peter Seligmann of Conservation International and who had just returned from one such expedition scuba diving in Costa Rica accompanied by his son and Stone Gossard, the guitarist for Pearl Jam. Gossard had been working with Conservation International to offset the greenhouse gas footprint of his band's world tours. It was after returning to Arkansas from that trip that Walton personally asked Scott to take the meeting with Ellison. As Lawrence Jackson, then executive vice president and chief people officer of Wal-Mart (he would be promoted the next year to CEO of global procurement) put it, "When fifty-one percent of your shareholders turn up on your doorstep one day and tell you to take a look at this, what would you do? . . . When he asks you to do something, you take it very seriously."[1]

So that gave Ellison clout. Then there was access. Normally, access to the CEO would be severely limited at a huge company like Wal-Mart. Not this time. One of his earliest conversations with Scott hit home the point that the only way the top executives within the company would accept sustainability as their personal responsibility, rather than foist it off on low-level subordinates, would be if Scott stayed directly and regularly involved. "You've got to own this, or it won't work," Ellison said. "The hardest part is getting the people who run the big lines of business, who have profit-and-loss responsibility, to think differently. Because once you think differently, you act differently."

Scott agreed, to the astonishment of his senior executives—the "direct reports" who answered to no one at Wal-Mart but the CEO. They included the head of the Wal-Mart Stores Division, the head of the Sam's Club warehouse membership stores, the CEO of Walmart .com, the CEO of procurement, the head of logistics—all the people who actually ran the company, powerful and busy and very, very skeptical. Yet Scott penciled in on his calendar an hourlong meeting once every week with Ellison. The subject: sustainability. No one else outside the company (and few, if any, inside) got an hour a week blocked out like that. The direct reports had no idea what was up at first, except that they were told to join Scott and Ellison every three months or so to report their progress on sustainability.

Doug McMillon, then the president and CEO of Sam's Club, recalled hearing about sustainability for the first time and thinking that Scott was giving him a job performance review. Lawrence Jackson recalls hating the meetings in the beginning, feeling his time was being wasted on some sideshow that had little to do with the real business of Wal-Mart, which was already consuming his life for sixty or more hours a week. He was not alone. But as Ellison knew, if Lee Scott was on board and backing up Blu Skye's agenda, no one could say no. They had to come to the meeting. And they had to listen.

SHORTLY AFTER HIRING BLU Skye, Scott called Andy Ruben, Wal-Mart's vice president for strategy (who as yet had no idea that his title was about to become vice president for strategy *and* sustainability), and told him to gather some data for someone named Jib Ellison who would be calling soon. Scott provided no explanation of who Ellison was or what he was doing at Wal-Mart, no intimation that a new environmental initiative was about to gear up. Ruben was simply told to get him a list of the codes that Wal-Mart used for its product departments in its stores (Department 10 was automotive, Department 40 was analgesics and upper respiratory, Department 82 was front-end impulse merchandising), along with information on two experimental "green" stores Wal-Mart had recently opened and a few assorted other bits of information.

Ruben, who was trained as an engineer and had worked as a strategy consultant in his native Chicago before coming to work for Wal-Mart in 2000, would be the first person at the company Ellison interviewed in depth. Like most Wal-Mart executives Ellison encountered, Ruben was skeptical about sustainability as a business strategy. In Ruben's experience, environmental programs were impediments, not assets. But as the months passed, working with Ellison started taking up 3 percent of his time, then 5 percent, then 10 percent, and suddenly he found himself reading Paul Hawken's 1993 book, *The Ecology of Commerce*, and finding resonance in the author's argument that corporations could and should restore and protect nature. He was soon converted to Ellison's view that enormous opportunities to realize Hawken's vision were there for the taking in the areas of waste and efficiency. Ruben became Wal-Mart's most ardent in-house supporter of the idea. He had, Ellison crowed, put on the lens of sustainability, and no matter how hard he might try, it would not come off. The two began working together like a pair of detectives, hunting for ways the company could cut waste, use less energy, or locate more sustainable products than those currently on the shelves.

They agreed that the key to convincing the rest of the company—from the executive suites to the midlevel managers to the rank and file who were in a position to point out waste and inefficiency at the grass roots level of the mammoth company—was to come up with a whole series of "quick wins." Kid Connection toys were a great start, but it would take much more for sustainability to become part of Wal-Mart Culture.

Figuring out what those quick wins might be, then convincing the company to pursue them, would end up requiring months of planning and buildup—a careful combination of exposure to new ideas and perspectives and an openness to outsiders that, despite Wal-Mart's size and global reach, was alien to the company's culture. Known in-house and industrywide as "the Bentonville Bubble," the company had a proclivity for ignoring critics, outside experts, and conventional wisdom. This had long been a source of strength for the company, stemming from Sam Walton's original decision to ignore the naysayers and to pursue his conviction that big discount stores could thrive in rural rather than urban settings. Lee Scott still speaks of simpler times when Wal-Mart was written off as a bunch of bumpkins in the Ozarks who could be left alone and who posed no threat to their competitors: "They ignored us, and we could focus on the core of our business."

The flip side of this inward focus was a kind of tunnel vision that left many in the home office incapable of accepting any criticism of Wal-Mart as constructive, and suspicious of outsiders bearing new ideas. This tendency was accentuated by the nature of the company leadership; most of the managers had risen through the ranks, having worked as hourly wage earners on the store floor. Though this meant that they had invaluable expertise as retailers and merchants, and no one knew better how to squeeze suppliers to lower costs to the bare minimum, they had little or no expertise when it came to sustainability: no one with training or experience in package design, fisheries management, waste management, or life-cycle assessment. Ellison would have to burst that bubble.

He started by hiring a former consulting colleague, Dave Sherman, who had cofounded a Virginia-based company called Sustainable Value Partners. He and Ellison put together a two-day "choice meeting" for Scott and twenty-five of the company's senior executives and rising stars. Peter Seligmann of Conservation International came to explain the environmental threats to the planet, why business as usual would accelerate the decline of nature and vital natural resources, and why that should matter to Wal-Mart. Company leaders listened to evidence in support of human-caused global warming, ocean acidification, the dangers of pesticides, and the rather horrifying consensus on the exhaustion of worldwide fisheries (90 percent of the large fish that inhabited the oceans at the start of the twentieth century were gone by the start of the twenty-first). The executives were invited to peruse the data on global energy use, economic and population growth, and the limits of natural resources and then to ask themselves: Can this way of life go on? Will business as usual even be possible in fifty years—or twenty, or ten? "Look at the numbers," Ellison told them. "What we're doing now is not sustainable."

Armed with data from the Union of Concerned Scientists that

described the environmental impact of 134 kinds of products, Sherman used sales figures to create rough estimates of the greenhouse gas emissions, water use, land use, air pollution, and water pollution for almost every Wal-Mart product sold. These "back of the envelope" calculations sufficed for getting started, although more exacting data would be sought later.

Several things became clear in Sherman's numbers. First, Wal-Mart's direct environmental footprint of its stores—the energy, land use, and transportation everyone thought of as Wal-Mart's footprint—represented less than one-tenth of its overall impact. Ninety percent of its impact on the planet came from its supply chain—the companies that sell the goods that Wal-Mart puts on its shelves. So any meaningful sustainability initiative would have to involve Wal-Mart's suppliers early on.

To make clear how important he considered this first meeting on sustainability, Scott told his top executives to shut down their laptops and cell phones. He argued that they needed to accept that Wal-Mart's future, its license to do business, was at stake. Still, he wasn't going to make it easy on the environmentalist. "Tell me why I should care about some endangered mouse in Arizona when I just want to build a store," he asked at one point. And Seligmann told him: about endangered species, about habitat protection, about ecosystems and how the loss of seemingly insignificant species can throw whole chains of life and interdependency into catastrophic failure mode, just as removing a few rivets from an airplane wing may not cause a crash—until you remove one too many. Destroy that species of mouse, and other animals who preyed on it may perish, soil in which the creatures burrow will no longer be aerated and will thus become infertile, invasive species of plants that were previously held in check might flourish, parasites that had once been eaten might run wild. Nature is hardy, but balances are delicate. Choices about building, design, location, and landscaping can make a huge difference—and not just for an endangered mouse but for Wal-Mart's bottom line.

Think about sustainability this way, the Wal-Mart executives were told: Your company generates a huge amount of waste, 9,000 tons of it daily in the United States alone: food waste, cardboard, plastic. Right now, the company pays people to haul most of it away. Some is recycled, the rest is put into a landfill, a growing environmental problem. That is the opposite of sustainability. The more sensible approach would be, first, to reduce the waste by making packaging and processing more efficient and, second, to recognize that the waste has value that can be recaptured instead of dumped in a landfill: recycled plastic, recycled paper, food waste used to make energy or compost. If Wal-Mart were sustainable, it would be *making money* from its waste, not paying to deal with it. That got their attention.

At the end of that first, two-day "choice meeting," Scott told his executives that Wal-Mart faced a decision: They could continue fighting the environmentalists and getting bad press and saying that the planet's deterioration was not Wal-Mart's problem—that it was not our responsibility, not part of our core business. Or they could do what the environmentalists and Ellison had suggested and take on a leadership role in sustainability. Couldn't Wal-Mart, which thought itself the most efficient company on the planet, find a way to turn sustainability into an opportunity for competitive advantage? Lee Scott's appeal came down to this: If anyone can do it, Wal-Mart can.

The vote was unanimous. They'd go for it.

NEXT, ELLISON WENT ABOUT recruiting evangelists in the company for his cause. He enjoys telling people that one of Blu Skye's core competencies is designing meetings. He smiles wryly, knowing how it sounds, knowing that the very word "meeting" in the corporate world can be a groan-inducing cliché. "The thing is," he continues, "nobody designs meetings like these."

The meetings are intended to astound—and enroll. When you're done, Ellison says, you're ready to sign up. Soon a procession of leaders from major environmental groups who had never before visited Wal-Mart—the National Resources Defense Council, Environmental Defense, Greenpeace—flowed into the Bentonville Home Office, where they discussed green issues for hours with company executives. To Ellison, it was Project RAFT all over again, bringing opposites together in a setting where the ground rules required they work together. And, to everyone's surprise but Ellison's, they found common ground. Even so, several of the environmental groups were so paranoid that their constituencies would accuse them of collaborating with the enemy that they agreed to come to Bentonville only if their participation was kept secret.

Then there were more intimate, visceral encounters outside the Bentonville confines, such as the meeting Ellison arranged in Sweden for Mike Duke, a senior vice president at the company who would succeed Lee Scott as CEO in 2009. While Duke was in Europe on Wal-Mart business, Ellison set up for the executive a day on a glacier, where he met with one of the world's premier glaciologists. Then he stayed the night in an ice hotel, where he heard how this part of the world was melting away bit by bit. Excited and humbled, convinced in a personal way about man's impact on climate, something he had doubted previously, Duke returned with a slide show to share with his colleagues and a new interest in sustainability.

Ellison also arranged for the executive vice president of apparel merchandising at the time, Claire Watts, to meet with cotton farmers in Turkey, at the center of one of the largest cotton-growing regions in the world, where the material for many of the clothes and other products sold in Wal-Mart originates. She visited a conventional cotton field, met the sharecroppers and their families, then crossed the road to an organic cotton field. The difference shocked her. The organic field was beautiful, a pleasure to walk through. The conventional field resembled a toxic wasteland. It stank. Her eyes burned from the chemicals. Cotton is one of the most intensively sprayed and treated crops when grown conventionally, coated with fertilizers, herbicides, pesticides. Huge amounts of fossil fuels are expended on conventional growing methods. And in the middle of that wasteland, Watts watched the sharecroppers' children play in the fields. Watts was not blind or ignorant. She had always known that cotton was a dirty business, that it demanded heavy chemical treatments. She knew it—but she had never seen it, had never been nauseated by the acrid stench. It was a brief visit, but she came away affected by what she saw and by what she realized Wal-Mart could do about it. She began working to commit Wal-Mart to buying organic cotton products and ended up negotiating deals directly with farmers to buy the cotton in bulk at Wal-Mart-style prices, then provide the cotton to manufacturers who supplied Wal-Mart. Within a year, Wal-Mart became the single largest purchaser of organic cotton in the world.[2]

Then there was the meeting on New Hampshire's Mount Washington that Ellison arranged for Scott. The river guide had decided it would be a good idea to trap the Wal-Mart CEO overnight in the bunk room of a science station in a mountaintop wilderness with some environmentalists and climate scientists as bunkmates. "I think you'll find it enlightening" was his offhand comment.

Scott had come to Boston to attend a stock analysts' meeting, giving Ellison an opportunity to waylay him for a side trip. The next morning, Ellison picked him up in a rented van, along with Andy Ruben, the new vice president for sustainability at Wal-Mart; Fred Krupp, the head of the Environmental Defense Fund; and Scott's bodyguard.

During the drive to the mountain, they stopped to spend the afternoon with a fourth-generation maple farmer whose family had been making maple syrup for a century. The farmer explained to Scott how his trees had been harmed by acid rain years ago, but as that threat eased and the maples recovered, climate change began affecting production and causing oak trees to begin to crowd out and displace the maple trees. The oaks were migrating—slowly, of course, but migrating nevertheless—to a climate they preferred. To the maples, they were an invasive species. Scott was fascinated: Who ever heard of migrating trees? Then the CEO of Wal-Mart sat down in the farmers' aged log cabin to have milk and cookies and commiserate over the uncertain future of farming, an industry just as important to Wal-Mart's bottom line as it was to his host.

Then they piled back into Ellison's van and headed up the mountain to visit the research station at the 6,000-foot peak. The Mount Washington Observatory is a major outpost for the study of climate change and renowned for having some of the worst weather in the world. It also has a storied environmental history: A century earlier, Thomas Edison and Henry Ford used the difficult terrain of Mount Washington to field-test a new electric car built with an Edison-designed battery that could travel as much as a hundred miles on a single charge—a breakthrough modern carmakers are still struggling to match. A *New York Times* reporter accompanied Edison and documented the journey, though Ford's and Edison's plans to change the world with a new electric car came to naught, defeated by the era's cheap and plentiful oil and expensive electricity. Now that same mountain was being used to study climate changes brought on, in part, by the ascendancy of gasoline-powered cars over electric ones.

At the summit, Scott, Ellison, and the others were joined by a Brown University professor of environmental studies, Steven Hamburg, and the young PhD students who lived and worked at the observatory. They shared a pasta dinner at a long wooden table in a cramped kitchen rich with the smell of fresh-baked bread. During dinner the researchers explained their climate research to the visitors. Afterward, the guests were jammed into bunk beds in a small dormitory, where there was nothing to do but chat. Not only did Krupp, the environmentalist, and Scott, the businessman, decide to work together, but Krupp agreed to open a branch office of the Environmental Defense Fund in Bentonville to partner with the company to make Wal-Mart part of the solution instead of the problem. Hamburg, meanwhile, suggested that Wal-Mart could use its stores to promote environmentally friendly products that would put a dent in the greenhouse gas emissions driving climate change. He thought a perfect choice would be energy-saving compact fluorescent bulbs that, if more widely used, would save billions of dollars and the energy equivalent of dozens of power plants. Scott would eventually accept that suggestion.

Scott, like his executives who went to Turkey and Sweden, returned home—as Ellison had planned and hoped—moved by what he had seen, felt, and heard. As never before, Wal-Mart's leaders had seen the face of climate change, pesticides, and air pollution—and it was the weathered face of a maple farmer, it was the vanishing snow lines of ancient glaciers, it was the clothing and skin of children dusky from pesticide residue. "You don't get that in a briefing paper," Ellison remarked to Scott. The CEO nodded.

While these field trips were under way, the consultants also formed teams of Wal-Mart managers paired with a few outside experts from Conservation International, the Environmental Defense Fund, and other groups to craft sustainability goals. Each team tackled a different part of Wal-Mart's business: energy, transportation, suppliers, waste, food and fiber, and packaging.

"Lee," Ellison told Scott, "some of these will be like picking hundred-dollar bills off the ground."

After the revelation that a small adjustment to the Kid Connection toy package could save millions of dollars a year, the possibilities suddenly seemed endless: Wal-Mart sells hundreds of thousands of products. Its private-label brands rival the size and customer base of some of the leading national brands in the country, from coffee to sour cream to car batteries to suitcases. If shrinking just one product's package could save millions of dollars and improve the company's environmental footprint, what would a systematic, storewide packaging transformation accomplish?

The story of the chicken box, more than anything else, seemed to answer that question and capture everyone's imagination as it spread through the company's ranks. Wal-Mart had been receiving its tons of frozen chickens in waxed cardboard boxes, a practice that dated back to Mr. Sam's early years. The waxed boxes prevented leakage but were no longer necessary because frozen chickens are now individually bagged for shipment. The problem was that wax boxes can't be recycled. Wal-Mart sells more chickens than any other retailer, and that meant a lot of wasted cardboard (for all its products, Wal-Mart goes through 15 billion pounds of cardboard a year in its U.S. stores).

One day the executive in charge of frozen foods called the chicken supplier to say, hey, is there some reason why we can't get regular boxes instead of waxed boxes? The supplier said there was no reason at all, except for one: "You never asked for the unwaxed boxes." So Wal-Mart made the switch to chicken boxes that could be recycled, diverting 2.5 million cardboard boxes from landfills every year. That meant that garbage Wal-Mart had paid to have a company haul away for many years suddenly became a valuable commodity that it could sell to a recycler—good for the bottom line, good for the planet. Sustainability had been staring company executives in the face for years, but they simply couldn't see it.

Just as impressive were the results of the transportation team. Walmart's transportation experts had always taken pride in operating one of the most efficient trucking fleets in the nation. Other retailers used contractors, but Wal-Mart had 7,000 of its own tractor-trailer rigs by 2004. They were well-maintained, modern vehicles. The drivers were well trained and were the best-paid rank-and-file workers at Wal-Mart. Scott initially felt that there was little to be gained from scrutinizing Wal-Mart's trucking operation, his old turf and the largest private fleet in the United States. But there were, it turned out, some large untapped opportunities.

Charged with finding new efficiencies, the transportation team's in-house experts seized on auxiliary power units as a solution. None of Wal-Mart's beautifully maintained diesel-powered trucks had APUs—small motors that generate electricity to power air conditioners and heaters while a truck is parked and drivers are resting or sleeping.

APUs are simple boxes easily installed on a truck. They are optional extras and add a modest amount to a $200,000 big-rig price tag. Without them, however, drivers had to keep the main engine on and idling all night while they parked and slept or when they had to wait to be unloaded at some distant warehouse. Immense amounts of fuel, carbon emissions, and money could be saved if Wal-Mart installed APUs on its trucks.

So a retrofit program was initiated, generating huge savings—$25 million a year, a quick payback on the cost of installing the APUs. Fuel usage was reduced by a whopping 8 percent—equivalent to taking 560 of those trucks off the road—and carbon dioxide emissions were cut by 100,000 metric tons.

Once again, the Wal-Mart leadership team wondered, first, how it could be that they had not seen this source of cost savings before—savings equivalent to the profits generated by $700 million in sales. Then they asked the next logical question: What else is out there that we've missed? What else can we do with our trucks? To help address these questions, Ellison brought in famed environmentalist Amory Lovins from the Rocky Mountain Institute, who had recently completed a study for the Pentagon on how to wean the military and the country from dependence on fossil fuels. Wal-Mart's transportation experts had been uncertain at first—they had invited Lovins in before and felt his ideas either were impractical for their business or had already been adopted by Wal-Mart. But this time, the mood was different in Bentonville, and his ideas were embraced. Lovins and his colleague, energy economist Odd-Even Bustnes—who ended up doing the bulk of the Rocky Mountain Institute's work with Wal-Mart—urged the retailer's transportation execs to think of each truck as a system. They should shift their focus from finding better motors, and consider instead what a truck has to do and what it has to overcome to do it—namely, fight wind resistance, rolling resistance, and weight. If you can find ways to reduce those obstacles, then the engines can be smaller and more efficient because they'll have less work to do. And this shift in thinking led Wal-Mart to embark on a quest for innovations in streamlining, on a new generation of tires to ease friction and resistance, and on hybrid systems, all of which contributed to fuel and dollar savings as their trucks were modified or replaced.

Wal-Mart ended up setting an ambitious goal of doubling, by 2015, the fuel efficiency of its trucks, which hovered around six miles per gallon at the time. Lovins predicted the move could end up saving the company $300 million a year.

Little by little, one executive after another, then one department after another, began to look at their operations with different eyes, looking for the most efficient, least wasteful, more planet-friendly alternative—looking for their APU, their chicken box.

Inefficiency and waste, it turned out, could be found everywhere. There was the shrinking of laundry detergent bottles that saved millions in shipping and materials costs. There were the inefficiently packaged bags of dog food that could be reduced in size by 50 percent, saving $1 million a year. Improving the shipping boxes for SudaCare Shower Soothers cold medicine allowed twenty-one cases to be stacked on every pallet instead of just three of the old ones, which meant that Wal-Mart could ship the same amount of the product on 28 trucks that had once required 196. A quarter of a million dollars was saved, along with 6,000 gallons of fuel and 66 tons of carbon emissions—just from the packaging of a single product.

Even the once-skeptical president of global procurement, Lawrence Jackson, became a convert. Jackson grew up in an impoverished section of Washington, D.C., and was, at the time, the highest-ranking African American at Wal-Mart. His doubts about the sustainability initiative faded as he began to see that Wal-Mart could be the perfect vehicle for diversifying and democratizing "green." Sustainable food, clothes, and technology products had been around for a long time, but the ones that were truly green, rather than just greenwashed, were expensive, premium niche products. Jackson was disdainful of them— the sorts of goods that people with disposable income could choose but that poor people could not. Sustainability was for the rich, not for the friends and family members he cared about back in D.C. The average shopping trip to Wal-Mart was sixty bucks, Jackson knew. Many people didn't choose Wal-Mart—they needed it. Now, he felt, Wal-Mart could give budget-restricted shoppers access to natural, organic, and earth-friendly products as no one else could. Sustainability Wal-Mart-style, Jackson realized, would not be elitist.

So Jackson became another one of Blu Skye's early evangelists. At a meeting of the board of directors, he heard a board member express reservations about the sustainability initiative. Shouldn't we be focusing on getting stock prices up? How is this going to help the bottom line? Jackson was ready. He reached into a pocket and pulled out a sealed plastic sandwich bag filled with a dirty-looking powder. He tossed onto the table. It landed with a thump.

"That's how much chemical pesticide goes into making that shirt you've got on," Jackson said. "One cotton shirt." It was a visceral demonstration (although the bag was a prop—it contained only sand). The board member, looking shocked, leaned back. He was wearing a crisp white shirt that, in the course of its manufacture, had been literally immersed in poison—a notion that, while not news to him, had never been illustrated in such an immediate fashion. Jackson's message was clear: getting rid of the chemical waste and selling a product that had not been so contaminated would bring new value to Wal-Mart's customer. "If you're a mother buying a shirt for your baby, which would you want to buy?"

The board member nodded. But he didn't go near that baggie.[3]

Later, Jackson and Andy Ruben flew to San Francisco to meet with Adam Werbach, the former (and youngest ever) president of the Sierra Club, one of America's most august environmental groups. He had just given a highly contentious speech to the Commonwealth Club in San Francisco in which he pronounced modern environmentalism dead. He decried the movement he had helped lead as a model based on regulation, litigation, and lobbying rather than celebrating nature and inspiring Americans. Environmentalism, as he saw it, had devolved into backroom negotiations by insiders on how much harm to nature would be acceptable. "Instead of a narrative for America, instead of a vision, we were preparing for maximum daily allowable loads of toxic chemicals."

The part of the speech that caught Ellison's attention was Werbach's suggestion that the environmental movement would do better to focus on clean, green, and sustainable jobs, businesses, and lifestyles. "What if we stopped defining global warming as an environmental problem," Werbach asked, "and instead spoke of the economic opportunities it will create?"

These were not new ideas. But Werbach, now chief sustainability officer for the global advertising firm Saatchi and Saatchi, had put his own spin on the business case for sustainability, framing it as a popular green movement that could recapture ordinary Americans' enthusiasm. Ellison thought it was such a great speech that he e-mailed copies to Lee Scott and Andy Ruben with a note suggesting they consider working with Werbach—another possible bridge between the company and the environmentalists who typically revile Wal-Mart. Soon Werbach, who had founded a small environmental consultancy, Act Now Productions, was sitting across a coffee shop table from two Wal-Mart executives. There was wariness on both sides. Werbach had been a green activist since the second grade, when he had petitioned to remove Ronald Reagan's notoriously antienvironmentalist interior secretary, James Watt, and the Wal-Mart team knew he had once called their company "a new breed of toxin." Jackson would later reflect that for his part, Werbach seemed to have been expecting "a couple rednecks with corncob pipes to show up instead of a black guy from Washington and a Jewish guy from Chicago." But the discussion went well and eventually led to Werbach signing on as another green consultant for Wal-Mart, enduring the charge of "sellout" by his peers. He, like Ellison, saw the potential for Wal-Mart to lead a green business revolution.[4]

Werbach took charge of designing an in-house initiative at Wal-Mart called Personal Sustainability Projects. The idea was that the company would support its employees' efforts to build sustainability into their daily lives—eating better, quitting smoking, walking or bicycling instead of driving, recycling at home, giving up fast food and junk food. Tens of thousands of Wal-Mart workers embraced these voluntary personal projects, another avenue for baking sustainable thinking into company culture. By 2008, participating Wal-Mart employees would collectively lose 180,000 pounds and 19,000 workers would quit smoking.

The presence of the outspoken Werbach at Wal-Mart, and his repeated statements that he believed the retail giant was sincere in its green ambitions, perplexed and roiled the close-knit landscape of major U.S. environmental groups. Most of them tended to view the retailer as Werbach had done up until 2005: as a company that would tear down nature just so it could sell a cheaper pair of underpants. "I thought they were the devil," he recalls simply. Many of his progressive friends and colleagues, already taken aback by his environmentalism-is-dead speech, were horrified that he would even meet with Wal-Mart representatives, much less go to work for the company, and Werbach tended to agree with them—at first. Then he took his first trip to Bentonville, an exploratory visit before he and Wal-Mart agreed to work together. To his surprise, he found a line of managers and career–Wal-Mart people waiting to meet with him, asking him why he thought their company was perceived so negatively when, internally, they said they prided themselves on always trying do the right thing. They kept asking: Why is there this disconnect? What can we do better? Werbach, who until that moment felt he probably would not work for Wal-Mart, began to wonder if coming to Bentonville might be one of the greatest opportunities to bring about environmental progress he had ever encountered. Ruben, Jackson, and even Lee Scott all told him that the company needed to hear outside views on these questions—even when the answers were not what Wal-Mart supporters liked to hear.

When Werbach and Wal-Mart agreed he would launch the Personal Sustainability Projects, which in a year grew from a pilot program in 120 stores to a companywide initiative, environmentalists derided his efforts to interest workers in sustainability at home and in their personal lives as inconsequential, even frivolous, in comparison with the enormous environmental concerns raised by Wal-Mart's business model and supply chain. Carl Pope, then executive director of the Sierra Club, dismissed Werbach's work at Wal-Mart with a quip: "It's rearranging deck chairs on the *Titanic*." But Werbach, whose consultancy expanded from ten to forty staffers through his work with Wal-Mart and was then bought out by Saatchi and Saatchi, sees it differently. He and his fellow activists had for years bemoaned the inability of Sierra and other green groups to attract the interest and support of Middle America. And here was Wal-Mart, putting him in charge of the largest sustainability education program in history. "I was training a million people on what green is, on what a carbon footprint is, on energy conservation. It was unheard of, and they loved it. These weren't people in grad schools, these were people making eleven bucks an hour, and there was a thirst for this information. I've done tons of organizing on college campuses, elite universities, urban areas, but I've never seen uptake like this." As the training went from store to store, employees would talk up their sustainability projects in their communities, Werbach said, and soon teachers would be calling to see how they could build a similar program into their curriculums.

The main reason the word "sustainability" is a widely understood term today, concludes Werbach, is that Wal-Mart made it part of the national conversation. "Wrap you head around that if you're a hemp-wearing environmentalist."[5]

The nature of these projects also provided valuable insight into what Wal-Mart might have to do to sell sustainability to large numbers of its customers. Americans live the least sustainable, most wasteful lives on the planet, consuming 25 percent of the world's energy and producing 25 percent of its waste with less than 5 percent of its population. Wal-Mart employees, who are demographically similar to most Wal-Mart customers—which is to say, women and men on tight budgets—chose sustainability projects geared toward personal health and well-being. Give up smoking, and it doesn't only clean your lungs and the air in your house, it also decreases the demand for an energy-intensive, heavily packaged agricultural product with no social benefit and enormous health costs. Give up fast food, or even cut your beef intake by a third, and you've lowered the demand for products that have been linked to obesity and that also produce an enormous carbon footprint. The takeaway for the entire corporate sustainability initiative: wherever possible, Wal-Mart should link sustainable products to health and well-being. Customers will be more likely to understand the value and embrace the product, even if they have to pay a bit more. Organic, pesticide-free baby clothes are a perfect example of a sustainability home run. Who, Ellison observed, wants to dress his or her baby in togs made with toxins?

Bit by bit, these sorts of insights, conversations, and conversions began to spread throughout the company during that first critical year. Even so, Scott could have decided at any time that, though sustainability was an interesting experiment, it was not really Wal-Mart's job or purpose to save the planet, and that it was time to get back to business. No one outside the company would have known. The actual number of employees dedicated full-time to sustainability was six out of 2 million—Ruben and his five subordinates. As far as the outside world went, there were no announcements about sustainability outside the Bentonville Bubble. The environmental groups had been brought to town in secret. There had been no public commitments. No press releases. Ellison had delivered the quick wins to validate his ideas, but that just meant it was time to do the hard work of taking these little demonstration projects as models for remaking the entire company. And it was not clear that Lee Scott would do that. He had had no epiphany of the type that Ellison and Ruben had experienced. He was understanding more, he was less skeptical about the warnings of environmentalists, he had even used Ellison's phrase, "lens of sustainability," but a big part of his commitment remained his desire to improve Wal-Mart's reputation. For Scott, it was still about defense. And a successful defense of Wal-Mart's image could be made on the low-hanging fruit already harvested. It could end with that. The press office could have a field day spinning those accomplishments to laud Wal-Mart as the greenest retailer on the planet.

Still, Scott wavered. He was a lifelong fisherman, and some of his earliest memories were of the rivers he and his father had fished. Now he had seen how pollution had harmed those same rivers and the life within them. That concerned him. He also had a granddaughter now, and he admitted that made him more thoughtful about the future— her future. Ellison had asked that favorite question of his that sticks in your mind, about what you'll tell your grandchildren when they ask what you did to make the world better. Scott had always known there was a connection between the visible deterioration of the environment and his work, but it had always been just a nagging sorrow in the back of his mind. It's not as though there was anything he could do about it. But now here was this damn river guide telling him that there really was something he could do after all—and that it would be good for business as well as good for his granddaughter.

If he did move forward as Ellison suggested, the Sam Walton purists and Wal-Mart old guard might see it as rank treachery. For Lee Scott to take the lead in an attempt to reinvent Wal-Mart as America's newly green giant would be arguably contrary to traditional Wal-Mart culture, with the founder's core principles, with the stockholders, with history. Yes, Scott had become CEO in part because he had learned how to make the company culture work for him rather than the reverse, how to get Wal-Mart to embrace things that seemed at first blush to be at odds with the company's values, and he would argue that sustainability fit Mr. Sam's prime directive of efficiency and cost-cutting. Still, committing fully to sustainability would be his biggest pirouette by far. Scott was becoming a believer, but a year in, Ellison still didn't know what would happen next, nor did the CEO. Ellison, in the end, could only suggest and advise. Scott was the one who had to act—and who had accept the risk. It was one thing for Scott to get rid of his aged Volkswagen—following Mr. Sam's tradition of the CEO driving an old, cheap car as a symbol of Wal-Mart frugality—and replace it with another sort of symbol, an eco-friendly Lexus hybrid. It was another thing entirely to hybridize the whole company.

Then Hurricane Katrina hit in August 2005, and, oddly enough, it was that disaster that pushed Scott to commit.

CHAPTER FIVE

Katrina in Slow Motion

It was one of the five deadliest hurricanes in U.S. history and the costliest natural disaster of any kind. After Hurricane Katrina plowed into the Gulf Coast on August 23, 2005, New Orleans was under water. Biloxi's waterfront casinos, hotels, homes, and landmarks had been tossed and splintered. The entire Gulf region was ravaged, with more than 1,800 men, women, and children dead and a million refugees driven from their homes.

When the government failed to mobilize, when the state and federal disaster officials seemed at a loss, and when President George W. Bush publicly praised the clueless head of the Federal Emergency Management Agency, who would soon be driven from his job,[1] Wal-Mart trucks swooped in to deliver food and water and batteries and hope.

Even before the hurricane made landfall, Wal-Mart stores in the region had stocked up with extra truckloads of bottled water, flashlights, batteries, and canned goods in anticipation of widespread shortages once the storm passed through. And the morning the storm hit, Scott met with his executive team in Bentonville to talk about how the scope of the company's response to the disaster should match its size. Scott had already pledged a $2 million donation to relief efforts, but he wondered aloud to his team if that figure should have been $10 million instead.

In a matter of days, Scott's question had become irrelevant. Wal-Mart ended up donating $17 million in cash and used its stores and trucks to haul in more than a hundred trailer loads of free merchandise, food for 100,000 meals, and 150 computers for Red Cross emergency centers. Scott, after touring the Superdome evacuation site in New Orleans with former President Bill Clinton, promised that a job would be waiting for every Wal-Mart worker made a refugee by the disaster. The assistance continued long after the first wave: Wal-Mart shipped another two thousand truckloads of clothes and supplies, donated another $9 million in cash disaster relief for Wal-Mart employees and their families, raised $7 million more from customer donations at Wal-Mart stores, and dispensed free prescription medications to storm evacuees who needed treatment but lacked the cash to pay for it. Amid the horror of the storm's devastation and outrage at the White House's decision to gut what had been the widely praised and effective Federal Emergency Management Agency, one headline in *The Washington Post* stood out: "Wal-Mart at Forefront of Hurricane Relief."

After years of being cast as a villain, Wal-Mart was now lionized. Larry King invited Lee Scott onto his CNN talk show to discuss the relief efforts. Two former presidents, Bill Clinton and George H. W. Bush, held a joint press conference to praise Wal-Mart. Clinton pointedly remarked that Congress ought to be guided by the company's example. Even Wal-Mart's critics conceded that the company had played a positive role in the crisis, although some asserted that the company's motivation was as much about repairing its tattered image as it was about rescuing the Gulf Coast. This take, put forth by the union-funded blog Wal-Mart Watch, was fueled by a *BusinessWeek* magazine story that revealed the efforts of Wal-Mart's Bentonville "war room" PR operation to capitalize on Katrina without appearing to do so. The war room operators had leaked information to conservative bloggers early on with details of Wal-Mart's Katrina efforts, providing Internet links to in-house blogs that Wal-Mart employees had been using to coordinate relief effort logistics in storm-ravaged Louisiana and

Mississippi. The conservatives loved the story's spin—private enterprise works, government doesn't—and from the bloggers, the story filtered into the mainstream press without its having to be trumpeted first in Wal-Mart press releases. Not exactly the most selfless scenario, but for most media observers, as well as the general public, Wal-Mart's actions mattered far more than its motivations. And those actions had eased suffering and saved lives.

Many of the most poignant aspects of Wal-Mart's relief efforts had nothing do to with PR spin. They began and ended at the store level, without any input from the Bentonville leadership. One Louisiana store turned itself into a shelter for police officers and rescue workers who had lost their homes in the storm. Another Wal-Mart worker used a forklift to break into a locked warehouse to get fresh water for the residents of a retirement home. And the assistant manager of the Wal-Mart in little Waveland, Mississippi, where more than fifty people died when a twenty-six-foot storm surge hit, ran a bulldozer through her flood-damaged store so she could collect supplies that local residents needed. She gave them all away in the parking lot. Later she broke into the store pharmacy to get medicine for the local hospital. She consulted with no one and didn't know if she'd be praised or fired. She just did it.

Scott, who had become used to being pilloried in the press, read the Katrina media coverage and saw, as he would later describe it, "Wal-Mart showered with gratitude, kindness, and acknowledgments." The McKinsey consultants had been right: nothing changes the way a company—or a person—is perceived more than doing something good. Of course, when it came to the sustainability issue, this cut two ways. On the one hand, the original reason for considering a green initiative—image repair—had been addressed by the Katrina efforts. Wal-Mart suddenly had approval ratings any politician would die for. Scott could shut the fledgling sustainability program down, mission accomplished, if he wished. On the other hand, the outpouring of gratitude to Wal-Mart for Katrina relief suggested that continuing to do good would generate even more public goodwill, along with the benefits to profit and planet that sustainability could bring if Ellison was right. Wal-Mart had stepped up and led in a way it had never done before. Why stop now?

A few weeks later, in September 2005, Ellison took Scott on a field trip to consider various farm methods used to produce Wal-Mart products. They first visited several huge factory farms in Kansas, where conventional and time-worn tilling methods were causing topsoil erosion, expending huge amounts of fossil fuels, and releasing large amounts of carbon into the atmosphere. Then they met with advocates of no-till farming, a way of planting and growing that leaves the soil largely undisturbed. Wal-Mart, it was suggested, had the clout to ask its suppliers to choose a no-till method. The benefits to the environment would be huge and immediate, Scott learned.

A year before, the idea of attempting to dictate to farmers the method of tilling fields would never have occurred to Scott. Now he was on a corporate jet thinking about it—and about compact fluorescent bulbs, maple syrup, climate change, solar panels for Wal-Mart supercenters, hybrid trucks for the fleet. Halfway to Bentonville he turned to Ellison and said it was finally time to commit. It was time to talk to the associates.

On October 24, 2005, Scott stood on the stage of the home office's packed auditorium. He was there to do something never done before in the history of Wal-Mart: deliver a speech via live video feed to every one of its 6,000 stores worldwide, and to its then-62,000 suppliers, too. He announced that Wal-Mart would be going green in the biggest way imaginable, embracing sustainability to become "the most competitive and innovative company in the world."

Scott is not known as a great speaker, but this time he hit an unexpectedly passionate note. There was none of the past defensiveness. No sarcastic jabs at critics. No extolling Wal-Mart as the future of American capitalism and friend of the common man. Instead, he explained his motivations in plainspoken but emotional terms. His speech alternately captivated and confused his audience in Bentonville and in the Wal-Mart workforce around the globe, and it would soon shock the rest of the world as well, for it was both unexpected and radical for such a famously conservative company. The title of his speech was "Leadership in the 21st Century," and at first is seemed to be a simple exercise in feel-good, inspirational reflection:

> You know, we are in uncharted territory as a business. You won't find any case studies at the Harvard Business School highlighting answers for companies of our size and scope. If we were a country, we would be the 20th largest in the world. If Wal-Mart were a city, we would be the fifth largest in America. People expect a lot of us, and they have a right to. Due to our size and scope, we are uniquely positioned to have great success and impact in the world, perhaps like no company before us.
>
> After a year of listening, the time has come to speak, to better define who we are in the world, and what leadership means for Wal-Mart in the 21st century. Nothing brought this home more clearly than Hurricane Katrina. Katrina was a key personal moment for me.
>
> When Katrina hit last month, the world saw pictures of great suffering and misery. At Wal-Mart, we didn't watch it, we experienced it. Some of our stores and clubs were under water. Associates lost their savings, their homes, and in a few cases, their lives. I spent time with a few of them in the Houston Astrodome. I saw the pain, the difficulty, and the tears. But I saw something else. I saw a company utilize its people, resources and scale to make a big and positive difference in people's lives.
>
> I saw how Jessica Lewis, the co-manager of our Waveland, Mississippi store, worked to help those in her community. When the flood surge swept through the store, it was a shambles. That night, though it was dark and flooded, she took a

bulldozer and cleared a path into and through that store, and began finding every dry item she could to give to neighbors who needed shoes, socks, food, and water. She didn't call the Home Office and ask permission. She just did the right thing. Just like thousands of our Associates who also did the right thing, a trait I am proud to say is bred in our culture.

During this time, we were asked by governments, relief agencies and communities to help. And look what happened. We were showered with gratitude, kindness, and acknowledgments. This was Wal-Mart at its best.

Katrina asked this critical question, and I want to ask it of you: What would it take for Wal-Mart to be that company, at our best, all the time?

What if we used our size and resources to make this country and this earth an even better place for all of us: customers, Associates, our children, and generations unborn? What if the very things that many people criticize us for—our size and reach—became a trusted friend and ally to all, just as it did in Katrina?

Until that moment, the speech had seemed a fairly conventional, if unusually emotional, appeal to his workers' better nature, as well as congratulations for a job well done in the midst of a crisis. But then Scott veered into uncharted territory: "We should view the environment as Katrina in slow motion."

At first, many of his listeners weren't sure they had heard Scott correctly. Had he just likened environmental concerns to the worst natural disaster in American history? Then, as he continued, it dawned on his audience that not only had he made that linkage, he was assigning responsibility for both its cause and its cure to Wal-Mart.

Environmental loss threatens our health and the health of the natural systems we depend on. . . . As one of the largest companies in the world, with an expanding global presence, environmental problems are *our* problems. The supply of natural products (fish, food, water) can only be sustained if the ecosystems that provide them are sustained and protected. There are not two worlds out there, a Wal-Mart world and some other world.

That's what we saw with Katrina: Our associates, customers and suppliers occupy the same towns, our children go to the same schools, and we all breathe the same air. These challenges threaten all of us in the broader sense, but they also represent threats to the continued success of our business.

During Katrina, I was reminded of the vision and innovation of Sam Walton. We became who we are by serving the underserved. The smart folks predicted we'd lose our shirt with a discount store in a small town. There is another crowd of smart people who think that if a company addresses the environment, it will lose its shirt. I believe they are wrong. I believe, in fact, that being a good steward of the environment and in our communities, and being an efficient and profitable business, are not mutually exclusive. In fact they are one in the same. And I can show you why.

Scott proceeded to explain the major environmental challenges that he believed had to be addressed. He put climate change at the top of his list. At a time when many companies were hewing to the U.S. Chamber of Commerce's line casting doubt on the science of global warming, Scott made it clear that he accepted the scientific case that human-caused greenhouse gas emissions were contributing to climate change and weather-related disasters, and that Wal-Mart needed to behave accordingly. Air pollution, water pollution and shortages, destruction of critical habitats, and the threat to the diversity of life completed his list of urgent environmental concerns.

Next he laid out a laundry list of the sustainability quick wins that had already improved Wal-Mart's environmental posture and that, he vowed, had convinced him and the Wal-Mart leadership that much more could be accomplished in service of both profit and planet. Many of those accomplishments—the reductions in packaging and the fuel efficiency gains—had not been publicized up until then. "The idea," Ellison would later explain, "was for Wal-Mart to get caught doing something good."

Scott ended with Wal-Mart's long-term environmental goals, which he said would be "simple and straightforward":

1. To be supplied 100 percent by renewable energy.
2. To create zero waste.
3. To sell products that sustain our resources and environment.

"These goals are both ambitious and aspirational," Scott said, "and I'm not sure how to achieve them . . . at least not yet. This obviously will take some time. But we do know the way."

TECHNICALLY, THE SPEECH HAD been for in-house consumption, aimed at employees and suppliers, but Scott knew the world was listening. His speech made headlines and confused the stock market (the company's share value dropped 3 percent in the next two days, but soon rebounded, up 11 percent within a month). Scott had shocked Wal-Mart's competitors, suppliers, investors, and critics in the environmental community. How do you react if you're the Sierra Club or Greenpeace and public enemy number one says, "Hey guys, you were right all along. Let's work together now"?

A number of the big environmental groups—some of which had taken part in the secret meetings in Bentonville—expressed interest in Scott's promises but withheld judgment, waiting to see if the company's actions matched the lofty rhetoric. This was the "cautious optimism" camp. "The fact is, Wal-Mart exists," said Gwen Ruta, head of the Corporate Partnerships program of the Environmental Defense Fund. "We might as well try and make it better."

Others offered harsher assessments, labeling the effort greenwashing and suggesting that Scott's "aspirational" goals of zero waste and all renewable energy were so far ahead of where Wal-Mart stood that they were essentially meaningless. What did promising a goal at some undefined point in the future to live off of 100 percent renewable energy mean for a company that had a completely nonrenewable energy footprint? What did even the concept of "sustainability" mean at a business that, at its core, seemed to define *un*-sustainability, with its stated mission to expand the number of stores (and countries with stores) every year, to roll back prices every year, and to persuade people to buy more stuff every year? How could that ever be sustainable? To Wal-Mart's toughest critics, Scott's aspirations seemed like mere happy talk from an environmental outlaw, part of a campaign to improve Wal-Mart's image rather than its substance.

Stacy Mitchell, a senior researcher at the New Rules Project and author of a book harshly critical of large retail companies, *Big-Box Swindle: The True Cost of Mega-Retailers and the Fight for America's Independent Businesses*, suggested that Wal-Mart's green initiatives were worse than greenwashing because they were genuine. And because they're real, she argued, they distracted many environmentalists and journalists from the reality that Wal-Mart is fundamentally unsustainable and always will be. Just the fact that its millions of U.S. customers must drive long distances to shop, she said, negates any reductions in carbon emissions the chain makes at its stores. "As a system of distributing goods to people, big-box retailing is as intrinsically unsustainable as clear-cut logging is as a method of harvesting trees," she would later write in *Grist*, the online environmental magazine.[2]

Other critics expressed concern for Wal-Mart's suppliers and vendors. The companies who made and sold things to Wal-Mart or provided services such as waste removal already likened themselves to battered spouses, always under pressure to lower prices, no matter how painful it might be. Now Scott was asking a whole lot more of them. They were expected to rethink their carbon footprint, their waste, their water use, and their energy consumption, and to be open about their impact, both good and bad. An expert on labor history at the University of California, Santa Barbara, Nelson Lichtenstein, suggested that the sustainability project was just another way of shifting costs and burdens from Wal-Mart to its suppliers—a shift that, historically, has led to pay cuts and poor treatment of workers. There's a reason why the standing joke among Wal-Mart vendors was that the only thing worse than not selling to Wal-Mart was selling to Wal-Mart.[3] The conservative *American Spectator*, meanwhile, echoed Lichtenstein's criticism, though the magazine expressed concern for shareholders rather than workers, arguing that Scott's "so-called sustainability campaign" was a form of "Russian Roulette" that was "betraying the legacy of Sam Walton." Asserting that Scott had lost his way if not his mind, the magazine bemoaned what it saw as political correctness gripping what had been the epitome of a disciplined business.[4]

Business analysts noted that, during the tenure of Scott's predecessor at the helm in Bentonville, Wal-Mart's stock price had risen twelvefold. Since Scott had taken over from David Glass, in the five years leading up to this big green announcement, the stock price had dropped a worrisome 30 percent (even as revenue and sales growth continued, albeit more slowly than in the past). Shouldn't the CEO be focusing on the core of his business, rather than distracting himself and his company with all this green nonsense? Was he worried about leaving a legacy instead of taking care of business?

Ellison had a different reaction to the speech: he felt like high-fiving Scott. He was jubilant. The wave of negative punditry and criticism was inevitable and expected, so far as Ellison was concerned—proof, in a way, that they were on the right track. History shows that visionaries and outliers are almost always mocked, feared, or attacked. The ancient Greek atomists were derided for suggesting that the universe was made of vanishingly small particles they called atoms. Galileo was imprisoned as a heretic for seeing the structure of the solar system accurately. Charles Darwin was (and still is) vilified for documenting the natural evidence of evolution. John D. Rockefeller was burned in effigy for donating land that would be used to create Grand Teton National Park, once an object of fear and loathing, today a national treasure. Now here was Scott, donning the mantle of the heretic, espousing ideas about business and environment that were on the cutting edge of the new century, suggesting that the old way of thinking about profit and planet as a dichotomy was the wrong way to think and a disastrous way to live.

"There's a simple rule about the environment," Scott told his workers, paraphrasing his first-ever conversation with Ellison. "If there is waste or pollution, someone along the line pays for it." Eliminating that waste and cleansing the environment, he argued, would serve the core company mission of always pursuing the everyday low price with the added component of doing good for the environment and the world.

Because he was addressing his employees, he also invoked the old icon of Mr. Sam and asserted that this new green thinking, this idea of sustainability with which he wanted to transform the business and the world, was in reality rooted in Wal-Mart Culture. The opportunities had been there all along, Scott said, but they just hadn't seen them. Now that the company's eyes were open, Wal-Mart had no choice but to go for it, Scott argued, because that's what Wal-Mart had always done.

"Sam Walton's dream to serve the under-served changed the world," Scott intoned. "His method was to go where other businesses feared to go. . . . In other words, we didn't get where we are today by being like everyone else and driving the middle of the road. We became Wal-Mart by being different, radically different."

Ellison was mesmerized by the speech, even though he knew what was coming. He saw his ideas, the fruits of their conversations, the trip to Mount Washington—the speech was infused with all of it. Even energy-saving lighting was in there, when Scott mocked his own initial skepticism about the profitability of sustainability:

A Wal-Mart environment program sounded more like a public relations campaign than substance to me. But we kept talking, and as I learned more a lightbulb came on for me . . . and that's a compact fluorescent lightbulb!

Scott had committed to transformation. More important, he had linked the sustainability effort firmly to Wal-Mart's culture—what he called its *radical* culture, which was the first time anyone in the home office used that particular word to describe Wal-Mart's business model. Scott had pledged in his speech a half-billion-dollar annual commitment to this transformation, an immense and unprecedented budget for sustainability.

Based on the early sustainability victories with packaging and the trucking fleet—and Ellison's promise that there were much more waste, efficiencies, and new insights out there to harvest—Lee Scott had dealt himself a high-stakes hand. His embrace of sustainability had been done so publicly and forcefully that it would be all but impossible to fold now. The world's biggest company had just gone all in.

CHAPTER SIX

Because Everyone Loves a Good Deal

Once the buzz over Wal-Mart's big green announcement faded, the hard work of making the rhetoric real began. A series of sustainability demonstration projects and three lofty goals had to be built into a systematic business strategy.

It was clear to Scott and Ellison that trying to train and deploy a full-time team of sustainability staffers, as some other companies had sought to do, would be a mistake at a business as immense as Wal-Mart. First of all, it would take an army of sustainability soldiers to do the job. Second, such an army, even if creating one were possible, wouldn't work. Sustainability, they agreed, had to come from the inside out. That's why Scott had agreed to be personally involved rather than handing it off to a subordinate who would not have outranked the direct reports. Sustainability gurus would have a similar second-class status, and they would end up merely hounding and shadowing the regular executives, managers, and workers directly involved in Wal-Mart's various lines of business. A ponderous and pointless sustainability bureaucracy plopped on top of those lines of business would fail.

There was a place for a sustainability officer, someone to coordinate across lines of business, to network with suppliers, and to evangelize innovations—Andy Ruben's job at the time. But a deep sustainability strategy had to be baked into the business, "into Wal-Mart's DNA," as Ellison liked to say. It had to catch fire with the buyers, salespeople, logistics managers, truck drivers, product designers, building and maintenance staff, and all the other hands-on Wal-Mart employees and managers worldwide. They were the ones who would be in the best positions to identify waste and inefficiencies. They had the best vantage points from which to recommend areas for reform. They had to be the sustainability army.

But how to get there? How could the tone and example set by the CEO's speech be used to burst through the "silos" that evolve in any large business—the individual divisions that become so big and powerful that they function like separate companies of their own, semi-independent towers competing for budgets, attention, and praise from the CEO and the board of directors? The immense company that, to outsiders, seemed so united and focused, had for years struggled with bringing its many parts together for common goals. The big divisions—the Sam's Club warehouse stores, Wal-Mart U.S. stores, and Wal-Mart International—had rarely been able to cooperate on big projects because of their different leadership styles, missions, and approaches to the marketplace.

Ellison and the growing number of consultants he had hired at Blu Skye seized on the idea of creating a series of teams within the company, each focused on a different product category or Wal-Mart system—seafood, jewelry, trucking, energy, waste, textiles, fourteen groups in all[1]—so that the entire range of activities and products within the company would be spanned. These teams would be called "Sustainable Value Networks." They would be made up of Wal-Mart executives, managers, and innovators from each of the three big silos and, more important (and more contentiously), large numbers of non-Wal-Mart people, with some of the outsiders even assigned to team "cocaptain" roles. Ellison argued that the teams had to include substantial numbers of suppliers, academics, scientists, and even the environmental groups and other nongovernmental organizations that had been Wal-Mart's harshest critics.

The only way to make progress and to discover new solutions, Ellison asserted, was to burst the Bentonville Bubble and welcome the outside world into the investigation of how Wal-Mart could become more sustainable. Wal-Mart had to network its way into this effort, rather than dictate as it usually did. If you want to sell environmentally friendly wood products, bring in the Rainforest Alliance people—they know, better than anyone, what needs to be done. Why not listen to them for a change? They'll share their data, their experts, and their opinions with the company for free and thank Wal-Mart for the opportunity. If you want to know if it's possible to substitute safe chemicals for harmful ones in detergents and window cleaners, don't do the research yourself or rely on the happy talk from manufacturers; bring in the EPA or the Sierra Club. Wal-Mart had expertise in many areas, but if company leaders wanted to have a conversation about organic cotton or heritage agriculture or why Europe's Restriction of Hazardous Substances Directive for electronics and other products was better than the United States', they would need to look elsewhere. They would need to say what Lee Scott told Jib Ellison during one of their early conversations: "I know so little about sustainability, I don't even know how much I don't know." Few things Scott said or did impressed Ellison more, because he knew from long experience as a consultant that few men or women in Scott's position, with that kind of power, ever willingly admitted they didn't have the answer.

The independent vendors, the trade associations, the big companies such as Procter & Gamble, the mavericks such as Patagonia, and the researchers and activists would provide the sustainable network teams with fresh eyes, expertise, and alternative views on the green opportunities that Wal-Mart was missing. The quick wins had eroded that bubble a bit, but bursting it entirely would mean inviting more than a few token outsiders in secret, as had happened during the initial demonstration phase. Blu Skye wanted to bring in dozens, even hundreds, to participate in engagements that would last not just a few days or weeks but months, perhaps years. The outsiders wouldn't just be observing or joining a few meetings. They would be team members of the Sustainable Value Networks. Their views would count. They would be partners.

This idea did not go over very well at first. Wal-Mart had spent forty-two years keeping out the rest of the world, particularly its critics. The company had played into the documentary filmmaker Robert Greenwald's hands by turning him away at the home office door; instead of interviewing Lee Scott, he roamed Bentonville and got candid shots of the razor-wired bunker the Walton family had constructed after the September 11, 2001, attacks. This only fueled the abiding, defensive, almost paranoid conviction in Bentonville that constructive criticism was a myth and that any sort of dramatic change, particularly if championed by outsiders, would be the undoing of Wal-Mart's four decades of success. A year before meeting Jib Ellison, Lee Scott had said Wal-Mart didn't believe in revolutionary change. During a speech on the leadership challenges of a global corporation at Webster University in St. Louis, he explained, "We are incrementalists at Wal-Mart. You don't see any new strategies building up. We had food, we added more food, then we added fresh food, and little by little, we incrementally developed into a supercenter concept."

But then Jib Ellison and Hurricane Katrina had come along, persuading Scott to launch the first serious challenge to the policy of incremental change and Bentonville isolationism that had served Wal-Mart so well for so long. Ellison's strategy for overcoming Wal-Mart's cultural resistance to the next stage in the sustainability project was to employ an old trick from his consultant days at Human Factors, adapted from a process called "appreciative inquiry."

Developed in the mid-1980s by Case Western Reserve University researchers David Cooperrider and Suresh Srivastava, appreciative inquiry is roughly the opposite of problem solving. The idea is to bring about a perceptual shift: that in striving to improve, organizations should focus not on what needs to be fixed but on what's working—and then build from there. Cooperrider and Srivastava found this shift to be surprisingly effective at "curing" failing organizations and leadership because of a simple tendency of human behavior: if you study problems, you see and find more problems; if you study successes, you see and find more successes. When Lee Scott asked his employees how the company could behave all the time like the Wal-Mart that had helped Hurricane Katrina victims, he posed a classic appreciative inquiry question.

An early proof of the process's effectiveness came when the Avon Corporation tried to combat rampant sexual harassment in its Mexico branch with a long series of workshops on the problem in the 1990s. This tactic failed to alleviate the harassment; disgusted participants started refusing even to show up. But then Avon hired an appreciative inquiry consultant to lead a different approach, in which pairs of workers were asked via the company newsletter to share stories of positive working relationships between men and women at the company. Hundreds volunteered, and the wide-ranging group discussions that followed revealed stories of shared leadership, career advancement, and overcoming stereotypes. The company then used these examples to expand similar opportunities and programs for workers. A dramatic drop in sexual harassment reports in the year that followed. By 1997, Avon Mexico received the Catalyst Award as the best place in the country for women to work.[2]

Other organizations that have used appreciative inquiry range from the U.S. Navy, which sought ways for low-level leaders with innovative ideas to be heard, to a New Jersey charter school seeking to redesign its curriculum with grassroots input, to the United Nations, which convened an appreciative inquiry summit of five hundred corporate, civic, and government leaders in 2004. The goal was to strengthen the oft-criticized United Nations Global Compact, which asks corporations to embrace sustainable and socially responsible practices. Among the accomplishments of the gathering were the adoption of a long-resisted international anticorruption program (the estimate of bribes paid that year by global businesses had topped $3 trillion) and a pledge by twenty major global investment companies with combined assets of $6 trillion to integrate environmental and social justice into investment analyses and decisions.

The technique has the added benefit of bringing antagonists together, forcing them to focus on their common ground rather than their differences—an intellectualized and water-free version of the "magic" of river-rafting trips. Ellison wanted to use appreciative inquiry to pave the way for acceptance of the outside experts he wanted to get inside the Bentonville Bubble. Dave Sherman, Ellison's first hire for the Wal-Mart initiative, and Sherman's business partner, John Whalen, who joined the Blu Skye consulting team a short time later, had worked with Cooperrider and had been among the first to adapt the process to sustainability projects in business.

Their first test had come when they brought environmentalists in secret to Bentonville, to meet with Lee Scott and his senior executives. Before launching that meeting's discussion of the case for sustainability and the evidence of a planet in peril, however, the group members had to take part in a classic appreciative inquiry exercise. Each Wal-Mart representative had to pair up with an environmentalist. Then they had to interview each other about their backgrounds, a high point in their careers, and a situation in which each of them faced a major challenge and had been able to accomplish something outstanding. Then the interviewers took turns sharing what they had learned with the rest of the group.

On the surface, these discussions provided an obvious biographical introduction for the members of the group. But the main purpose was the revelation of the common ground these disparate sets of leaders shared, despite the negative preconceptions each faction held of the other. The Wal-Mart people saw the environmentalists in a different light. The critics they had tended to dislike and dismiss for years, it turned out, were leaders of complex multinational organizations, with pressures, concerns, and constituencies not all that different from Wal-Mart's. Their organizations' purposes might be different, but they faced similar challenges: people issues, budget crises, messaging, litigation. The greens, for their part, could no longer think of Wal-Mart as a faceless monolith. They had met people they liked and, more important, could imagine a collaboration they would not have considered in the past. The humanizing effect of this simple exercise changed the discussion that ensued over the next two days, as Blu Skye led the group into the second of the four stages of the appreciative inquiry process.

Stage two is when the group moves from common ground to common goals and a shared vision—as in, what should the future look like for our children and grandchildren? With the right facilitators in the room to guide the session, the consensus reached during these first two stages can appear more magical than rational (there's a reason the United Nations hired Cooperrider to jump-start progress on the Global Compact). In this case, the magic of that meeting led the Wal-Mart leadership to seek outside help from green groups, while representatives from the Natural Resources Defense Council and the Environmental Defense Fund pledged a long-term commitment to help the company pursue its unlikely sustainability crusade.

The technique that led to this shift may seem simple, even obvious, but it runs contrary to the conventional problem-solving approach most businesses and CEOs employ. Common sense would suggest that when companies arrive at the point where they need to hire an outside consultant, they want to engage in some intensive problem solving, not some feel-good process. Thousands of consultants make many millions of dollars every year pursuing the problem-solving model—what Ellison calls "the-smartest-guy-in-the-room consulting." A team arrives at a corporation in crisis, interviews everyone in sight, identifies weaknesses and problem areas, and develops a cogent, comprehensive plan for correcting the flaws, fixing the problems, and moving on. But the strategy often fails, because the dysfunctional company culture that created the crisis in the first place is still there. Ellison likens the result of this type of consulting to going on a diet plan. The dieter sticks to the plan of low calories and exercise at first, loses some weight, then falls off the wagon and gains most of it back. That's because a diet plan—or a new corporate strategy—treats just the symptom, not the underlying causes.

As Blu Skye and Wal-Mart set out to create Wal-Mart's fourteen Sustainable Value Networks, with their mix of Wal-Mart insiders and outsiders and their "countercultural" mission, the structure and agendas were built around the appreciative inquiry method. This task often fell to John Whalen, the soft-spoken business consultant and adherent of Sufi mysticism, who has an uncanny ability to turn a meeting of hostile stakeholders into a collaboration fest. One of the networks he worked with early on was devoted to examining the chemically intensive products carried by Wal-Mart: cleaners, detergents, bug spray, and other items that raised concerns about chemical ingredients that could pose risks to human health and the natural world. The goal was to make these products more sustainable—which meant making them less toxic.

If any area at Wal-Mart needed the appreciative inquiry approach, chemicals were it. The subject has long been touchy in business and industry, dating back to the revelations about environmental damage and human health risks associated with the then-rampant pesticide use made public in Rachel Carson's *Silent Spring*, published the same year the first Wal-Mart opened, 1962. The entire chemical industry, along with the U.S. Department of Agriculture, vilified Carson for, as one industry spokesman said, advocating a "return to the Dark Ages, [so] the insects and diseases and vermin would once again inherit the earth."[3] Carson was, of course, vindicated, but the chemical industry has lobbied hard and successfully to keep its business largely unregulated. Contrary to popular belief, there is almost no outside safety testing of the chemicals commonly used in the products sold at stores such as Wal-Mart. Of the 80,000 chemicals currently registered for use by manufacturers in the United States, only 200 have been tested by the Environmental Protection Agency, and only 5 have been banned since

1976. Yet many times that number are known to be harmful. Nervous manufacturers worried that Wal-Mart was trying to impose its own regulation on chemicals.

Whalen began with a disarmingly simple question for the group of retailers, manufacturers, chemical industry representatives, and environmentalists on this network team: What would success look like when it comes to chemicals in products? The answer: Success would be a store where there were no warning labels.

Whalen had deftly pointed the group members away from debates over which chemicals were harmful and what limits were acceptable, and instead had them start out by brainstorming what it would take to have a store where no products were toxic and no labels needed skulls and crossbones on them. Were there chemicals used in products that were legal but nevertheless bad for our bodies and nature? Of course. And of those, were there alternatives that would do just as good a job without doing harm? Indeed. In a short time, the team identified two common pesticides and a common ingredient in detergents that had already been banned in Europe for their health risks and toxic qualities yet remained in wide use in the United States.[4] All three of the chemicals could easily be replaced with more benevolent compounds—even the chemical industry representatives agreed it could be done. It hadn't happened because the U.S. government hadn't required it and because, absent such pressure, change of that sort is costly and therefore avoided. But a solution soon emerged in discussions: What if Wal-Mart could reward manufacturers for making the switch by featuring the greener projects with prominent displays and shelf space, thus guaranteeing more sales and more profits? In that case, the manufacturers said, we'd do it. Being green would then be a competitive advantage: the environmentalists would get rid of chemicals that are killing wildlife and contaminating water supplies; product makers would have a legitimate claim of doing good while getting a better deal from Wal-Mart; and Wal-Mart would get to sell a better, safer product at no additional cost to the company or its customers. The win-win was so attractive that the initially contentious team members agreed to get started on a larger list of twenty chemicals of concern that could be removed from products.

By 2008, Wal-Mart was acting ahead of federal regulators on some chemicals of concern, banning from its shelves baby bottles containing the common plastic ingredient BPA (bisphenol-A), which has been linked to a host of disorders in lab animals, including impaired fetal and child brain development, hormone disruption, increased obesity, and increased risk of prostate cancer. The baby bottle manufacturer Playtex immediately agreed to stop using the substance, as did the water bottle maker Nalgene. (Unfortunately, BPA has been a ubiquitous product ingredient since the 1950s, used in everything from the linings of food and beverage cans to the receipts that come out of store cash registers; government tests have shown that 93 percent of Americans have the stuff in their urine.)

The work of the chemicals team provided the sort of result that began to win over the doubters at Wal-Mart. They had feared that the Sustainable Value Networks would amount to little more than another layer of bureaucracy, meetings, and paperwork. And for what? To let in a bunch of outsiders who want to ask us uncomfortable questions? But when those uncomfortable questions led to tangible results in the first few months, the initiative received an important boost. Soon internal champions for the concept emerged. One of the first was at Sam's Club: Matt Kistler, then the vice president of packaging and innovation (who, in his previous position at Kraft Foods, had watched his sustainability ideas get shot down). His early work on sustainable (and profit-boosting) packaging later made him the logical successor to Andy Ruben as the senior vice president for sustainability and head of Wal-Mart's eight-person sustainability office. Another early champion, Mary Fox, Wal-Mart's senior vice president for apparel, became one of the first merchant leaders at the company to create a sustainability position on her own staff, and (with Blu Skye's help) issued a sustainable apparel "best practices" handbook to apparel suppliers for energy, waste, and water conservation practices she wanted them to adopt for clothing sold at Wal-Mart. This not only informed apparel makers that sustainability would help determine their place at Wal-Mart, it also made life easier on them: manufacturers knew exactly what they could do both to be more sustainable and to stay in favor with Bentonville. A third and pivotal early champion of Blu Skye's efforts, though he was at Wal-Mart for just a few years, was Tyler Elm, then Wal-Mart's senior director of corporate strategy and business sustainability. Initially skeptical, Elm quickly came to view the network idea as essential in hammering home the idea that sustainability isn't something you do in addition to your "real" job. Elm, who is now an environmental consultant himself and who is credited with coining the term "sustainable value network," began telling his colleagues that sustainability had to be "the new way of doing your existing job." He also emphasized to Wal-Mart managers, and to outside suppliers who asked to join the networks, that this wasn't about charity or doing good for the sake of doing good. The networks' main purpose was to find ways to make sustainability make economic sense for the business. Doing good was the side benefit, not the driving force.[5]

Elm's framing became the company's de facto sustainability policy: doing good because it's good for business. This sort of thinking allowed the Sustainable Value Networks to take off as the road map for Wal-Mart's green makeover—and a model for other companies embarking on the same quest.

Aside from Chemicals Intensive Products, there were two waste-related networks: Operations and Procurement, which focused on waste produced by the stores and warehouses; and Packaging Innovations, charged with shrinking packaging and converting it to reusable and recyclable materials—one of the areas that had the potential to produce very large returns. Four networks revolved around climate: the Greenhouse Gas Network for energy use; the Sustainable Building group for green store construction; Global Logistics, which covered trucks and shipping; and Alternative Fuels, to advance Wal-Mart's renewable energy goals. The remaining seven networks related to product lines: Forest Products, Textiles, Electronics, Jewelry, Food and Agriculture, Seafood, and China.

Each network had a top executive as a sponsor and one or more network captains chosen from the ranks of senior managers with reputations as top performers within Wal-Mart or Sam's Club. Blu Skye attached at least one of its own consultants to each network as well, and some also had specialists from the Rocky Mountain Institute, the National Resources Defense Council, the Environmental Defense Fund, Conservation International, and others. Some were paid; many worked for free. Hundreds of suppliers, government officials, nongovernmental organizations, Wal-Mart critics, and even competitors that had developed strong green credentials joined the various network teams. The networks were free to figure out their own priorities, meeting schedules (usually once a month), and which projects they would undertake to pursue sustainability within their areas of responsibility.

Network members had to devise a list of projects divided into three types: the now-familiar "quick wins," which could be accomplished in a year or less; "innovation projects," which would take between one and three years using emerging technologies and practices; and "big game changers," which were long-term projects with the potential to transform whole industries and "tilt the playing field" to favor sustainability. Game changers were intended to push market forces to work for sustainability rather than against it.

The teams used Blu Skye's take on an appreciative inquiry method known as the "4 Ds" to get organized: Discover, Dream, Design, and Deploy. The discover phase was essentially a team research project, and it provided some sobering and sometimes horrifying information for the networks to consider at the outset. The seafood team, for example, learned that 90 percent of the fish species we eat have been overfished into oblivion. And at least a quarter of the remaining fisheries are depleted and under stress. As with so many other products,

Wal-Mart sold more seafood than any other company, including many fish on the environmental red list of endangered species.

The electronics network learned that the United States generates 2.1 million tons of e-waste every year and that 75 percent of the power that home electronics and appliances use is devoured while the devices are switched off—a phantom energy drain known as "vampire electronics" that cost Americans $5.8 billion a year.

The forest products network received an estimate that, every second of every day, a section of forest the size of a football field is cut down. That means, every day, 86,400 football fields' worth of trees disappear from the earth.

The China network learned that economic development in China has meant that the country saw the 648 million people who had been living in poverty there in 1981 drop to 218 million in 2001, the greatest reduction in poverty at any time in history. But in the process, China also became the world's leading consumer of coal, steel, grain, and meat and surpassed the United States as the largest greenhouse gas emitter. The newly industrialized China—which Wal-Mart's outsourcing had helped create—was now home to six of the world's ten most polluted cities.

The jewelry network found out that mining enough gold for one ring generates 20 tons of mine waste.

The packaging team learned that the largest source of solid waste in the United States—fully one-third of the waste stream—comes from packaging. That's eight hundred pounds of packaging a year for every man, women, and child in the country—boxes, wrapping, polystyrene foam, packing chips, plastic loops for six-packs, soda cartons, tape, ties, and those impossible-to-open plastic blister packs.

The global logistics teams learned that Henry Ford's Model T averaged 25 miles per gallon a century ago. In 2004, the average U.S. passenger car got 20.8 miles to the gallon. If the country raised its fuel efficiency by an average of 2.7 miles per gallon—which would still mean the average car got worse mileage than the Model T—the annual saving would be equal to the United States' combined oil imports from Kuwait and Iraq.

The Chemical Intensive Products network learned that blood samples showed that a typical American's body contained about two hundred chemicals that didn't exist a century ago. *Indoor* pollution from common household chemicals was estimated to cost billions of dollars a year in health care costs.

Though this baseline information did not suggest specific projects or strategies, it showed just how seriously out of whack—how unsustainable—American life had become: collapsing fisheries, impossible amounts of packaging waste, modern fuel efficiency that couldn't even rival that of the Tin Lizzie. That portrait could have been paralyzing but for the next stage in the process, the second "D"—the dreaming of solutions. What if Wal-Mart carried electronics that didn't suck electricity when idle? Or jewelry mined without immense amounts of waste? Is there a way to use packaging that avoids the landfill, to sell natural food and clothes at a reasonable price *and* devoid of harmful chemicals, to obtain seafood in a manner that ensures that there will be fish in the sea to feed future generations? Would such products have extra value for customers? Would they cost more than conventional products? Or would the efficiencies and reduction in waste behind their production make them cost less if a buyer the size of Wal-Mart took an interest in them? Would it pay, for instance, for Wal-Mart to send teams of engineers to assess the efficiency of suppliers' manufacturing plants—to invest in energy audits, gambling on the possibility that the resulting savings would more than make up for the cost through lower prices?

The answer was yes to many of these questions. During the very first plant visit by the Greenhouse Gas network, the team showed one of Wal-Mart's suppliers, Dana Undies, how to cut electricity use by 71 percent in its 65,000-square-foot factory. Jim Stanway, Wal-Mart's senior director of energy services and captain of the network, was stunned when it became clear just how much could be accomplished

and how easily it could be done. "What we found out there was staggering. And that's only the beginning."

Who knew that U.S. manufacturing in this day and age wasted
so much energy due to poor lighting and inefficient machinery? Just
dusting air-conditioning and refrigeration coils in factories and large
buildings could save hundreds of millions of dollars a year. Fixing
inefficiencies would pay for itself in a year or less in many cases. If
done nationwide, enough electricity would be saved to avoid building
dozens of power plants. Worldwide, the number would grow into the
hundreds, perhaps more. Add renewable energy, and the picture grows
even brighter. Do the same with houses and businesses, all of which
are massively inefficient, and the impact on carbon emissions would be
off the charts. Stanway and his network realized this approach could
buy the world the time needed to wean itself from fossil fuels and the
environmental damage they cause.

With that, a new business model suddenly occurred to Stanway and
others at Wal-Mart: a business based on carbon. Or, more precisely, a
business built on getting rid of the carbon emissions and other greenhouse gases driving climate change. To the surprise of many inside and
outside Congress, Wal-Mart executives took the work of the Sustainable Value Networks to Washington and appeared not once but twice
to testify on Capitol Hill in favor of climate change legislation, most recently in 2009. The company continues to call for "meaningful legislation to slow, stop, and reverse the growth of greenhouse gas omissions."[6]

Wal-Mart wanted a plan that would regulate greenhouse gases
through a market-based cap-and-trade plan. Stanway envisioned a
system that would reward companies that made, promoted, and sold
products that helped reduce carbon emissions. Wal-Mart would be
able to collect huge numbers of carbon credits with its green products, and those credits could be bought, sold, or traded like stocks and
bonds. Stanway saw climate legislation as a gold mine for companies
with strong sustainability programs: "There's obviously an enormous
number of credits to be harvested there."

This position is exactly the opposite of the argument put forth by the opponents of climate change legislation, who have branded it a business burden and job killer. Wal-Mart, however, saw opportunity, and Stanway, Ruben, and Scott have bemoaned the paralysis in Washington over climate. Stanway predicts that sooner or later legislation will come to put a price on carbon emissions and that Wal-Mart will be ready. He foresees an economic incentive in cap and trade that would mean lower prices for green products, higher prices for dirty ones—the incentive that Wal-Mart, and most American shoppers, understand best. The right policy could usher in a new retail revolution that would make sustainability the most marketable, sensible, and fashionable feature of any product. Because everyone loves a good deal.

CHAPTER SEVEN

Cotton, Fish, Coffee, and Al

As the sustainability work intensified throughout 2006, several of Wal-Mart's sustainability value networks began to stand out for their rapid progress and for proposing game-changing ideas and goals. One in particular was the textiles network, which focused its most intensive efforts on cotton, the pure, white, soft, natural fabric that turned out to be the dirtiest secret of the apparel world.

Cotton fiber is ubiquitous. It is the number one nonfood crop in the world. You cannot get through the day—you cannot make it out of your house—without encountering cotton. The sheets you sleep on, the pajamas you sleep in, the towel you dry yourself with are made wholly or in part from cotton. The swabs for your ear, the bandage for your cuts, the socks on your feet—cotton. Blue jeans, Oxford shirts, Chambray shirts, curtains, car seats, diapers, washcloths, T-shirts, and underwear are most often made of cotton. Coffee filters, fishnets, and bookbindings all use cotton. It is by far the most important and often used plant product on the planet, accounting for 40 percent of all fibers used by humans.

Cotton's usefulness extends beyond fabric. Cottonseed oil is edible and is all over the supermarket shelves, found in thousands of packaged baked goods, snacks, and other foods. The seeds are used for livestock feed. Even gunpowder contains the fiber in the form of nitrocellulose, also known as "guncotton."

Cotton is also the dirtiest crop on the planet. It is grown on only 2.5 percent of cultivated land on Earth but is treated by about 16 percent of the chemical insecticides used in world agriculture, more than any other crop.[1] Some of these chemicals are extremely toxic and known to cause cancer and birth defects. One, the carbamate insecticide Aldicarb, is so poisonous that it is banned for home use in the United States. A single drop in concentrated liquid form absorbed through the skin can kill a person. Sixteen states have reporting finding it in groundwater supplies. As little as a tenth of one percent of the chemicals applied to cotton actually reach their intended targets—the bugs and other pests that afflict the growing plant—with the other 99.9 percent ending up in the soil, in grazing areas, in water supplies, and in the atmosphere.[2]

Growing cotton also exhausts the nitrogen in the soil, which is why, for 6,900 of the 7,000 years humans have cultivated the plant, growers periodically left fields fallow or rotated vegetables or legumes in place of cotton to renew nitrogen in the soil. Modern conventional cotton farmers bypass this natural limit by treating their fields with massive doses of fossil fuel–based synthetic nitrogen fertilizers. This technique allows them to grow cotton year-round, year after year. The same synthetic fertilizers have also boosted food crop production while reducing the risk of famine throughout the twentieth century. But synthetic fertilizers have major drawbacks. Their continual use can cause toxic chemicals and heavy metals to accumulate in the soil over time. Rainwater runoff of synthetic fertilizer is a significant contributor to eutrophication—the creation of oxygen-starved dead zones in lakes and oceans. The Gulf of Mexico has such a dead zone covering 8,500 square miles, a surface area large enough to hold eighteen New York Citys. Dependence on synthetic fertilizers also leaves the industry dependent on dwindling supplies of natural gas and at the mercy of rising fossil fuel prices. And then there is the large climate impact: according to the U.S. Environmental Protection Agency, the spreading of synthetic fertilizers on fields leads to more than 165 million metric tons of greenhouse gas emissions every year. The nitrous oxide released by the fertilizer is three hundred times as potent a greenhouse gas as carbon dioxide.

The cotton footprint doesn't stop in the field. Processing and dyeing generate large amounts of contaminated wastewater and employ innumerable chemicals, heavy metals, and petroleum products—all to bring to market that thick, soft towel or brightly colored T-shirt. Producing cotton from start to finish requires immense amounts of fresh water—about 3 percent of global freshwater supplies every year, in a world where water is increasingly scarce and expensive.

Kim Brandner, the senior brand manager for sustainable textiles at Wal-Mart and captain of the textiles network, told his team members that cotton provided a huge opportunity for improving Wal-Mart's environmental footprint. The problem was lack of information. The life cycle and "chain of custody" of cotton were a mystery. The textile network's first mission, then, became breaking down the supply chain, uncovering its inefficiencies and waste, and exploring alternatives to conventionally grown, chemically intensive cotton. Brandner wanted to find a way that made economic sense for Wal-Mart to nurture what was then a rather pitiful organic cotton industry, which contributed barely one-tenth of one percent of worldwide cotton production.

Diana Rothschild, a former Wal-Mart analyst who went to work for Blu Skye and was assigned to the textile network, understood how unusual it was for Wal-Mart to perform this sort of investigation of the cotton process. Tracing the product trail from the grower to the ginner to the spinner, then on to the knitting, weaving and dying, and packaging, and ending with the wholesaler, the warehouse, the Wal-Mart shelves, the consumer's home, and finally the landfill, was difficult and uncomfortable—and far outside the Wal-Mart buyer's normal "need to know." Many of the production stages for a single cotton product took place at different locations, sometimes in different countries, expanding the environmental impacts. "This was so eye-opening, exploring the life of a cotton T-shirt," she would later recall.

"In the past, no one thought to look beyond the supplier who sold the shirts to Wal-Mart. . . . But that's the only way you can see the impact and the only way you can see the opportunities to do it better."

One of the surprises for the network members was how that cotton environmental footprint broke down: 20 percent of the overall impact came from growing, and another 20 percent came from processing. The remaining 60 percent—mostly in the form of energy use and waste—came *after* the manufacturing process was complete, through shipping, consumers washing their cotton products, and the eventual disposal in landfills of worn-out products. (The toxic chemical impacts to the environment, which were almost completely tied to the growing and processing stages of bringing cotton to market, were the principal exception to the 20–20–60 percent breakdown.) The biggest carbon footprint came at the end of the line. These figures suggested that, in addition to cleaning up the production of cotton, sustainability would be enhanced if Wal-Mart could also influence the life of products after selling them.

The network teams focused on consumer education, fiber-recycling programs, removal of chemicals in detergents that created ocean and river dead zones, and promotion of laundry detergent formulated for cold water. Energy research contributed by the environmental group members of the team revealed that 90 percent of the cost of running a washing machine came from heating water; washing with cold water would reduce greenhouse gas emissions from this mundane household activity by an order of five—which adds up, given that Americans wash 35 billion loads of laundry a year. If everyone in America washed clothes in cold water, it would be like taking 2 million cars off the road, according to the network's calculations. At the network's recommendation, Wal-Mart began promoting cold-water formulations of detergents online and in stores, and asked suppliers to reformulate more brands of laundry soap for cold water. But ingrained behavior is tough to change: as of mid-2010, a number of surveys showed that only 22 to 29 percent of Americans washed all their clothes in cold water.[3]

Cotton was one of the first products—but not the last by any means—that suggested Wal-Mart would have to look at the complete life cycle of its products, from field to factory to home to landfill. That meant finding ways to get not just growers, producers, and Wal-Mart itself to become more sustainable, but customers, too. The network put the "sustainable consumer" part of the cotton project into the "game-changer" category, because changing the ingrained habits of large numbers of Americans has always been a long-term and diffi- cult proposition. In the past, Wal-Mart's efforts to get customers to bring old computers and electronics back to Wal-Mart for recycling had failed abysmally because, it turned out, they didn't want to be inconvenienced when they could just (illegally) stuff them into their trash cans.

The highest priority for the textiles network after completing the "discover" stage of its work became organic cotton, which seemed to offer Wal-Mart the greatest potential for immediate results, as well as the possibility of pushing the industry in the long term toward more sustainable methods. Organic cotton is grown without chemical insec- ticides and herbicides, synthetic fertilizers, and other toxic substances. The quality tends to be high—and so does the price. Organic cotton was a niche product in 2005, with just over a half-billion dollars in global sales—too little for economies of scale to bring costs and prices down. Growers had difficulty finding buyers at times, which meant that the risk of converting conventional cotton fields to organic re- mained dauntingly high.

At the time, organic products were fairly scarce in Wal-Mart stores, although cotton was the one category where the company had some prior experience. And it had been a good and profitable experience, making the company receptive to experiment further with organics. In the spring of 2004, before the sustainability initiative began, a buyer for Sam's Club stores, who for personal and health reasons preferred to purchase organic food and clothes for herself and her family, placed an order for organic cotton yoga suits from the small Seattle-based

Greensource Organic Clothing Company. Made of cotton from a Texas organic grower with a reputation for strong environmental standards, the high-quality fabric yoga tops went for $10 apiece. The matching pants were $14. These items were not typical for Sam's, and the membership warehouse stores did nothing unusual to promote the yoga suits. There was no signage telling customers that they were sustainable or organic, just the product labels.

But customers loved them. They sold out in record time—190,000 yoga suits within ten weeks. This was not expected. The yoga suits were nicely priced for high-quality recreational apparel, but they were not as cheap as the nonorganic sweat suits sold at Wal-Mart and Sam's Club. Low prices generally convince Wal-Mart customers to make a purchase. When the textile network members looked at the sales, they concluded that Wal-Mart shoppers would purchase organic goods even if they cost more than conventional clothes because of the added value they perceived—so long as the organic alternatives were still affordable.

Rebecca Calahan Klein, the founder and president of the nonprofit Organic Exchange in Oakland, California, was invited to join the textile network and collaborate with Rothschild on analyzing the business case for organic cotton. Klein had been working for five years to find markets for organic cotton, urging retailers to move away from conventional cotton and the third of a pound of unhealthful chemicals that accompanied every conventional cotton shirt sold in America. This had been a difficult battle with many barriers. The fabric industry favored conventional cotton. Processors had to keep the two types of cotton separate to avoid contamination and so charged more for the lower-volume organics. Lower volumes also meant higher processing costs for growers, even those that had worked hard to build efficient, sustainable cotton farms. While conventional cotton's price varied wildly, between $.35 a pound and a $1.10 a pound, depending on quality and country, organic cotton tended to be at the high end when it came to quality and averaged at least $.20 more a pound than conventional, Klein told her network colleagues. In its early years, the Organic Exchange focused on premium retailers such as Nordstrom and Nike, encouraging them to build a market for organic apparel through their customers. As a group, their customers were more likely to accept a higher price tag for green goods. But given the small size of that market, it was hard for organics to gain a foothold and build up to a scale where costs would come down and they could be more competitive with conventional Big Cotton. Klein proposed that a company with Wal-Mart's scale could make buying decisions that altered that calculus in a big way. The yoga suit success showed that the customer base was there.

The tricky part, she said, was that it would require Wal-Mart to do business with suppliers in a different way. It takes producers three years to make the switch from conventional growing to organics. Fields have to be free of chemicals at least that long before an operation can be certified as organic. The first few years of establishing an organic operation are the most expensive for the cotton grower. At the same time, any cotton grown during those three years is known as "transitional," which means it is worth no more than conventional cotton. Those three years are so expensive that many growers who would like to go organic refuse to do so for fear of risking financial ruin. Wal-Mart, Klein suggested, could reduce that risk by promising to purchase and resell transitional cotton goods from growers and use those fabrics for its private label apparel brands. Better yet, Wal-Mart could make multiyear buying commitments with growers switching to organic, instead of the usual one-year deals that go to the lowest bidder. A five-year commitment would reduce the start-up risk and encourage more farmers to produce organic cotton.

The problem was that Wal-Mart didn't make five-year deals with suppliers of any kind. It didn't make two-year deals. Everything was annual. Sam Walton's business model depended on it. Suppliers had to make an annual pilgrimage to Bentonville to meet buyers in the famously shabby little deal rooms at the home office to arrive at

the terms of the next year's contract. That almost always involved a
demand that the supplier cut prices. Again. The suppliers then had a
decision: they could meet Wal-Mart's price-cut demand, or the retailer
would take its business elsewhere. This has long been Wal-Mart's advantage. No matter how unreasonable the price-cut demand might be,
no sales manager for a company making underwear or barbecues or
dish soap wants to come home and say, "Sorry, boss, but we lost the
Wal-Mart account. There goes 30 percent of our sales for the year."
That sales manager would come back to work to find a pink slip and a
cleaned-out desk. The company's survival would be threatened. Better
to cut costs, lower quality, or outsource than risk losing so much business. This dynamic has let Wal-Mart prosper, but it is not the sort of
formula that would encourage the fashion industry to invest in organic
and sustainable practices.

An enthusiastic advocate for organics, Klein gamely offered a
compelling portrait of a future world where clean cotton ruled, then
outlined the reasons why a radical departure from Wal-Mart's usual
buying practices would make sense for the business.

"Your current business model is literally built on cheap oil and
cheap water," she said. "Conventional cotton exists on fossil fuels.
How sustainable is that? What happens if the price of oil goes up five
percent? Fifteen percent? What happens if China decides it wants
clean water for its people more than it wants to help Wal-Mart make
money?"

Given the inevitable increases in energy costs and the growing
middle classes in such key cotton-growing countries as China and
India, the cost of conventional cotton will likely rise in the foreseeable future. The supply could become less reliable, particularly in the
quantities Wal-Mart requires, she argued. Smart business strategy
requires planning for future supply interruptions, and sustainable
resources are the best hedge against this type of scarcity. Organic
cotton, with its much smaller footprint, would be relatively immune

to cost pressures. Whoever had a lock on a steady organic supply would have an enormous competitive advantage. And in the interim, there was already a willingness among Wal-Mart shoppers to pay a reasonable premium for organic clothes.

There were also external costs to consider—the unpleasant side of business decisions that, nevertheless, ought to be part of decision making, Klein argued. The ecological damage caused by fertilizer, pesticide, and herbicide runoff at conventional factory farms is a classic example of unaccounted-for external costs. Worldwide, the legal use of these chemicals does trillions of dollars' worth of damage to fisheries, habitats, climate, and human health. There are hundreds of thousands of deaths due to pesticide poisoning each year, she said, and millions of nonfatal poisonings. "It's awful and harsh and horrible to think about it, but it's an effect, and it's not pretty. Organic growing is one way to address that cost."

Right now, the external costs of cotton (or any other product, for that matter) are not borne by the chemical companies, farmers, or retailers, nor are they reflected in the price paid by consumers for a cheap T-shirt. Governments, taxpayers, health insurance customers, and families are subsidizing these immense hidden costs. Klein suggested that Wal-Mart was in a position to do better.

When she joined Wal-Mart's textiles network, Klein wasn't sure how she and her ideas would fit in. Many of her friends and colleagues in the organics business were dubious of the retailers's sincerity and suggested that it would just use the Organic Exchange's progressive reputation as greenwash. And though it was true that some of the Wal-Mart representatives on the network team at first seemed to be wondering what they were doing in the same room with Klein, she gave them credit for being in the room at all and for the respectful, thoughtful attention with which her ideas were received. She, in turn, became convinced that Wal-Mart could become a force for good in the textiles market, as the team went to work designing a program through

which Wal-Mart could support the expansion of organic cotton farming in the world. And, of course, profit from it.

By the end of 2006, Wal-Mart had agreed to make a unique arrangement with organic cotton growers, buying their transitional
cotton and making a five-year commitment to purchase their fully organic cotton at a good price, removing enough risk for organic growers
in Texas, Turkey, and elsewhere to expand their operations.

With a single purchase, Wal-Mart became the largest buyer of raw
organic cotton in the world. By the beginning of 2010, the amount of
organic cotton grown worldwide had expanded five times from what
it had been when Wal-Mart made that first purchase. That same year,
Wal-Mart switched from dealing directly with growers and concentrated on ordering increasing amounts of finished organic cotton products, becoming the world's largest purchaser of organic textiles as well.
Meanwhile, Greensource, the small manufacturer of those first Sam's
Club yoga suits, had become a regular supplier of organic baby clothes,
bedsheets, and other products for Wal-Mart (and also Macy's, Sears,
and Kohl's), racking up $50 million in annual revenues to become the
eighth largest organic clothes maker in the world.

When conventional cotton growers showed up in Bentonville to
protest statements by Scott and others about the environmental harm
caused by the industry—Scott had bragged that Wal-Mart's organic
cotton purchases had taken the equivalent of two Boeing 747s filled
with pesticides out of the environment—Brandner invited them to
join his textile network, too. There wasn't enough organic cotton in
the world to supply Wal-Mart, he said, so there was a need to create
cleaner, "environmentally preferable" conventional cotton, too. With
the cotton industry representatives' help, the network created a supplier scorecard that all textile manufacturers and suppliers would have
to answer before Wal-Mart would buy from them. The scorecard reveals their products' origins, the chemicals used, the amount of energy
consumed, the amount of recycled fiber put back into products rather

than landfills, and any pollution and efficiency measures involved. Because Wal-Mart buyers would use the new scorecard when choosing products to stock Wal-Mart's shelves, cotton growers of all types—organic and conventional—who wanted to do business with Wal-Mart would have an incentive to become more sustainable.

IF ORGANIC COTTON WAS a no-brainer for Wal-Mart, seafood sustainability proved to be a more difficult challenge. The network's "dream" for the future, based on the dire information that team members from Conservation International presented on dwindling sea life, called for a radical change in the business of seafood. They suggested Wal-Mart, which buys $750 million worth of seafood a year (wholesale), should use its market leadership to help stabilize and then restore dying ocean fisheries, end practices that are leading to extinctions, and push for international agreements for wise management of the global "ocean commons"—the vast areas of sea, habitat, and life in international waters that are now being exploited at unsustainable rates. The alternative, marine scientists informed the network members, would be to continue with business as usual—and watch the collapse of every species of wild seafood within the next fifty years.[4] Long before that, supplies of wild fish will fall far short of demand, and prices will skyrocket.

Wal-Mart's seafood sustainability network leaders decided the most immediate and effective way to begin dealing with that grim prospect would be to push Wal-Mart suppliers to become certified for sustainability, relying on the independent Marine Stewardship Council for wild, sustainably caught fish and the seafood industry–sponsored Global Aquaculture Alliance for farmed fish.[5] The goal was for Wal-Mart to purchase wild fish exclusively from sustainable sources by 2011 and to use only certified sustainably farmed shrimp by the same deadline. No specific goals for other types of farmed fish were made public.

Substantial progress would come quickly: within a year, about 20 percent of Wal-Mart's suppliers had been certified and ten different types of wild seafood bore the Marine Stewardship Council's blue Eco Label. Still, few insiders expected the retailer to reach the 100 percent certification goal anytime soon. And though some network members wanted the company to address the massive environmental problems associated with salmon farms—a highly profitable industry Wal-Mart had helped create by becoming the primary customer for cheap farmed salmon from Chile—Wal-Mart did not include farmed salmon in its specific sustainability goals.

A common misconception about fish farms is that they are inherently sustainable because they take pressure off of wild sea life, thereby alleviating extinction threats and overfishing. But this is true only of farm-raised herbivorous fish, such as freshwater tilapia. Farmed carnivorous species such as shrimp and salmon consume two to four times the amount of seafood protein that they produce as food—the very definition of an unsustainable industry. Aquaculture ponds also can do enormous harm to coastal ecosystems, their pens packed with fish swimming in foul water filled with waste, feed, and massive amounts of antibiotics to counter the disease threat from such crowded, unhealthful living conditions. Coastal areas of Chile have been devastated by salmon farms, which create anoxic ocean dead zones and can spread diseases to wildlife. Thai shrimp farms, where Wal-Mart obtains most of the 50 million pounds of shrimp it sells every year (40 percent of its total seafood sales), have been notorious polluters as well. As the global demand for shrimp has quadrupled since the 1990s, ecologically vital mangrove swamps have been ripped out and replaced with shrimp ponds that spew chemicals and waste. Mangroves have root systems that stabilize coastal areas and provide buffer zones against tsunamis; as habitats, they provide nurseries and food for up to 80 percent of the sea life we eat. An estimated 35 percent of mangroves have been destroyed by aquaculture and other human development in the last quarter century—a rate that rivals the disappearance of tropical rain forests.[6] Vandana Shiva, one of India's most prominent environmentalists, calculates that the average shrimp farm creates jobs for fifteen farmers and fifty security guards, while displacing as many as fifty thousand people through loss of traditional fishing and agriculture.[7]

Despite such grim findings, the seafood industry had resisted certification and sustainability reforms in the past for both wild-caught and farmed fish, objecting to the presumed added cost of sustainable practices, as well as the fees that certifying organizations charge to monitor fishing and farming operations. Fishermen in particular feared that their catches would be limited and their profits reduced.

But resistance on the wild-fish side of the industry had begun to weaken by the time Wal-Mart began its sustainability work, as fishermen suffered the effects of shrinking fisheries. Many were forced to go out to sea longer and farther than ever before to make their catches. More than 13 billion gallons of fuel were being burned every year—1.2 percent of global oil consumption—to catch the 80 million tons of fish consumed yearly. Peter Redmond, then the Wal-Mart vice president and divisional merchandise manager of deli and seafood who captained the seafood sustainability network, told his team members that the scarcity and cost issues had made it difficult to find reliable, high-quality supplies of seafood to stock Wal-Mart stores. Suppliers were sneaking poor-quality fish into shipments or reneging on price agreements and demanding more money. Others sold to someone else at the last minute if that customer agreed to beat Wal-Mart's price.

Redmond felt sustainability certification would provide a means of restoring certainty and quality to the industry. Wal-Mart would encourage better practices by favoring the most sustainable seafood companies in the business. Some seafood companies saw this as a market opportunity opening up, as buyers such as Wal-Mart—and their shoppers—were increasingly drawn to the certified sustainable label. Others accepted the network's argument that fishing sustainably can be more efficient and therefore can provide a cost saving over time. Using more sustainable netting techniques that reduce the bycatch of unwanted fish lets fishermen spend less time and money on sorting edible fish from waste. An even simpler way to use sustainable fishing to lower costs is to switch gears and go after alternative species of fish that are more plentiful and therefore require less fuel, time, and effort to catch. Finally, to be sustainably certified, fish must have a documented "chain of custody" tracing their journey from hook or net to sale. Such transparency tends to produce very short chains of custody with higher-quality fish that command better prices for the fisherman. Uncertified fish have no documented chains of custody beyond the honor system, which in the past meant that Wal-Mart got stuck with fish that had changed hands five times or more as it was frozen, thawed, and refrozen; its quality diminished each time it was passed along and resold.[8] For Wal-Mart, sustainability was the perfect tool for boosting quality.

Still, by 2010, only 55 percent of the wild-caught seafood sold at Wal-Mart was certified sustainable, and twelve of the twenty-two redlisted seafood species were still being sold in the seafood aisles.[9]

On the farming side, following the recommendations of the network's environmental group members, Wal-Mart told its shrimp suppliers that in order to sell their shellfish in its stores, they would have to meet a tough list of requirements intended to lower the environmental impact of their operations and submit to a certification process that takes three to six months. Among the requirements: contaminated wastewater from shrimp pens that previously was dumped in ocean and rivers had to be treated with filters, settling ponds, and paddle wheels that oxygenate the water. Monitoring of the filtered discharge is required to protect water quality. Antibiotics previously dumped into shrimp pens by the barrel were banned. The farms were required to pay workers the prevailing local wage. Finally, three mangrove trees had to be planted for every one that was torn out to make way for a shrimp farm.

Some environmentalists thought these standards were not tough enough. Others expressed concern that the small family farms that make up more than half of the Thai shrimp business would be driven out of business and that Wal-Mart would make all its purchases from a few conglomerates. Shrimp farmers were encouraged to pool their resources through co-ops, but the company did end up doing most of its shrimp business with a few large producers. By 2008, all of Wal-Mart's farmed shrimp had been certified sustainable.

Wal-Mart considers the embrace of sustainable seafood practices by its suppliers a big win, even a game changer, but the results of this seafood initiative overall are not as clear-cut as efficient trucks and power-sipping lightbulbs. Sustainable seafood has some fine print attached. Even when wild seafood is caught in a sustainable manner, the rest of its product life cycle may be terrible for the environment: wild salmon caught in Alaska and sold in Wal-Mart is routinely frozen and shipped in bulk to China, where it is thawed, gutted, filleted, packaged, and refrozen, then shipped back to the United States for sale—an energy-intensive, greenhouse gas–emitting supply chain that makes no sense but for the low labor costs in China.

Salmon farms selling to Wal-Mart were still not certified in 2010— indeed, less than half the total seafood, farmed and fresh, sold in Wal-Mart that year bore a sustainability label.[10] But the only way Wal-Mart seemed able to stock its popular year-round offering of frozen salmon at about $5 a pound has been through cheap foreign salmon farm imports that produce such pallid, unnatural-looking fish that they have to be dyed to resemble salmon. There wasn't enough wild salmon to fill the demand Wal-Mart had created.

As a result of these intractable problems, Wal-Mart's seafood network reached a conclusion that seemed both logical yet surprising for a company that had so long embraced the notion that market forces were best left unfettered: the company would encourage and support greater worldwide government regulation of fishing and aquaculture—the only way to be certain that ocean life, and the business that depends on it, can be sustained.

OTHER SUSTAINABLE VALUE NETWORKS began racking up a range of quick wins, innovations, and game changers. Divisions within Wal-Mart—which, under Mr. Sam, had competed with one another on sales and cost cutting—now sought to outdo one another on sustainability.

After one of the waste networks analyzed trash patterns at Wal-Mart stores, the company installed baling machines in every one to collect plastic and paper waste for recycling rather than sending it to the landfill. Instead of paying a waste company to haul it away, Wal-Mart began making more than $3.5 million a year from recycling its trash.

At the jewelry network's suggestion, Wal-Mart launched the "Love, Earth" eco-friendly jewelry line, complete with a Web site that allows buyers to track each piece of jewelry, by serial number, to see how and where it was mined and what its environmental and social impacts were. This was one of the first experiments with full product transparency at Wal-Mart not just for internal use but for customers and the public as well. But for the bulk of the $3 billion of jewelry sold annually at Wal-Mart, such information is notoriously scant. The network's relatively modest goal for the retail chain—to have similar transparency for 10 percent of all gold, silver, and diamond jewelry sold at Wal-Mart—has been met only for gold as of 2010. The jewelry industry, generating huge amounts of waste and using massive amounts of water, has proven to be a difficult area for Wal-Mart's sustainability efforts, with the only marked successes coming from packaging. Wal-Mart jewelry is now packaged in 100 percent recycled materials, which are then recyclable by the customer. Not even the suppliers selected for the "Love, Earth" line—the mining giant Rio Tinto and the Denver-based Newmont Mining Corporation—can be considered sustainable. Wal-Mart instead uses the vague term "responsible mining," reflecting the companies' compliance with legal licensing requirements.[11]

Wal-Mart trucks were further improved, with streamlining of the bodies and trailers to cut wind resistance, better tires, and more efficient loading methods. Combined with the auxiliary power units, these measures cut fuel use by at Wal-Mart by 25 percent, surpassing the initial goal Lee Scott set for the first round of improvements. By 2020, those changes will save Wal-Mart an estimated half-billion dollars. Better planning, routing, and loading of freight on the trucks made the fleet even more efficient, allowing Wal-Mart to ship 77 million more cases of goods a year while driving 100 million fewer miles (figures are for 2009, compared to the baseline year of 2005, when the sustainability efforts began). That reduction in miles led to a 143 million metric ton reduction in carbon emissions. Since 2005, the Wal-Mart trucking fleet has increased its efficiency by 60 percent. The goal set by the transportation network is a 100 percent increase by 2015.[12]

A new design for Wal-Mart stores matched the trucks' makeover, reducing energy consumption by 30 percent—with low-energy LED lighting in cold cases, closed freezers (instead of the old-style open ones), the use of heat generated by refrigerated cases to heat the store, and "daylight harvesting," which employs skylights during the day to light the aisles and reduce the lighting bill in each of the new stores by up to 70 percent. Electric lights in these stores are dimmed by central computers in Bentonville that measure the sunshine in every Wal-Mart store in the United States. "Closed-loop" CO_2 refrigeration systems were installed in new stores as well, reducing greenhouse gas emissions from refrigerants. Leaks from older chemical refrigerants are a source of greenhouse gas hundreds of times as damaging as carbon dioxide. Old stores were systematically retrofitted with most of these improvements, too, netting a 25 percent reduction in their energy usage. A small number of prototype stores experimented with other technologies, including solar panels and wind turbines in the parking lots and rainwater harvesting for use in irrigation and cooling systems. Motion sensors were installed in cold cases to shut off display lights when customers weren't near. The surprising result: the lights were off 80 percent of the time.

The agriculture and food network pushed through a program for buying locally grown produce throughout the Wal-Mart chain, reducing shipping costs and the distance food had to travel between farm and plate. Locally grown tomatoes became a staple at many Wal-Marts. Cilantro, typically shipped from California, could just as easily be grown in Florida, and Wal-Mart found farmers willing to plant the herb. Now stores in the eastern side of the United States are supplied by cilantro farms in Florida instead of the West Coast. Reducing food miles became a priority—a multiple win for sustainability, efficiency, cost, and local economies. And in the case of produce, that meant better-tasting veggies and far less spoilage. Huge amounts of waste occur when food goes bad or expires on shelves. American food producers, retailers, and consumers throw away an estimated 27 percent to 40 percent of our food supply every year, a colossal waste of resources and energy (the energy spent growing the wasted food every year is greater than all the energy derived from U.S. offshore oil drilling).[13] The food network concluded that Wal-Mart should pursue a zero-food-waste-to-landfill goal. Expired but still edible bulk foods that were trashed in the past are now donated to nonprofit groups to feed the hungry. Given the size of the Wal-Mart footprint, that means *127 million* pounds of food for the hungry in just one year. Other food waste goes to composting companies to be resold as organic mulch, turning trash into products that Wal-Mart then sells in its gardening department.

Wal-Mart's decision to purchase Toshiba laptops that met more stringent European environmental standards—following a trip to the manufacturing plant provoked by Jib Ellison—became the catalyst of a much larger initiative. In exchange for making longer-term buying agreements with suppliers, Wal-Mart persuaded other computer makers to strip out toxics and heavy metals voluntarily in U.S.-bound electronics. By July 2006, every computer and monitor Wal-Mart sold met the higher European environmental standards, even though the U.S. government hadn't passed a comparable regulation. The entire industry cleaned up within another year, not just for equipment sold at

Wal-Mart but everywhere. (Wal-Mart had less success with pilot programs for recycling e-waste—dead computers and other electronics. It tried rebates, prepaid mailers, special recycling days, and promotions, but none of those attempts to keep hazardous e-waste out of landfills worked well, as customer participation was poor.)

Sometimes a breakthrough in sustainability would arise from personal connections, as with Wal-Mart's efforts to purchase sustainable coffee, sparked by Blu Skye consultant Dave Sherman's unrelated doctoral work on social entrepreneurs. One of his interview subjects for his thesis was Paul Rice, founder and CEO of TransFair USA, a fair-trade organization based in Oakland, California. It would be hard to find a more unlikely partner for Wal-Mart; Rice had graduated from Yale University in 1983, then spent the next decade helping Nicaraguan peasant farmers form cooperatives in order to get a fair price for their coffee and other crops—finally transforming ten cents a pound into more than a dollar back in 1990. He later formed TransFair to persuade American companies to buy responsibly from co-ops of small farmers abroad rather than from large agribusinesses that often try to rip off those same farmers. When Sherman happened to mention to Rice that, in his day job, he worked on sustainability for Wal-Mart, the activist begged him for an introduction. Sherman put Rice in touch with Matt Kistler, then still working at Sam's Club. Kistler, in turn, had a particular interest in fair trade, having been shot down in his old job at Kraft Foods when he proposed working with a group such as TransFair to bring fair trade organic coffee to market. Kistler's boss at the time felt there was no market for fair trade—a position Kistler and Rice would soon disprove at Wal-Mart with a successful new line of fair-trade coffees.

Wal-Mart coffee buyers worked with Rice to set up a new arrangement with a Brazilian coffee company that buys directly from farmers. The supply chain on coffee had always been byzantine, moving from coffee growers to brokers to roasters to packagers to wholesalers and retailers. Many of these middleman steps added costs to the coffee but little real value, and out of a $90 billion industry, only ten cents on the dollar ended up with the farmers trying to eke out a living growing coffee. As many as 30 million families around the world depend on the backbreaking work of growing coffee for a living, and many end up selling beans below their own cost while others up the line get rich.

Wal-Mart's and TransFair's approach, however, eliminated half the supply chain, allowing the large Brazilian coffee company Café Bom Dia to deal directly with farm cooperatives certified as producing organic fair-trade coffee, which meets much higher environmental and social justice standards. Organic fair-trade coffee earns more for the growers with less environmental impact. It's grown in shade, without chemical pesticides, and without further clearing of rain forest, which is critical in Brazil, where deforestation was declared a national emergency after satellite tracking showed that more than 10,000 square miles of rainforest had been cut down in 2004.[14] Sustainability is further enhanced by roasting the beans locally, reducing their weight by 20 percent at the source, thus lowering energy and shipping costs. Wal-Mart partnered with the U.S. Agency for International Development to provide $2 million in grants and training to five thousand small family coffee farms that had demonstrated a commitment to organic fair-trade coffee and produced superior-tasting coffee as a result. The Rainforest Alliance environmental group, which has a representative on the Wal-Mart food and agriculture network, has certified as sustainable several of the brands of coffee Wal-Mart marketed this way in addition to TransFair's approval.

As a result, Wal-Mart could sell normally pricey organic and fair-trade coffees at a bargain—under $6 a pound. Yet farmers also earned more than in the past, creating an incentive to increase the acreage of coffee grown sustainably and organically. This worked so well that TransFair and Wal-Mart set up similar programs for fair-trade tea, bananas, and fresh roses.

Overall, Wal-Mart's food network figured out how to double the company's total organic food offerings within a year, introducing a thousand new products and becoming the largest seller of organic milk practically overnight. Organic advocates were divided by this move, fearful that Wal-Mart's low-price pressures would bankrupt organic farmers or reduce quality. But over time, the idea that organics could be sold to a much larger customer base—similar to the democratizing of sustainability that Lawrence Jackson yearned for—won over many critics who had long worried that organics were too elitist a product. Organic products, while eschewing pesticides and chemical fertilizers, are not necessarily better on the sustainable front than their conventional counterparts; producing them can use just as much energy and water and generate just as much waste and carbon. Still, Wal-Mart's entry into the organic market led large food companies to develop new lines of organic *and* sustainable products, from cornflakes to cooking oil, so they wouldn't be left out of this new opportunity. With only a 10 percent price premium for the organic label, Wal-Mart had the ability to mainstream the sale of organic food in a way that had never been possible before. As one supplier of organic dairy products who was taken to task by his peers for dealing with Wal-Mart said, "I don't want to be David. I want to be Goliath."

WAL-MART VICE PRESIDENT MATT Kistler, who would take over Ruben's job as head of sustainability in 2007, led the effort to create a packaging scorecard to drive, as well as measure, the goal of reducing the packaging of all 329,000 separate items sold by Wal-Mart by 5 percent. That reduction, similar to the original Kid Connection toy package reduction, would save the company an estimated $3.4 billion a year.

Wal-Mart told all its suppliers that they would have to answer the scorecard questionnaire to reveal who had wasteful packaging. The short answer: almost everyone. Participation in the scoring was begrudging at first. Here was big-daddy Wal-Mart trying to tell suppliers how to run their businesses, demanding more paperwork and research and calling for changes to long-standing business practices.

But soon the manufacturers saw that the scorecard could provide them with a path to cost savings and increased profits. A child car seat manufacturer, which had always shipped its products in giant corrugated boxes, killed the box and put its seats in a reusable, zippered plastic bag that showed off the product on the shelf and could be used by customers to protect the seat when flying or storing the car seat. It provided extra value for customers while cutting costs and environmental impact. The seats could be shipped nested in a third less space, using a third of the trucks and fuel.

Wal-Mart's scorecard also persuaded Apple, Inc., to shrink its iPod package and to make it from 100 percent renewable materials. The Sam's Club's private-label apple juice, Member's Mark, started using packages produced using 11 percent renewable energy from a hydro-electric-powered plant. Wrapping for vegetable trays and some other produce was switched from petroleum-based plastic to corn-based biodegradable polymers. Wal-Mart calculated that the first four products "wrapped in corn" saved 800,000 gallons of gasoline and 11 million pounds of carbon emissions that would have been expended in the production of regular plastic.

"None of this would have happened without that scorecard," Kistler told the four hundred members of the sustainable packaging network. This was by far the largest of the network teams, given that everything at Wal-Mart comes in some kind of package. "Everything flows from asking the question."

Then there was Hamburger Helper, the inexpensive boxes of noodles and flavoring used to turn ground beef into a full-course casserole by adding meat, water, and milk. Wal-Mart's questionnaire led product designers at General Mills to think about how to shrink the package for Hamburger Helper, which debuted in 1971 and became a best-selling fad in the mid-1970s. They hit on the simple idea of using straight noodles instead of curly ones. Straight noodles took up less room in the box than curled ones, and the box could then be shrunk by a fifth. What happens when a popular product shrinks its box? Every year, 890,000 pounds of paper fiber are saved and 500 truckloads leave the road.

Not to be outdone by Kistler's Hamburger Helper, even Lee Scott competed in the sustainability scoring game. He made Small & Mighty All, the concentrated small bottle of laundry detergent that packed the same cleaning power as the big 100-ounce bottles, his VPI—"Volume Producing Item." Wal-Mart executives—from store managers up through the CEO—competed with one another by selecting a favorite item to promote, then doing everything they could to drive sales volume. Scott decided to throw his weight behind the concept of small detergent bottles, which the packaging network wanted the entire detergent industry to adopt.

Unilever, the manufacturer of All, had tried more than a decade earlier to introduce a similar concentrated detergent under its Wisk brand. The effort was a disaster. Consumers saw big bottles for the same price as the small ones and chose the big ones, even though all they were carrying home was more water. When Unilever approached Wal-Mart a year or so before the sustainability drive and asked for help with trying the smaller bottles again, the retailer told the company to forget it: been there, done that, didn't work.

But now Wal-Mart intended to go all out. The network's experts worked with Unilever on packaging that would make it clear why the small All was best. Each label, front and back, now has a picture of small and large detergent bottles with an equals sign between them. Wal-Mart gave the little bottles prime shelving real estate, both eye-level shelves and "end caps," the high-visibility positions on the ends of each aisle. Scott appeared on *The Charlie Rose Show* on PBS and hawked Small & Mighty All on national television, and Ellen DeGeneres devoted a segment of her show to the product. She staged a mock game show entitled "Lighten Your Load," in which contestants brought in their dirty laundry and demonstrated that one tiny bottle would provide enough detergent for thirty-two washing machines set up in the studio back lot.

This time around, customers got it. The real value was in small, not large bottles. Sales were brisk. It didn't take long for Procter & Gamble and other detergent makers to realize what they had to do to get a share of that premium shelf space. The laundry detergent industry was transformed, with every manufacturer pushing its eco-friendly, concentrated formulations. The reduction also meant fewer and smaller shipping cartons and truckloads. Wal-Mart estimated that, in three years, the reduction saved 125 million pounds of cardboard, along with a half-million gallons of diesel fuel, 95 million pounds of plastic resin, and 400 million gallons of water used to dilute the detergent to fill the bigger bottles. "Lee pushed me," the chief executive of Procter & Gamble, A. G. Lafley, told *The New York Times*. "We totally, totally changed the way we manufacture liquid laundry detergents in the U.S. and, now, around the world."[15]

At this point, Scott and other Wal-Mart leaders began to realize that sustainability wasn't just a way of being cleaner and more efficient. It also seemed to be driving innovation. It led to better products, better packaging, better shipping and labeling. And none of those green innovations cost Wal-Mart anything. For the most part, the innovations only increased profits. Even suppliers, who had incurred some upfront costs in order to modify packaging or reformulate products, found that many of the changes lowered their costs over time and ended up more than paying for themselves.

Scott also helped promote the greenhouse gas network's plan to boost the sales of compact fluorescent lightbulbs by slashing prices and vowing to sell 100 million of the bulbs in a year. The environmental impact of meeting that goal would be dramatic: a saving to consumers of $3 billion in electricity bills and 20 million metric tons of greenhouse gases. Scott wanted Wal-Mart to push the power-saving bulbs into more American homes.[16]

Shortly after Scott first mentioned CFLs in his first sustainability speech, Oprah Winfrey devoted a show to climate change in which she, two environmentalists, and the actor Leonardo DiCaprio discussed the energy-saving lightbulbs. Wal-Mart put on demonstrations of the bulbs in stores, displayed them prominently (raising them from the no-man's-land of the bottom shelf to eye level), and put up signs explaining why each CFL would save consumers $40 in electricity bills over the life of the bulb even though their price at the cash register was more than that of an incandescent light. They even put them in ceiling fan displays in the lighting department so that people would get used to seeing the spiral shapes in their fixtures. Meanwhile, the chemical intensive network brainstormed new CFL designs with manufacturers and the Natural Resources Defense Council with the goal of reducing the mercury content of the bulbs, their one environmental drawback. Low-mercury-content CFLs debuted at Wal-Mart a few years later.

This campaign for more sustainable lighting did not come easily. Major lightbulb manufacturers, led by General Electric, which had been promoting its own green initiative called Ecomagination, long resisted a full transition to CFLs. The century-old technology of incandescent bulbs is wasteful, costly to use, and should have been consigned to obsolescence long ago. Engineers have called incandescents "heaters that put out a little light," because only 10 percent of the energy that goes into the bulb produces light, with the rest wasted in the form of heat. But they were cheap to make, and GE, Sylvania, and other bulb makers made a lot of money churning out incandescent replacements for the burned-out bulbs in America's billion-plus residential light sockets. CFLs lasted up to ten times as long—about eight years. It was the better and less costly technology for the environment and for consumers, but it wasn't as profitable for bulb companies to make a product that took so long to wear out. Consumers were already using and had accepted the primitive incandescent bulb.

The bulb makers told Wal-Mart to slow down. Wal-Mart told the bulb makers it was going with CFLs one way or another, with the U.S. bulb makers or without them. It could always create its own private-label bulbs and buy them elsewhere. This is the sort of argument Wal-Mart rarely loses. General Electric and other suppliers acquiesced. Selling some bulbs at Wal-Mart was better than selling no bulbs.

Within a year, Wal-Mart had surpassed its CFL sales goal, reaching 137 million bulbs sold. That's more than one for every household in America. By 2010, that number had nearly tripled, saving Wal-Mart customers an estimated $10 billion in electric bills over the life of the bulbs. Still, America trailed the rest of the developed world in adopting the cleaner, cheaper technology.

But Wal-Mart's advocacy helped unite Congress and political parties to pass lightbulb efficiency legislation as part of the Energy Independence and Security Act. Although there are critical loopholes—colored and three-way "specialty" bulbs are exempted—the law begins a phaseout of incandescent bulb sales in 2012 and mandates that all general-purpose lightbulbs be at least as efficient as current CFLs by 2020.

As the Sustainable Value Networks continued hunting for ways to embed sustainability projects companywide, Jib Ellison and his Blu Skye consultants designed Wal-Mart summit meetings for industry, academic, and environmental leaders around the country on CFLs, packaging, and sustainable textiles. There Wal-Mart suppliers were asked to help find new green innovations and to join the sustainability effort. Refusing meant facing the risk (unstated but nevertheless feared) of disappearing from Wal-Mart's shelves. The packaging conferences have become an annual affair, as have the semiannual sustainability "milestone" meetings in Bentonville to measure progress, which began as small quarterly meetings between Scott, his direct reports, and Ellison, but grew rapidly.

At a key early milestone meeting in July 2006, more than eight hundred Wal-Mart managers and executives from around the world arrived in Bentonville for briefings on the latest work of the sustainability networks. It was the first really big public meeting on Wal-Mart's green efforts, with a few journalists and several celebrity guests invited, including former Vice President Al Gore, there to screen his then-new climate change film, *An Inconvenient Truth*. Gore could have been too much for conservative Bentonville, but Ellison designed the meeting well. He made sure that before Gore took the stage, the audience heard from Reverend Jim Ball, who wove an environmental message into his evangelical sermon. Ball ran the Evangelical Environmental Network and *Creation Care* magazine, and had launched a national "What Would Jesus Drive?" campaign to hammer home what he saw as a biblical imperative for Christians to be environmentalists—and to take action on global warming. Ball's message was the perfect setup for Gore, who followed his film by addressing the gathering and answering questions with sentiments and arguments that sounded a lot like the preacher's.

The audience, who at the start of the film seemed uncertain, appeared rapt by the end. Some were in tears. In his talk, Gore likened the Wal-Mart sustainability push to the post–World War II work of the Allies, whom he described as using the moral authority and vision they had gained from struggle and victory to lift up and rebuild their adversaries once the violence ended. They made friends and partners of former enemies, he reminded them. He then addressed his audience directly: "And by taking this climate crisis on frontally and making this commitment, you will gain the moral authority and vision as an organization to take on many great challenges. . . . Doesn't it feel good to have this kind of commitment? Don't you feel proud?"

And there in the heart of red-state America, in a county where Gore lost two-thirds of the vote in his 2000 bid for the presidency, the new vicar of global warming received a standing ovation.

That same month, *Fortune* magazine put a picture of Lee Scott on its cover, posed in a cornfield in shirtsleeves, carrying a bucket overflowing with gorgeous garden vegetables. The headline read, "Wal-Mart Saves the Planet." Beneath that, the subhead demurred: "Well, not quite. But CEO Lee Scott's green campaign, which started as PR, is becoming a force of nature."

The bemused Andy Ruben later reflected to a University of Arkansas audience, "If Jib and I had sat down and said, 'What will two years later look like?' and I said, 'Jib, I can see in two years that Lee Scott is on the cover of *Fortune* magazine and the title is 'Wal-Mart Saves the Planet,' that would have been a joke. And then it happened."

Wal-Mart had even updated its slogan. The change was not made because of the sustainability efforts, yet it seemed to reflect this new mission anyway. Gone was the familiar "Always the Low Price." Now it was "Save Money. Live Better."

At a 2007 summit of Wal-Mart supplier CEOs, Scott said his company was in the sustainability hunt for the long haul. "It is not a fad, it is not a marketing ploy," he told them. And he expected suppliers big and small, name brands and unknowns, to join the effort to cut waste, improve efficiency, remove harmful chemicals, and reduce packaging—both because it made sense for the bottom line and because it would serve customers better. Then came the threat: suppliers who disposed of waste improperly or used harmful chemicals would be banished from Wal-Mart's shelves. "What in the world would make Wal-Mart think that the person who is willing to compromise the environment knowingly wouldn't also be willing to compromise on quality to meet a price point?"

Wal-Mart's threats, no matter how veiled or implied, have a history of motivating suppliers on price, and they have had a similar effect in spurring sustainability efforts. However, there have been few instances in which Wal-Mart carried out this threat and "fired" a supplier for sustainability failings—the ending of imports in 2009 from grossly unsustainable Chilean salmon farms is one known example, and that came only after a ruinous disease outbreak and after Wal-Mart spent years trying to improve suppliers' environmental practices.

Receiving this warning in the audience in Bentonville were four hundred CEOs and other senior executives from Procter & Gamble,

Sony, 3M, General Mills, SC Johnson—a who's who of major American corporations. "We make no claims of being a green company," Scott told them. "We're not saying we're better than anyone, we're not saying we're doing it right. What we're saying is that we recognize an opportunity to make a difference in this world, make a difference for our customers, for our shareholders, for our associates, and it is worthwhile to do. . . . We are simply getting started."

Humbling reminders that Scott was right, and that Wal-Mart still had a long way to go, were easily found. At the November 2007 sustainability milestone meeting, a middle-aged woman who had been hired as a Wal-Mart store employee by Sam Walton stood up with what began as a testimonial for the company's new Personal Sustainability Project. This program, she said, had inspired her to take charge of her diet, health, and environmental footprint as an individual. But then she chastised the company on pay and benefits and asked why it was that she could go to the employee cafeteria at Sam's Club and buy a supersized slice of pizza and soda for $2.50, while a salad and a bottle of water cost twice as much. If part of sustainability involved better health, diet, and lifestyles, she suggested, this pricing didn't seem right.

Sam's Club lowered the prices of its salads and water the next day.

THE FOLLOWING SUMMER, JIM Stanway, the head of the greenhouse gas network, grew frustrated. He was at a loss on how to proceed, for there was one big piece of the puzzle missing from his daunting task, which was to reduce Wal-Mart's carbon footprint companywide.

There were many things in the works or already accomplished to address the footprint of Wal-Mart's stores, distribution centers, and trucking fleet. Those fixes had been relatively easy to figure out and improve, because they hit Wal-Mart's sweet spot by helping lower costs even as they lowered the company's carbon footprint. The curly-haired British transplant had developed a shorthand mantra to explain this win-win: "Carbon equals energy. Energy equals money. Cutting carbon saves money." If every member of Congress in Washington would just learn that little ditty, as Stanway saw it, the United States would have passed groundbreaking climate legislation long ago.

Wal-Mart was the largest private purchaser of electricity in the United States—its stores consumed more power every year than a city of 3 million—and Stanway was finalizing contracts to purchase millions of dollars worth of renewable energy allotments to help green up that power supply. The efficiency retrofits of existing stores were under way, air-conditioning and heating systems were being upgraded, superefficient lighting systems were being installed. Solar energy systems were going up on rooftops of Wal-Mart facilities in California and Hawaii—only a couple dozen so far, because they were not yet cost-effective. But add a climate bill and cap and trade, Stanway promised, and he'd be slapping solar cells on every store he could. Even so, energy consumption at Wal-Mart facilities would soon be reduced by the promised 25 percent, maybe more, and there were opportunities to achieve more efficiencies in the future.

All that was good, it was measurable, it was real. But it was peanuts, Stanway complained. And it wasn't enough. The gains Wal-Mart was realizing in stripping carbon out of its direct operations only allowed the company to run in place, because the two hundred new stores it opened around the world every year added to the company's footprint as fast as Stanway could find ways to trim it back.

The real gains, he knew, the big returns that would far exceed anything realized so far, were not in the operation of the stores. They were in the supply chain. They were in the individual products. Take out the carbon systematically, and the company's climate footprint would plummet. At the same time, theoretically, costs should go down as well.

It was a simple idea, it made perfect sense, but there was a problem: How could it be measured? What was the greenhouse footprint of the stuff Wal-Mart sold? What did a pair of blue jeans do to the climate? A bunch of grapes? A pair of lady's stockings? Or an Alaskan salmon fillet twice frozen and shipped to China before landing in a freezer in the Newark Wal-Mart? How about a lawn mower? It had hundreds of parts, sourced from all over, from who knew where. So did one lawn mower have a smaller footprint than another? Did it matter if some its parts were steel or aluminum or plastic? Nobody knew. Nobody could tell him. There was no transparency. And if you couldn't compare, if you couldn't know what a specific product was doing to the climate, you couldn't decide what to buy and what to change. Blu Skye had helped gather estimates of the greenhouse gas emissions of whole in-dustries, which was helpful, but they didn't differentiate among brands and products and types.

Then it came to him: one night, as he sat in his kitchen, it occurred to Stanway that he needed a pilot program. Just a few simple, everyday items to see if the carbon footprint could be figured out by product. He looked around and decided on seven common items: milk, beer, soda, soap, DVDs, toothpaste, and vacuum cleaners. Everyone uses them. Wal-Mart sells them by the truckloads every day, rivers of beer and soda, mountains of soap and toothpaste. Why not start simple?

He put in calls to the major companies that sold Wal-Mart those products and asked them to figure out their carbon footprints. They knew how and where they made their stuff and sourced their parts. And if they didn't, well, it was time for them to find out. He repeated his mantra: Carbon equals energy equals money. Take the carbon out, and you save money. And really, wasn't this just another iteration of Sam Walton's old stricture about squeezing cost out of product? Only this time, the results would help save the planet, too.

For the first time since the sustainability initiative had begun at Wal-Mart, the most die-hard and suspicious environmentalists—even those who had distrusted the company's motives and sincerity all along and disdained those who "betrayed" the cause by working with the retailer—admitted that this idea excited them. While the government dithered and elected officials debated whether there was any need for action on the climate at all, Wal-Mart planned to dig deep into the greenhouse gas emissions of the consumer culture and do something about them. One constant critic, Greenpeace's research director, Kert Davies, told reporters, "Wal-Mart has the power to coax suppliers into changing. They're taking on a daunting task, which is pretty cool. . . . Wal-Mart is forging new ground."

So thirty companies involved in producing those seven types of products agreed to participate in a pilot carbon disclosure project, including giants such as Coca-Cola and Twentieth Century Fox. It was a challenging question. Some suppliers, including Fox, already had carbon studies under way and were eager to participate. Others would have liked to say no way, they didn't have the time or money or staff for such a task. But the operating assumption has always been that you don't say no to Wal-Mart if you are a Wal-Mart supplier. Not if you want to stay a Wal-Mart supplier. Just about every sustainability consultant in the business—and plenty had opened for business in the past year, hoping for a piece of the Wal-Mart pie—started getting calls from the affected companies, many of which were puzzled and worried about this latest demand from Bentonville.

The suppliers of one major product, however, ended up galvanized rather than repelled by the request. After an initial phase of skepticism and resentment at these new marching orders, Stanway's questions led them in a new direction, stimulating thoughts about innovation and cooperation where there had been hardly any in a hundred years. Stanway's request had the unintended consequence of launching the transformation of an iconic American product, a sea change that, though still a work in progress, is being looked at as a model for the country, if not the world, for moving an entire industry toward sustainability.

Wal-Mart, Blu Skye, and the American dairy industry had set out to turn milk green.

PART III

Beyond the Box

Economists think they are so smart, but they don't consider the services nature performs for us. They call those services "externalities." In other words, they don't care. . . . But try to figure out what it would cost us to do what nature does for us. . . . It adds up to $33 trillion.

—DAVID SUZUKI[1]

CHAPTER EIGHT

The Cow of the Future

Syracuse, New York
October 2009

The dairy farmers who assembled on a cool autumn morning at the Syracuse Holiday Inn arrived with little enthusiasm for the sustainability summit. They were suspicious and skeptical of the process, the purpose, this kitchen-table climate mandate from Wal-Mart, and pretty much everyone in the room who didn't milk a cow for a living.

There were the milk processors, the nemesis of dairy farmers. They almost never met or talked to one another, unless it was to argue about prices. Then there were the feed growers, the truckers, the retailers with their cases full of dairy products, always complaining about prices and how they barely broke even on milk. There were the bureaucrats who enforced regulations that hadn't changed since the Great Depression and the utility company guys who always had a reason why the farmers' renewable energy ideas wouldn't work. And then there were the politicians, the academics, the Wal-Mart guys and their fancy consultants from San Francisco, swooping into upstate New York to show the locals how it was done—how they were going to find answers for complex problems that the dairy industry had been trying and failing to solve for years. Yeah, right.

The dairy farmer who had been drafted to make the keynote presentation at the start of the summit eyed the unfamiliar faces and asked, "What are we supposed to do, sit around and sing 'Kumbaya'?"

It was October 2009, and for the second such summit meeting, the supposed culmination of a year and a half of planning, study, and work on dairy sustainability, this beginning seemed less than auspicious.

This event was to be another of Blu Skye's appreciative inquiry type of meetings, this one billed as "the system in a room," a process put to work when Blu Skye and Wal-Mart formed the Sustainable Value Networks. The idea was to have every part of the product's supply chain, from farmers to retailers to consumers and critics, involved in charting a new vision for dairy products, a reinvention of the humble gallon jug of milk. Everyone who touched the milk before it lands in a child's glass had to be involved—the whole system in one room. If there were barriers to success somewhere in the system, a reason why greener packaging or renewable energy had been blocked, the people who had the power to do something about it were right there to explain why—and, possibly, to do something about it. No memos, no voice mails, just face-to-face communication in a setting where unreasonable and arbitrary arguments could be called out.

At first, the discover-dream-design-deploy conversation had a fifth "D": desultory. There were plenty of sustainability ideas tossed around and ways in which they might move forward. But there was little agreement. Academics argued with farmers, state agriculture officials squabbled with environmentalists, people started looking at the clock. But this was normal, expected—part of the process. The Blu Skye consultants said a little "rapid prototyping" might help break the logjam, a seemingly spontaneous suggestion that was anything but. (This is why appreciative inquiry works and can be replicated—there's always a plan, and techniques that get results.) They herded everyone into a side room, where they had set up tables with an assortment of art, modeling, and building materials. There were pipe cleaners and clay, scissors and markers—the rapid prototyping setup turned out to be your basic kindergarten assortment. If dialogue isn't working, the consultants suggested, build something. Make a model. Show everyone what your vision of a sustainable future for dairy looks like.

At first no one quite knew what to do, unsure if this activity was useful, fun, or silly. After an awkward pause, one person finally dived in, a woman from the New York Agricultural Environmental Management Program, a last-minute but fortuitously enthusiastic addition to the attendees' list. She grabbed some clay and fuzzy pipe cleaners and started building. As everyone watched, a little town began to take shape, a community with dairy farms at its heart. The others joined in. The dairy farms in this model town produced large quantities of manure, but in this idealized community they weren't a source of environmental concern but a source of energy. Advanced digesters converted manure into methane used to generate electricity for the entire town, a town lit up by cow power. This turned a major source of climate-warming greenhouse gas into renewable energy. The by-product of the manure-to-methane process was a rich compost, destined for community vegetable gardens. Schools, homes, and businesses sent their food waste back to the dairy power station to make more energy instead of landing in a landfill. Habitats once threatened by excess manure were protected, water quality improved because there was no more runoff, jobs were created and supported, and greenhouse gases were rolled back, equivalent to taking 100,000 cars off the road in a mere ten years. All of it a result of one imaginary farm town's decision to extract value from what had been considered waste and pollution.

The simple power of this vision gripped the group and changed the dyspeptic dynamic of the meeting. Somehow seeing it laid out made it achievable. It wasn't far out, was it? It could be done, couldn't it? The technology was there. The need was there. Certainly the manure was there. What was missing from the puzzle besides leadership? Wasn't that leadership right there in the room?

The groups broke up into teams, drawing mockups of future *Time* magazine covers to show what the world could look like in 2020. The power grid representative and the dairy farmer who had reluctantly given the keynote address laughed together over a silly skit one group put on called "I Have Gas." Someone from the utility company volunteered to be the captain of a project to build cow manure power plants for smaller dairies, because there had to be some way to make this work. An artist Blu Skye employs to make real-time graphic renditions of its meetings with markers and whiteboards drew the entire ideal town in detail and listed the things that needed to happen to make it brick and mortar—and who in the room would take responsibility for one or two or more of the action items listed.

Then Blu Skye sprang a surprise it had arranged in advance: the governor of New York called to pledge his support for legislation to pave the way for making that silly little pipe cleaner and Play-Doh model, dubbed "Dairyville 2020," into something real, something that would turn an environmental negative into a positive, a homegrown energy industry developed from nothing, a model for the future.

DAIRY PRODUCTS ARE UBIQUITOUS in America. No class of products is more widely sold, no trip to the supermarket is complete without its purchase, few refrigerators in the country lack some dose of dairy products, be it butter, cheese, ice cream, sour cream, cream cheese, yogurt, or milk. The U.S. dairy industry has $100 billion in annual sales, creates hundreds of thousands of jobs, and represents nearly 10 percent of total U.S. farm sales. There are about 59,000 dairy farms in the United States, small and large, with a total of 9 million cows producing 180 billion pounds of milk each year.

But U.S. dairies are in trouble. Dairy farmers are perpetually on the brink of financial ruin. Retailers often only break even selling milk. Milk is the most regulated product in the nation in terms of health and safety, and those well-intentioned regulations, essentially unchanged since before the Great Depression, have left the industry locked into century-old technology and addicted to a hodgepodge

of subsidies that keep dairy farmers on life support while stifling innovation. Tom Gallagher, the CEO of the umbrella trade association
that represents a majority of American dairy farmers, Dairy Management, Inc., can't resist a bitter observation: "Good government
has been the barrier to our success."

Still, even without old-school regulatory gridlock, Gallagher
admits that his industry has been its own worst enemy time and again,
no outside help required. Dairy's image has taken a beating for health
and environmental concerns arising from the use of growth hormone
and antibiotics to boost milk production. The packaging, meanwhile,
is so tired and colorless that industry insiders deride the look of supermarket dairy cases as "the great white-out." And most recently, the
cow has become the four-legged poster child for global warming, a
source of greenhouse gases that rivals, and in some measures exceeds,
carbon emissions from the world's cars and trucks. All in all, the image
is not the one dairy farmers care to promote.

Gallagher, backed by a fifteen-cent tithe that goes to the Rosemont,
Illinois, headquarters of Dairy Management for every hundred pounds
of milk sold by member dairies, is in charge of creating, promoting,
and selling the image of milk. It was Gallagher's idea to launch an Innovation Center for U.S. Dairy at Rosemont. He hoped to "rebrand"
milk in the public's imagination as a tool for achieving better nutrition and health and a hedge against childhood obesity. But in terms
of marketing, presence, and consumer appeal in the grocery store and
the drive-through window, sodas and other sweetened beverages with
their empty, fattening calories continued to dominate.

Then, in the fall of 2007, Jim Stanway's call for greenhouse gas
footprint data for milk landed on the desk of Erin Fitzgerald, Gallagher's energetic young director of strategic planning. She turned to
her boss and said, "This is it! This is what we need."

The sustainability imperative from Wal-Mart may have drawn
reactions of resignation and dread in other quarters, but Fitzgerald's
take was enthusiastic. She saw "this kick in the butt," as she called

it, as just what the dairy industry needed to pull together all the disparate, feuding, uncompromising elements of the milk business—the farmers, the processors, the feed growers, the giant industrial dairies, and the smaller grass-fed operations. Wal-Mart sold a lot of milk, so the industry couldn't just say no to a request it might otherwise have blown off. To Fitzgerald, this project looked to be the catalyst to bring about the rebranding of milk as the healthy, green drink of the twenty-first century.

Fitzgerald reasoned that the Wal-Mart question would unite the members of the dairy business over an environmental matter for the first time ever (other than banding together to lobby against some regulation they didn't like). Responding to Stanway required an industry-wide analysis. It would be crazy to try to figure it out piecemeal, each dairy, processor, and grower trying to calculate its own greenhouse gas emissions. That would be costly and inefficient. Given the typically overworked and financially stressed lives of dairy farmers, it just wouldn't get done. Better to all work together through Dairy Management to figure out every sector of the dairy industry's footprint—and then, because Wal-Mart would demand it anyway, they could take the initiative and use those data to remake the industry. If Stanway's "carbon equals energy equals money" proposition proved true, Fitzgerald suggested, the dairy industry had a lot of money hidden in those 9 million cows. People had been toying with "cow power" for years, trying to convert those natural sources of methane into usable energy. The technology existed. It was mature and tested, in use on a handful of dairy farms large enough to afford the $1.5 million investment. Theoretically, it could scale up industrywide, but it just never had. The leaders of the American dairy industry had never pushed it en masse, never done the lobbying or investing needed to make it succeed. Now Wal-Mart was forcing the industry's hand.

Fitzgerald came to Dairy Management from a medical supply conglomerate, where she had been finance manager, but she had grown up on an Ohio farm and brought a persuasive passion to the dairy sustainability cause. It seemed so clear to her that the incentives that govern the dairy industry "are all crazy." Every time she ticks off the points in her argument, she gets into a lather. The government decided a half century ago to subsidize cheddar—no other cheeses, just cheddar. The laws are still on the books, so more cheddar cheese than anyone needs is produced every year and wasted every year. Other cheese makers? They're on their own. Up to 30 percent of the milk shipped to markets each year ends up thrown away after expiring on the shelves, a phenomenal amount of waste—wasted processing, wasted energy for refrigeration, wasted diesel fuel burned to transport hundreds of tons of milk that will nourish no one and generate no income. If three out of ten iPhones had to be destroyed rather than sold and used, or 30 percent of flashlights or basketballs or cornflakes or any other product, such waste would be fatal. The companies would go bankrupt. Investors would flee. But with dairy products, that's just the way it is, it's accepted, it's been that way for decades. It's how the industry is structured, in part because of its unbreakable tie to the venerable pasteurization process for sterilizing milk and the limited shelf life that process confers. "Our practices encourage waste," Fitzgerald laments. "Farmers are paid to waste. It is absolutely insane."

Her pitch is simple. Wal-Mart's sustainability push has come at the best possible moment for dairy. America is in a health, energy, and environmental crisis. Waste is no longer an option. And who is in the best position to address health and energy and environment all at once? In Erin Fitzgerald's view, it's the farmer. That should be the new paradigm for rebranding milk, she told her boss. "We can compete on health and environment. Coke can't. Flavored water can't. Gatorade can't. This is where we can innovate and win."

A business's embrace of sustainability as a core strategy, rather than as an ancillary act of social responsibility or marketing cleverness, always seems to begin with such a moment. Fitzgerald realized it when Wal-Mart asked for dairy's carbon footprint, and her impassioned argument left Gallagher convinced as well. He would try to

persuade his large and conservative board of directors—dairy farmers, for the most part—that sustainability wasn't a Communist plot
but a golden opportunity. Fitzgerald would work with the sustainability gurus at Wal-Mart and ask if they could suggest someone to
guide them over this unfamiliar terrain. That request led the dairy
industry to the same place where Wal-Mart had started, Blu Skye
Sustainability Consulting.

THE FRACTURED LANDSCAPE OF the dairy industry in the United
States seemed well suited to the appreciative inquiry method Blu Skye
had employed with Wal-Mart. Ellison tapped John Whalen to help
launch the dairy effort with his calm and reassuring style and diplo-
mat's knack for turning arms-crossed adversaries into allies.

The start was rocky when Gallagher took Whalen and Blu Skye
veteran Dave Sherman to dinner with some of the farmers on Dairy
Management's board of directors. Whalen recalls that when the topics
of sustainability and climate came up, these third- and fourth-generation dairy men grimaced as if they had just been served sour milk.
"Excuse me," one finally said, "the deed on my land is dated 1789.
Don't you tell me about what's sustainable."

Whalen understood his point of view. If a farm had been in the
family for centuries and was still a going concern, the owners must
know quite a bit about taking care of animals, resources, and the land.
Long before it became trendy and fashionable to talk about sustainability and "going green," these multigenerational family dairy farmers had been, to use the traditional term for sustainable agriculture,
husbanding their lands and herds. They had been in for the long haul,
mainstays of a business that, though most take it for granted, delivers
fresh product every day, all over the nation, week in and week out.
That product is nutritious and tasty and doesn't make people sick.
They felt they were doing pretty well, better than many businesses.

But whenever someone talked to them about the environment or sustainability, it always ended up being about something regulatory and costly—and about someone who didn't know their business telling them how to run their business. The men gathered at this dinner table resented Wal-Mart and its out-of-town consultants. They'd rather be left alone.

But Gallagher was not deterred. He had expected this reaction, and he had an answer for it: the carbon footprint issue is not going to go away—this is just the beginning, he told his board members. Our customers—meaning Wal-Mart—want it. Surveys of consumers show that at least a fourth have begun to consider the sustainability or "greenness" of products in making their food-purchasing decisions.[1] Sustainability is more and more being linked in people's minds with wellness, with the idea that if it's good for the planet, it's good for me and my children. And people think this way not because it's trendy but because it's true.

Dairy belongs in that conversation, Gallagher said, because this debate is going to proceed with or without us. "Either we're at the table, or we're on the table."

In dairy's case, the goal was to propel an entire industry forward, not just a single company, but the principle was the same as it had been for Wal-Mart: the early-mover advantage was there for the taking. Big dairy could use sustainability to reduce its costs and drive innovation. In the end, Gallagher persuaded his recalcitrant board members that they needed to do more than just set into motion a plan to measure dairy's carbon footprint, as Wal-Mart requested. They also needed to put that information to use by crafting a plan to make the dairy industry sustainable, and to create value for their businesses at the same time.

The Blu Skye consultants then became the green research arm of the American dairy industry, immersing themselves in all things bovine. They sought out leading farmers, researchers, and dairy critics for their expertise on cow diet and digestion, biogas energy, alternatives to current pasteurization technology, and the good, bad, and ugly facts about manure. They ranged as far as Denmark and South Africa in search of cutting-edge milk-producing technology, genetic research, and novel packaging. Meanwhile, they recruited the Wal-Mart-funded Applied Sustainability Center at the University of Arkansas to make measurements of emissions at dairy farms, feedlots, barns, and processors—a multiyear life-cycle assessment of dairy to reveal the true carbon footprint of milk. The university was a natural choice, as its researchers had already undertaken similar studies of the life cycle of global cotton growing. In the interim, Blu Skye made ballpark estimates using existing research to produce a carbon snapshot of fluid milk's entire journey from udder to kitchen table, from the grain crops fed dairy cows to enteric methane—cow burps—that contribute to climate change. They couldn't wait two years for the hard data from the University of Arkansas. The estimate would be close enough to make informed choices on which sustainability projects made the most sense to start first.

The initial estimate of the carbon footprint for fluid milk in the United States (not counting cheese, butter, ice cream, and other non-liquid dairy products) was 28 million metric tons of greenhouse gases a year, roughly the equivalent of the emissions of 5.1 million cars. The question then became: What can be done to take as many of those 5.1 million cars off the road as possible?

The largest share of those emissions—9.8 million metric tons, 35 percent of the total—comes in the form of cow methane emissions. Burps account for more than a third of the greenhouse gases coming directly from dairy cows.

The next biggest source of climate-warming gases—21 percent—comes from manure, which U.S. dairy cows generate at a rate of more than 1 billion pounds a day. Methane, whether in the form of burps or the emanations from decomposing manure, is far more damaging to the environment than the more common greenhouse gas carbon dioxide, one of the by-products of burning fossil fuels. Methane, pound for pound, is twenty-three times as potent a greenhouse gas as CO_2.

Another 12 percent of the industry's carbon footprint arises from the production of feed for dairy cows. The main, though not only, greenhouse culprit in feed crops is the nitrous oxide emissions from chemical soil fertilizers—the same problem associated with all conventional industrial agriculture. Nitrous oxide is even more damaging to the climate than methane—310 times as potent a greenhouse gas as carbon dioxide. The chemical fertilizers used in industrial farming also require massive amounts of fossil fuels to produce, adding more to the dairy carbon footprint.

Then there were smaller but significant percentages of emissions from the more than one thousand plants for pasteurizing and processing milk in the United States (7 percent of total dairy greenhouse gas emissions), packaging materials and manufacture (another 7 percent), transportation of the milk (3 percent), and refrigeration (3 percent), with the balance (7 percent) coming from the gasoline and electricity consumed by farming.

Fitzgerald and Gallagher told Blu Skye that revealing all of the sources of the dairy industry's climate footprint—not just the cows—was critical if dairy sustainability were to stand a chance. Every part of the milk supply chain had to accept its share of responsibility for emissions and for the campaign to reduce the dairy industry's carbon footprint. If the farmers were painted as the sole bad guys, that would be the end of the project. It was fine if the cows were the main source—no one would be surprised by that. But the farmers wouldn't stand for being the only ones who had to take the heat for climate change.

In June 2008, dairy industry leaders, Wal-Mart, and others met at the University of Arkansas's Applied Sustainability Center for a first-ever dairy sustainability summit. Two hundred fifty representatives from every side of the national dairy industry convened for three days to consider these new greenhouse gas data and to come up with a road map to greener milk. Blu Skye had sought out dairy experts worldwide and assembled a long list of possible opportunities to carve cost, inefficiency, and waste out of the system. There were short-term projects and longer-range, riskier ideas, but it was the economics of green that got the most attention. Blu Skye estimated that a full commitment to its sustainability recommendations would add a quarter-billion dollars to the industry's bottom line in combined savings and new revenues. That's the equivalent of selling 86 million gallons of milk, full retail price, added to the profit side of the ledger sheet for making dairy greener.

Energy conservation and efficiency were a particular area of interest because they provided the sort of "low-hanging fruit" opportunity that had first hooked Wal-Mart on sustainability. Energy audits of dairy farms and milk processors got under way to identify waste. It was discovered that modernization, conservation, and more energy-efficient equipment could cut power bills and related carbon emissions by an estimated 40 percent industrywide. Forty cents out of every dollar being paid to the electric company was wasted. That got even the crustiest farmer's attention: carbon really was money.

The problem of cow burps, the greatest greenhouse gas source in dairy farming, posed a far tougher challenge. Capturing the enteric methane in bovine belches is impractical, like trying to chase down every car's tailpipe emissions, except that you can't put the equivalent of a catalytic converter on a cow. Instead, the dairy farmers seized on the simple question Blu Skye posed: Why do cows burp so much? And is it natural for them to do so? No one knew, but the idea of altering their diet and identifying some kind of easy-to-digest "low-carbon feed" created excitement at the summit.

Cows' natural diet is grass. Their unique, multichambered stomach is built to digest it. Grass is an ideal nutrition solution favored by smaller and organic dairies because it's cheap, provides a marketing advantage (milk from grass-fed cows sounds—and is—natural), and has a much lower climatic impact than planting, growing, and harvesting grains, corn, and other crops, which require fertilizer and energy inputs. With the right grazing management, just having pastures lowers a dairy's carbon footprint. Even many large dairies use pasture feeding as a supplement. Dairy farmers have argued for years about the taste and nutritional value of milk from grass-fed cows versus grain-fed. So one of the projects proposed at the summit was to study whether a grass diet could lower the levels of enteric methane and to determine the ideal grazing management practices to reduce carbon emissions.

Larger dairies with thousands of cows to feed often find it difficult or impossible to rely on grassy pastures alone year-round, so they feed their cows a diet of grains—primarily soybeans and corn grown specifically as feed. The nonnatural diet may make cows' digestion less efficient, which then causes more gas. No one in the United States had ever studied this link between cow nutrition and cow burping in depth, so a Wisconsin veterinarian and dairy owner at the summit volunteered to lead a study of all sorts of other diet regimens that might lower the methane emissions from cows. One promising avenue for these low-carbon feeds is the addition of flax to cows' diet, which not only would add beneficial omega-3 fatty acids to cows' milk but could also reduce cow burping by as much as 40 percent. Studies in Europe, not yet replicated in the United States, suggest that adding fish oil to cows' diet can have a similar impact. Australian researchers have been experimenting with an encapsulated feed that moves farther into the cow's digestion system before breaking down, reducing methane production. It also has the unintended benefits of reducing cholesterol levels in milk and making cold butter easier to spread.

Another goal set at the summit aimed to reduce greenhouse gas emissions at the 35 percent of U.S. dairies that grow their own feed. No-till farming, replacing synthetic fertilizers with manure, and transitioning to more pasture feeding would reduce the overall dairy carbon footprint by an estimated 4 percent—the equivalent of taking 180,000 cars off the road. That reduction could be doubled with wider adoption of no-till farming by growers who sell soy and corn feed to dairy farmers. No-till farming has an added benefit: it's a form of carbon sequestration that could be used to generate income through carbon trading, although the collapse in 2010 of America's only carbon market, the Chicago Climate Exchange, has made this more difficult.

Perhaps the most controversial sustainability project approved at the summit took a swipe at the nineteenth-century art of pasteurization. This energy-intensive process of heating milk to kill germs before bottling it or using it in other dairy products has long been a sore point for dairy farmers. Developed by the pioneering French microbiologist Louis Pasteur to prevent wine from turning to vinegar, pasteurization is costly and limited in terms of shelf life compared to more modern alternatives. But the government has been inflexible for most of a century on the practice, allowing only two variations: HTST (high temperature, short time) pasteurization, which heats milk to 170 degrees for about fifteen seconds, then immediately cools it; and ultra-pasteurization, which heats the milk to 280 degrees—well above boiling—for only two seconds, followed by rapid chilling. Most milk in the supermarket uses the lower-temperature method, which provides a refrigerated shelf life of about two weeks. Most organic milk, however, uses the higher-temperature method, which provides a refrigerated shelf life of about two months and far less waste as a result. The higher-temperature method produces a kind of caramelized taste different from what most consumers expect, although some milk drinkers prefer it. Both kinds of pasteurization change the taste and texture of raw milk, which is so unfamiliar to all but a few American consumers that the "real" taste of unaltered milk is considered too exotic and rich.

An alterative method of sterilizing milk, not approved for human consumption in the United States but adopted in other countries (and for animal use in the United States), uses ultraviolet light instead of heating and rapid chilling. The UV method is far less energy-intensive—consuming as little as 8 percent of the power required for conventional pasteurization—so the savings in terms of cost and climate would be huge if adopted by U.S. dairies. A South African dairy-processing executive spoke at the summit about his country's long use of the technique, sparking considerable interest among U.S. dairy farmers.[2] The process can produce "shelf-stable" milk that can be shipped and shelved without refrigeration when vacuum packed, a particularly valuable feature in the third world and a huge cost saving anywhere.

What has the dairy industry most excited is the potential of UV to go beyond merely reducing the carbon footprint for processing milk. When combined with the HTST pasteurization currently used with most milk in the United States, ultraviolet can produce refrigerated milk that can last for two months, just like organic milk but without the flavor change. This could represent a quantum leap in the potential for saving energy and eliminating costly waste, as nearly 30 percent of dairy products are discarded at the store or at home because of exceeded expiration dates or spoilage. That means 30 percent of the energy used to make milk and bring it to market is wasted. Sixty-day milk would eliminate much of that waste, and the greenhouse gas emissions related to it.

With a shelf life four times greater, more variation in milk packaging could be used: the "great whiteout" of the supermarket cold case could become a thing of the past. Any sort of packaging could be used. And the United States' copious supplies of milk could be exported as never before to parts of the world suffering from hunger, particularly where refrigeration is not available.

Spoil-proof milk isn't the only high-tech, futuristic project on tap: the summit participants also decided to pursue a "Cow of the Future" project, intended to alter the cow itself rather than just its feed, in order to reduce its gassiness. One line of research seeks to produce a vaccine to combat the burping of greenhouse gases—a kind of climate change inoculation that would work like a bovine version of the over-the-counter gas remedy for humans, Beano. Australian researchers have been experimenting with swapping the digestive tract bacteria in cows for different but similar organisms that produce less methane inside cows' stomachs. Enteric methane was reduced by 80 percent in the test tube this way and by a less dramatic but still substantial 30 percent in animal trials.

The Cow of the Future project would also look at breeding. Could a different breed of cow produce as much milk as the currently favored breeds while emitting less methane? And would conventional animal husbandry lead to such a cow of the future, maybe some untested combination of Holsteins, Jerseys, and other lesser-known breeds? Or would more laboratory genetics be required—test-tube cows? Dairy farmers are wary of anything that could be labeled a "Franken-cow." Consumers' concern over genetically modified organisms, as with the uproar over the use of growth hormone to boost milk production, could be disastrous for milk sales. Still, the farmers would love to use a bit of science to develop a more sustainable cow that burped less while producing more milk with a higher nutritional value.

The greatest enthusiasm, however, was reserved for cow power. Producing energy from manure has its share of complexity and risk compared to something as straightforward as energy audits and conservation grazing. But the potential returns for the environment and for the dairy industry's bottom line were the greatest of any of the sustainability ideas at the summit.

THE AVERAGE DAIRY COW produces up to 150 pounds of manure a day. When this output consists merely of cow patties in a pasture, they may be messy, but they pose no great climate change threat. But at industrial-scale dairies, where thousands of cows are kept in large barns and pens, the enormous and constant flow of manure is mixed with water into a slurry that channels the goo into storage lagoons. There the manure breaks down through the process of anaerobic decomposition—without oxygen. This process, similar to what happens inside the cow's stomach each time it burps, produces reeking emissions of up to 75 percent methane. The remainder is mostly carbon dioxide with a touch of nitrous oxide. It's a greenhouse gas monster and the dairy industry's second largest source of greenhouse gas after cow burping.

The beauty of manure power is its use of proven technology, the anaerobic methane digester. Digesters have the potential to solve several nationwide problems: what to do with the 400 billion pounds of cow droppings produced every year, as well as what to do with the harmful methane emitted from the gigantic slurry ponds. But it's not just a waste solution. It also makes energy and money in the process. It's a win-win-win.

The actual digester is a sealed concrete box that can be almost any size, from experimental small-form digesters of hot-tub proportions to double-sized Olympic pool–scale monsters. Manure goes in, other organic waste (for example, restaurant and household garbage) can be added, along with some heat, and then nature takes over. A mixture of methane and other gases referred to as biogas is produced by the anaerobic decay and pumped out, while inside, a safe, sterile, odorless compost or fertilizer material is left behind. You can even make fiberboard and other lightweight construction materials out of it.

The gas can then be burned to generate electricity on-site to power the dairy and flow into the utility grid, just as with rooftop solar panels or wind turbines. Or the biogas can be purified and turned into biomethane for use as fuel in vehicles or in any system that can burn natural gas. Purification was once too costly a process to be economically viable, but researchers at the Western Washington University have recently developed an efficient refining system that produces fuel that would deliver energy equivalent to a gallon of gasoline, but for only $2.50 a gallon. The whole process not only stops harmful greenhouse gas emissions but creates a renewable energy source that can displace fossil fuels and their greenhouse gas emissions. The digester does double duty as both a fuel source and a dairy carbon footprint reducer.

Scaling up dairy power from manure could provide electric power for farm communities across the United States that now rely on coal-burning power plants. If U.S. beef cattle ranches (with ten times the number of cows as dairy farms), pig farms, and chicken farms made a similar investment in digesters—and these industries are all following the dairy sustainability initiative—manure could provide more than 3 percent of the country's total electricity needs. That's more than all the solar, wind, and geothermal energy electricity generated in the United States in 2010 combined. Even though burning cow biogas releases some carbon, it's still cleaner than coal, so using all that manure to its full potential could reduce power plant greenhouse gas emissions nationwide by 4 percent.

Even if the dairy industry goes it alone, it still owns 10 percent of the overall U.S. manure-methane pie. With digesters fully deployed, that could produce more than 10 billion kilowatt hours of renewable energy that, if used in place of coal in American power plants, would eliminate 10 million metric tons of carbon emissions every year. Dairy cow power alone could provide the electricity for a million homes a year.

Other countries, Denmark among them, derive substantial portions of their electricity from manure digesters. Norway runs eighty municipal buses on biogas (though the Norwegians are using human waste). A worldwide effort to make digesters a common sight wherever livestock is raised would not only bring electricity to areas where it is either too expensive or too difficult to deliver reliably but also have a huge impact on climate. Worldwide, according to a study commissioned by the United Nations, livestock accounts for 18 percent of global warming emissions but only 1.5 percent of gross domestic product. Livestock emissions are a greater contributor to climate change than the world's cars and trucks. A subsequent UN study that separated the life cycle of the global dairy industry from the larger population of livestock found that milk and other dairy-related products contributed 4 percent of all human-created greenhouse gas emissions.[3]

One dairy farmer, Mike McCloskey, a leading advocate of digesters, uses this process to power his massive dairy farm in Indiana. He says his experience is evidence that the cost of installing digesters is justified by the payback. McCloskey, something of a legend in dairy circles, owns Fair Oaks Farms in Indiana. With its 30,000 cows, Fair Oaks is a veritable Disney World of combination megafarm and theme park, with a birthing center open to the public that guarantees that visitors will witness the live birth of a calf any day they come by. Fair Oaks grows the grains and grasses for its cows right at the farm, processes and bottles the milk on-site, and makes cheese and other dairy items at the farm, selling the products on-site as well as through retailers. McCloskey has found an entrepreneurial model that works, that depends on size and diversification, and that, for its size, has a carbon footprint far smaller than that of other comparable dairy farms.

Another pioneering farm, Hilarides Dairy in California's Central Valley, uses the manure from its 10,000 cows not only to provide electricity for the dairy itself but to power a pair of eighteen-wheel tractor-trailers with biogas equivalent to 650 gallons of diesel fuel a day. The state Air Resources Board gave the dairy a $600,000 grant to convert its trucks to methane burners to help demonstrate the concept. Theoretically, the manure from all 1.7 million California dairy cows could produce nearly 15 billion cubic feet of methane annually, enough to power 2 million vehicles for a year. Treating other animal and human waste in this way could provide a substantial portion of the state's energy needs.

Based in large measure on the potential benefits of digesters, the dairy industry has pledged to reduce its carbon footprint by 25 percent by 2020. Yet daunting barriers remain. Despite real-world demonstrations of this huge opportunity to create a new renewable energy industry, there were fewer than one hundred dairy digesters in operation in the country in 2008, although there are at least 1,300 dairy farms large enough to make digesters economically feasible. That number could double if smaller dairies pooled resources for a communal digester, and double again if experimental small-scale digesters now being developed prove viable. The cost and complexity of the digesters available in the United States, legal and market barriers that prevent dairy farmers from selling their electricity at anything close to market rates, and lack of government and industry support have relegated digesters to the role of expensive novelties and toys for sustainability zealots.

As with all sorts of non-utility-generated renewable energy sources, the economics of cow power in the United States are crippling. Utility companies have, for the most part, refused to purchase the electricity created by digesters (or home solar panels or windmills) at a market rate. They are not legally required to do so and have little incentive to support policies that would encourage non-utility-controlled sources of power to flourish. Renewable energy has taken off in countries that have established a more equitable payment for farmers and other small-scale generators, using a regulatory framework called a "feed-in tariff." This simply means that if you feed electricity into the grid, you earn a market rate. Germany, with a fraction of the sunshine that the United States receives, leads the world in solar generation because of its feed-in tariff system, but the U.S. utility lobby has successfully opposed an American version of the program. Hefty connection fees to link a digester to the grid further discourage adoption of the technology. Many farmers simply can't afford the capital outlays. A large digester makes much more methane than is needed to provide electricity for the average dairy farm, which provides an economic incentive to invest in such a system—but only if farmers can get a decent payback for the energy they generate.

Instead, dairy farmers have flared off excess methane, wasting valuable fuel. Others have just let the manure decay and damage the environment. Whole cities could have been powered, whole fleets of trucks could have been fueled. Instead this source of fuel and electricity sits and rots.

The purpose of the second dairy summit in Syracuse in 2009 was to break the barriers to widespread adoption of methane digesters and cow power. The state of New York had been chosen as the test bed and

launch pad for dairy power, beating out California, which had regulatory roadblocks that officials would not ease to permit rapid development of methane digesters.

In the wake of a national call for more renewable energy by the
Obama administration, the possibility of ramping up the technology
for using methane from cow manure as fuel seemed obvious. Once all
the poop power jokes had run their course, the potential to build an
entire new line of business around what had been a troublesome and
costly waste material became abundantly clear.

The result was the inspirational Dairyville 2020 model, followed by
a commitment to ramp up methane digester installation in New York
State to more than equal the number currently in operation nationwide. All that was needed after that meeting to set the plans in motion
was strong federal support: grants, loan guarantees, and incentives for
utilities to support, rather than deter, manure-based renewable energy.

Two months later, at a press conference during the Copenhagen
Climate Conference, U.S. Secretary of Agriculture Tom Vilsack
stood with Erin Fitzgerald at his side and announced an agreement
between his agency and representatives of the dairy industry to use
grants, loans, incentives, and new rules to increase cow power and put
Dairyville 2020 on the map—first in New York, then nationwide.

"This historic agreement, the first of its kind, will help us achieve
the ambitious goal of drastically reducing greenhouse gas emissions
while benefitting dairy farmers," Vilsack said. "Use of manure-to-elec-
tricity technology is a win for everyone because it provides an untapped
source of income for famers, provides a source of renewable electricity,
reduces our dependence on foreign fossil fuels, and provides a wealth
of additional environmental benefits."

Within the month, the first round of construction of new methane
digesters began. By then five hundred energy audits had been per-
formed by Fitzgerald and her team, and carbon emissions at dairy-
processing plants were already decreasing. Meanwhile, trials of new,
low-carbon feeds and testing of UV pasteurization were under way.

Fitzgerald even appeared at a major trade conference with Dairy Management's display constructed entirely out of manure.

A suggestion from Jib Ellison, a question from a Wal-Mart executive sitting in his kitchen, the power of appreciative inquiry, an assortment of pipe cleaners: these unlikely ingredients had combined to bring the balkanized dairy industry together to remake itself into a renewable energy powerhouse. Wal-Mart is big, but even that mammoth company is only a piece of the retail sector. Dairy had become the first entire industry in the United States to commit to going green.

CHAPTER NINE

One Index to Rule Them All

F ive years from now, this is the vision: You walk into a store, pick up a pair of blue jeans, and check the tag. It has three scores on it, each ranging from 1 to 100: one for sustainability, one for health, one for social and ethical factors. The tag shows the industry-average scores for all blue jeans and how much better or worse the pair you're holding happens to be. The scores are colored red for below average and green for above, just to make things clear and simple—a whole new take on comparison shopping, accomplished with a glance. Want deeper information? Just swipe the tag's bar code with your smartphone, and up pop separate sustainability scores for carbon emissions, energy use, water conservation, deforestation, waste, and number of miles the materials in the jeans had to travel. If it's health you're most interested in, tap that icon instead for information on pesticide levels, organic growing information, and the relative safety of the chemical dyes used in the jeans. Social/ethical score details might reveal grades for labor conditions, wages and benefits, fair trade, or the manufacturer's philanthropic giving. Web links could let you drill down into the data even farther, taking you to photos of the field where the fabric was grown, an interview with the farmer, or a video of the factory in China where the pants were dyed and cut. Perhaps there's a note on what the Sierra Club has to say about the company or the chemicals in the jeans—or information from the American Cancer Society or Oxfam. As much or as little information as a consumer could want is available to you for your purchase, peeling back the whole impact and life cycle of those jeans, including how recyclable they may or may not be when they are worn out. Information on all the hidden, external costs that manufacturing those jeans imposes on nature, taxpayers, consumers, and public health is no longer invisible. When you shop for jeans, that information is staring you in the face.

Now imagine such a tag on every product in a store the size of Wal-Mart—basically everything you buy, from eggs to electronics. What would that mean? Can it be done? *Should* it be done?

Wal-Mart certainly seems to think so. This is the vision of business transparency that got a group of corporate leaders and environmentalists so excited during a Blu Skye whitewater trip on the Tuolumne River in the summer of 2009, when they called it the next Industrial Revolution. Putting Wal-Mart muscle behind a multi-industry sustainability index that could benefit competitors as much as Wal-Mart itself had been Matt Kistler's vision—the project wouldn't exist without him. But it had taken two years of work and planning just to get it from the idea phase to a point where the real work of building such a far-reaching tool could begin, a task that had fallen largely to Kistler's director of strategy/sustainability, Rand Waddoups, with help from Blu Skye. They believed adding such information to the world of commerce would transform the old adage "Let the buyer beware" into "Let the buyer be informed." Companies would have to compete not just on a product's price and features but on sustainability, health, and ethics, too. Such information wouldn't just drive consumer behavior, it would also guide the choices of the business world before consumers even saw a product—perhaps its most powerful aspect. Companies could use the same information to eliminate previously hidden waste and inefficiencies, thereby bolstering sustainability (and profitability). Manufacturers would try to beat the scores of their competitors. Retailers would use the scores to select which products to sell and promote. The universe of sustainability measures that would generate a return on investment would expand, driven by competition and the laws of supply and demand. A new market force would come into play—a market force for being good.

That's the hope, at least, behind The Index, Wal-Mart's most ambitious—and most controversial—sustainability project to date.

It's ambitious because it's so much bigger than even Wal-Mart and goes so much farther than extracting waste and inefficiency from a product or a store. The Index seeks to accomplish something never before attempted in any systematic way: measuring the true impact of our consumer culture while giving manufacturers, retailers, and shoppers a tool and an incentive to lower that impact. Mike Duke, the former engineer who would take over as Wal-Mart CEO in February 2009, described the logic behind The Index in an engineer's terms: "If you can't measure it, you can't manage it."

The Index is controversial because it amounts to Wal-Mart using its size and clout to impose on the business world what amounts to a sweeping regulatory scheme. Had the government attempted to mandate such an index as a public service, the cries of "socialism" and "job killer" from free-market purists and champions of deregulation would have politicized it immediately. And that's assuming any government this side of FDR would have the courage to measure the more unpleasant consequences of our consumer economy, then use that information to alter the way we manufacture and consume. After all, the government didn't even bother to test the safety of chemicals in baby pacifiers and other children's toys that, after decades of use, were found to be linked to hormone disruptions, premature puberty in girls, asthma, and other ailments.[1] Wal-Mart is stepping in to fill a conspicuous vacuum, though its motives are not altruistic. The company, as with all its sustainability efforts, believes it will profit from The Index, although in this case, Wal-Mart has taken pains to craft a multi-industry "level playing field" that, in theory, any company, including rival retailers, can use to gain competitve advantage.

In the past, the most obvious barriers to such a project as large and complex as The Index would have been the technology and the data gathering. Now, however, both of those pieces are nearly in place. The technology to make in-depth sustainability information on individual products accessible to all is rapidly becoming ubiquitous, as an estimated one out of every two Americans will own a smartphone by the end of 2011.[2] The process of gathering the data has been under way in one form or another since Wal-Mart launched its sustainability effort in 2005, beginning with a series of scorecards and questionnaires to its suppliers. In 2009, an independent industry and university consortium started a more detailed and scientifically rigorous analysis of the life cycle and sustainability of products—the consumer "detective work" that is supposed to form the heart of The Index.

Still, barriers to success remain that have no such straightforward solutions. One looming, we-won't-really-know-till-we-try-it question is whether enough consumers will put the information to use for The Index to matter. Wal-Mart uses its Bentonville supercomputer complex to track the buying patterns and preferences of Wal-Mart shoppers, and the data suggest that most of them will choose the more environmentally friendly alternative if the price is competitive (or even a little higher) and it doesn't inconvenience them. But whether that behavior will translate into significant numbers of Wal-Mart customers relying on The Index and their smartphones to buy greener dog food, batteries, and shampoo is anybody's guess. Americans have a long history of lagging behind the rest of the world on even the most seemingly commonsense green ideas and products, clinging to gas-guzzling SUVs long after the rest of the world went to gas-sipping compacts, despite the recession.[3] The United States has also been slower than Europe, Canada, Australia, and Mexico to adopt the demonstrably cheaper, better CFL lightbulbs. In 2009, about 10 percent of the light sockets in U.S. homes had CFLs in them; Japan by then had passed the 80 percent mark.[4] David Cheesewright, the bicycle-commuting CEO of Wal-Mart Canada, calls this consumer behavior in the United States and Canada "the great conundrum."

"I can't think of a single instance where a person says, the reason I come to your store is because of what you're doing on sustainability. They come for the prices, they come for the assortment—but they don't come for sustainability," Cheesewright says. "If you raise the subject they say, 'Yes, that's important, but I don't know what I can do about it as an individual, I just want someone else to do it for me, and I don't want to pay anything for it.' That, unfortunately is the typical sort of message you get from consumers."

Cheesewright adds that his company is not discouraged by this attitude because of all the other, internal benefits sustainability brings to the business—and because Wal-Mart is convinced that the next generation of customers will have a very different attitude.

The other barrier to creating a meaningful sustainability index is deciding exactly what it will measure and score. Those choices will determine whether it will be truly revolutionary or just another ho-hum entry in the hundreds of green and eco labels that have been slapped onto so many products in recent years—"a Tower of Eco Babble," as a leading university researcher on the sustainability index project, Jon Johnson, puts it. The Index will be useful only if it can bring unrelenting transparency, revealing the bad information along with the good. Will, for instance, The Index measure the quality and durability of goods, which tend to be Wal-Mart's weak spot? High-quality goods that last a long time are inherently more sustainable than cheaper, flimsier ones. Will Wal-Mart or its suppliers want to disguise or leave out that sort of potentially unflattering information from the scores? Or will the company be willing to take its lumps and do what it expects its suppliers to do when they score low on a sustainability measure: improve?

"We've had that conversation with Wal-Mart, because we faced it ourselves years ago," recalls Rick Ridgeway, the head of sustainability for Patagonia, which has something like a Web-based mini-index of its own products called "The Footprint Chronicles." Ridgeway and Patagonia, after years of refusing to go to Bentonville, are working closely with Wal-Mart on the apparel portion of The Index. "We kind of warned them, if you go down this path and you really commit to it, it's going to force you to completely shift your business model. Eventually you'll have to move away from the 'everyday low prices' model and move to the 'everyday high quality and durability' model."

Ridgeway expected them to object to such talk and to insist that Wal-Mart need not change its core mission to improve its sustainability. But he recalls instead that Lee Scott and his senior leadership said they understood that there would be a gradual change in the retailer's emphasis, perhaps by offering alternatives for Wal-Mart customers—products that emphasize higher quality but less cost of ownership because of their longer life. Such a shift is by no means imminent or certain, Ridgeway says. "But that's the path they're on now. And maybe they'll drag the rest of America with them. . . . We can hope."

IF WAL-MART'S FIRST GREEN phase, Sustainability 1.0, focused on what it could do inside the company with energy, efficiency, and waste and Sustainability 2.0 focused on greening the Wal-Mart supply chain, Sustainability 3.0 is about transforming whole industries. It moves the process beyond fixing individual products and procedures (although that work continues), to redirecting entire economies toward sustainability. Jib Ellison sketched just such a progression on a notepad for Lee Scott in 2005, arguing that Wal-Mart occupied a unique position for making history. At the time, few at the company, including Scott, envisioned anything so dramatic. Even talking in such sweeping terms made Scott nervous. He just wanted the company to do better on the environment and do it cost-effectively—notwithstanding Ellison's constant refrain, "You're not thinking big enough."

By mid-2008, with the planning for The Index under way, Ellison no longer felt the need to say that, as the sustainability projects had gotten successively larger and more ambitious. Instead, he brought Bill McDonough back to Wal-Mart to speak at a sustainability milestone meeting. The architect and coauthor of *Cradle to Cradle* (with Michael Braungart) designed Wal-Mart's first prototype green store in the early nineties but had not been back to Bentonville since. In the ensuing years, he had built his career around championing a vision of buildings and products that incorporated their end of life into their design, so they could be completely recycled, put nothing in landfills, and leave nothing harmful behind—in McDonough's terms, moving from "cradle to cradle" rather than "cradle to grave."

He used his speech before an auditorium crowded with Wal-Mart employees to challenge the company to do more—to stop trying to be less bad and try to be good. It's a crucial difference, he noted. If you get into a car to go to Mexico but take off toward Canada at a hundred miles per hour, that's bad. If you slow down to two miles per hour, that's *less* bad, "but you're still going in the wrong direction." Emitting less toxins, less carbon, less waste are all laudable goals, McDonough said, but they still amount to slowing down a car going the wrong way.

He used wall-to-wall carpets as an example. Old carpeting can be recycled and made into new carpeting, yet 3.5 billion pounds of it end up in U.S. landfills every year. This is due mainly to the common use of carpet-backing material made of polyvinyl chloride (PVC) plastics, which have toxic chemicals in them and can make recycling more difficult and expensive (as well as emit carcinogenic gases inside the home). McDonough has worked with several large floor covering companies, Interface and Shaw Floors, that have eliminated polyvinyl chloride (PVC) plastics from their products. The PVC-free carpeting is infinitely recyclable, McDonough says, with no dangerous household emissions. That, he said, is being good.

When he studied the 8,000 chemicals commonly used to process and dye clothing, McDonough says, he found that only 38 of them produced safe, healthy, ecologically sound clothing without carcinogens, endocrine disruptors, or other harmful chemicals. It is staggering how bad for the environment, animal life, and human health so many of the other chemicals are, he said, yet you can make textiles using just those few safe chemicals if you choose to do so. A Swiss textile maker, Jacob Rohner AC, has found that it can produce fabrics suitable for upholstery and fine apparel with only completely safe and healthy chemicals—and with a 20 percent cost saving, according to McDonough. There are no more toxic and hazardous substances that require special handling at the factory, no more regulatory burden of permits and paperwork. When government inspectors sampled the wastewater being discharged by the plant, they thought the equipment was broken, because it showed nothing harmful. Wal-Mart, he said, could ask its suppliers tomorrow to begin a shift toward making clothes with only safe chemicals. Make the clothes you sell good rather than just not as bad as before, he urged.

Of course, there was no way Wal-Mart was going to call up its apparel makers the next morning and order them to reduce thousands of chemicals to thirty-eight. The transition would be too big, too radical; the massive retooling it would require, the transitional costs and delays, would be beyond daunting. Most of the apparel Wal-Mart sells is made at least in part in China, where Blu Skye and Wal-Mart were working in unprecedented partnership with suppliers just to achieve some first, halting progress on sustainability. Wal-Mart had just held a massive national summit there for the CEOs of China's enormous and rapidly growing industrial sector, with Lee Scott in the Nixon-goes-to-China role—the first meeting of its kind for China's new capitalists. The challenge was enormous: the textile plants that dyed and wove fabric and cut clothes for Wal-Mart were the size of whole towns. Blu Skye consultant Adam Hyde reported seeing chemical-laced wastewater pouring out of some of the factories, coloring rivers, killing aquatic life, and contaminating surrounding land.

The 2008 Summer Olympics in Beijing had offered an opportunity to begin to clean up some of that pollution, as the Chinese government did not want to be embarrassed during the influx of international visitors and media attention. A Blu Skye and Wal-Mart team got permission to help Chinese suppliers improve their operations, equipment, and chemical formulae to lessen their environmental impact. At the summit, Scott extracted a commitment from Wal-Mart's top two hundred China-based suppliers to adopt permanent sustainable practices and energy efficiency. The Chinese manufacturers and government also agreed to regular audits by Wal-Mart of pollution, energy use, and waste—and also working conditions, a first. After years of criticism and numerous sweatshop scandals, Wal-Mart had put into place a certification process for enforcing stringent environmental and ethical standards against child labor and other abuses for all its suppliers worldwide. Factories that failed to comply, Scott had said, would be banned from making products for Wal-Mart.

It will be a long time before the Wal-Mart "car" is completely turned in the right direction. But Scott and Ellison believe that The Index will accelerate that change while rewarding past sustainability gains with high scores. Maybe a factory won't be able to reduce 8,000 chemicals to 38 in the foreseeable future, but perhaps it could cut them in half, and the prospect of earning a better score on a new sustainability index would help force that change. Wal-Mart would respond by selling products from that high-scoring factory instead of the manufacturers that did little to make their operations more sustainable. The next year, those sidelined manufacturers would have an incentive to outdo their competitors so they would score higher on The Index— and get back onto the Wal-Mart shelves. Thus the race to the top will begin, Ellison predicts, driven in the right direction by transparency.

WORD OF WAL-MART'S WORK on The Index became an open secret throughout the retail industry in the year before it was formally announced, arousing the usual mixture of interest and dread among Wal-Mart's suppliers. News of the project finally leaked to the press, and the story broke first online at *Slate*'s The Big Money Web site, then in

The New York Times on the day before the scheduled announcement.
Wal-Mart, it was reported, was trying something "audacious beyond
words." Whether that audacity was in the name of something good or
bad, the leaks piqued interest well beyond the normal reaction to an
announcement from Bentonville. The auditorium at Wal-Mart headquarters was packed.

The Index had been Lee Scott's project, the capstone of the sustainability program that defined his nine-year tenure leading Wal-Mart. But
he had recently retired, and though he still sat on the company's executive board and was present for the announcement, it fell to his successor
as CEO, Mike Duke, to launch the project publicly on July 16, 2009.
Duke said he wanted to make it clear both inside and outside Wal-Mart
that the new CEO believed in the sustainability path Scott had chosen
and that, if anything, he planned to accelerate progress. He pointedly
reviewed the many perils the planet faced from pollution, waste, and
climate change—a deliberate jab at global warming skeptics, who had
been gaining ground of late. But parts of his speech sounded defensive,
as if he were anticipating objections to Wal-Mart's continued focus on
sustainability during a recession. Tough economic times demand more
sustainability, not less, he asserted. He observed that the economic
downturn has changed Americans, made them more frugal, less willing
to consume and spend, more apt to save—saving being the only truly
sustainable strategy in life. When they do spend, Americans want their
purchases to last—yet another form of sustainability. Business has to
adjust to this new reality, he said, and The Index will be a big part of
Wal-Mart's adjustment to this frugality. "This is the new normal. I don't
think this is a short-term thing."

Before a crowd of Wal-Mart employees, academics, environmental
groups, suppliers, and media reporters, Duke outlined the company's
plan to measure the footprint of every product it sells—and, with
luck, every product, period. More surprising than The Index itself was
Duke's explicit invitation to Target, Tesco, Costco, Best Buy, Kroger,
Safeway and others—Wal-Mart's fiercest competitors—to join the

project. He asked them to contribute data, resources, and ideas and to help build a shared industrywide standard for measuring, and thereby managing, sustainability. "This is not a Wal-Mart standard," he stated. "It's a universal standard."

He said that The Index will drive innovation and cost savings even more than past sustainability efforts, because it will make the true qualities and costs of products transparent to both businesses and consumers. "When businesses aren't transparent, they really can't have the trust of their customers," he argued. "It will become the foundation of what we do in the future."

There would be three phases to The Index project, he explained. First was a questionnaire going out that day to Wal-Mart suppliers, all 100,000 of them, a sort of written exam on energy, waste, and ethics:

Have you measured your corporate greenhouse gas emissions?

What is [sic] your total annual greenhouse gas emissions reported in the most recent year measured?

Please report the total amount of solid waste generated from the facilities that produce your product(s) for Wal-Mart.

Do you know the location of 100 percent of the facilities that produce your product(s)?

Do you invest in community development activities in the markets you source from and/or operate within?

Have you obtained 3rd party certifications for any of the products that you sell to Wal-Mart?

There were fifteen questions in all.[5] Duke described the questionnaire as "simple," but a better word would have been "basic." The process and its implications for manufacturers and wholesalers was anything but simple. Beneath their bland and grammatically challenged corporate jargon, the fifteen questions were pointed. Answering them could, for some companies at least, be laborious and uncomfortable. Duke made it clear that Wal-Mart expected its suppliers to provide unvarnished answers on transparency, trash, water, and carbon footprint and whether their sourcing and manufacturing operations left communities and workers better or worse off. The stated goal of the questions was to allow Wal-Mart to get a snapshot of its suppliers' sustainability at the companywide level—with sustainability broadly defined to include not just energy, carbon, water use, and waste but health and social impact as well. The unstated implication was that, if a supplier's answer was "no" to, say, question number one—"Have you measured your corporate greenhouse gas emissions?"—it had better get busy finding a better answer. "It will make us all much stronger businesses," Duke promised suppliers who enthusiastically participated in the effort. Then came the inevitable Wal-Mart big stick: "Not participating, obviously, could go the other way. We'd seek participation from *all* of our partners in this effort."

In Wal-Mart-speak, you're a partner if you're on the shelf. You're not a partner if your products get taken off the shelf. Duke has the easy demeanor of a favorite uncle, but no "partner" in the room for this big announcement could have missed the threat: Wal-Mart buyers were going to start using that information come annual contract time.

The second step Duke outlined for the project was the formation of an independently governed Sustainability Consortium charged with constructing the product database that would form the backbone of The Index. While Wal-Mart's questionnaire was an internal attempt to estimate the sustainability of its suppliers as whole companies, the consortium had a much more involved and time-consuming task: analyzing the life cycle of individual products, tracing them from raw materials to the final product to their end of use. Cereals, cell phones, window cleaners—the entire consumer universe awaited a sustainability diagnosis.

Duke made it clear that this database would not be the usual honor-system reporting exercise used by annual corporate reports on sustainability, which were heavy on slick marketing but short on revealing anything negative about a company's footprint. That sort of reporting had put a company such as British Petroleum into a favorable public light as a socially responsible oil company in the past, despite its enormous carbon footprint and long series of environmental problems, culminating in the Gulf of Mexico oil spill in 2010, the worst in history.[6] By contrast, Duke said, the Sustainability Consortium would produce open, multisourced, peer-reviewed data devoid of hype.

The codirectors of the consortium would be sustainability experts from Arizona State University and the University of Arkansas (already knee-deep in sustainability research for Wal-Mart and its suppliers), with advisers from Harvard, MIT, Duke, Berkeley, Cambridge, the University of Texas, and the University of Michigan. Wal-Mart would provide the start-up money for the consortium, but Duke said that other companies would join in (and help pay for) the project, so that it would remain "open and collaborative." Founding members of the consortium already on board included the green products manufacturer Seventh Generation, as well as companies not normally associated with environmentalism: the agribusiness and biotech giant Monsanto, the chicken company Tyson Foods, cleaning products maker Clorox, and the privately owned commodities and livestock giant Cargill. Other confirmed participants were Dairy Management, Inc., Waste Management, Disney, SC Johnson, Procter & Gamble, PepsiCo, the computer makers Hewlett-Packard and Dell, and a dozen others. The list seemed impressive, but Duke had been unable to persuade any Wal-Mart competitors to sign on before the launch—only companies already in business with Wal-Mart. (However, in the next several months, the electronics retailer Best Buy and grocery store chain Safeway joined, and the presence of competitors of Wal-Mart convinced more companies to take part in the project.[7]) The member companies paid up to $100,000 each to join and become part of the steering committee setting policy for the project; government agencies and nonprofits got a cheaper rate, $10,000. (Only one environmental group took the offer up: the World Wildlife Fund.)

Finally, Duke said, the third step would be creation of the public "consumer-facing" index—the tags and smartphone apps for shoppers to use to compare products and companies. That would take several years to roll out and would happen in stages, a few product categories at a time—electronics would likely come first, because that industry was farther along on sustainability than others. The form of the scorecard, tag, or label had not been decided upon, but the goal was clear, he said: to "put the consumer in charge."

"We'll help to create a new retail standard for the twenty-first century," Duke confidently predicted. "There's no doubt about it."

Despite the public optimism, behind the scenes there was internal dissension from the start among the companies who joined the consortium. Not everyone wanted their products' score made public with a big red or green tag (to be precise, it was the red tag of nonsustainability they didn't want). They would prefer to use the data inside their business so they could make their products greener and improve their scores. Others companies, however, which were already investigating and improving their environmental impact through Wal-Mart's earlier initiatives, felt confident that they'd fare well and wanted to get their scores out in the real world as quickly as possible.

Some of these companies were already talking up examples of what they could accomplish through The Index. Stonyfield Farm, the leading U.S. producer of organic yogurt and a major supplier of Wal-Mart, reexamined old assumptions. The company had always based its effort to improve Stonyfield's carbon footprint on reducing energy consumption at its production plants. But after analyzing the footprint of its suppliers, company officials were stunned to learn that energy was a distant fourth place on the list of greenhouse gas sources. The milk used to make the yogurt was first, followed by packaging and distribution—all far worse culprits than the energy used to make the yogurt.

(Those findings mirrored the research done by Blu Skye for Dairy Management for the mainstream milk business; the organic dairy industry has a different trade organization.) Stonyfield switched the focus of its sustainability efforts to the same sort of packaging reductions and more efficient trucking that Wal-Mart has used, leading to a projected 40 percent reduction in carbon emissions from transportation and savings of about $2 million a year in costs. The company also worked with its organic dairy farmers to start, in 2009, feeding cows with flax and other feed rich in omega-3 fatty acids to reduce methane from cow burps. If The Index were to launch that day, Stonyfield expected, those measures would help it score far above the industry average.

Wal-Mart showed off its own "index-ready" products from its thousands of private-label items, redesigned with sustainability in mind, complete with videos documenting improvements in the products and their impact. One was the Great Value house-brand sour cream, reformulated with all natural ingredients, reduced packaging, and milk made from dairies where the manure generates electricity instead of climate change. Photos and videos that would be available through a smartphone swipe if The Index were already in place showed production facilities, a manure digester in action, and an interview with a dairy farmer who celebrated the virtues of cow manure power but complained of the lack of government and industry support needed to make the technology ubiquitous. The other "index-ready" product, with similar multimedia material, was house-brand Deli Pizzas, sold in a familiar cardboard pizza box made of recycled cardboard from Wal-Mart's own trash—at a Pratt Industries paper mill in Indiana that generated nearly half of its power from the waste left over from recycling. Wal-Mart estimates that 125,000 trees and 40 million gallons of water have been saved through this recycling program.

Part of Wal-Mart's plan for The Index, Duke and other Wal-Mart leaders made clear, was to push for similar sustainability gains for all its private-label products—which are usually the least costly in their categories and account for about 20 percent of sales. This was a natural choice for the company. Wal-Mart could control the suppliers of its own brands far more than it could command national brands or the manufacturers that supplied Kroger, Walgreens, and other companies with their own private-label goods. From environmentalists' perspective, this plan was ideal, another way of forcing companies to compete to be the most sustainable. However, some retailers had to wonder why they should even get involved at all in an effort where it seemed that Wal-Mart had a head start and the home-court advantage. Only about 10 percent of Wal-Mart's suppliers had the necessary information to answer all of Wal-Mart's questions,[8] and that lack of information about their environmental footprint left many companies leery of how they would score on The Index. Others, meanwhile, scrambled to try and catch up on building sustainability into their project. A cottage industry of "supplier readiness workshops" sprang up around the country for companies that sell products to Wal-Mart but found the questionnaire and the sustainability push daunting.

Public reaction to The Index announcement was mostly positive. There were enthusiastic press accounts, optimistic assessments by some environmental and scientific groups—often wildly optimistic, considering that years would pass before tangible results appeared—but there was also the usual skepticism from others. After all, this was Wal-Mart.

Some Wal-Mart critics fretted over this latest pronouncement from the mother ship in Bentonville, yet another costly demand suppliers would have to meet to stay in the retailer's good graces. Others questioned the need for yet another green label on store shelves and suggested that The Index would replicate resources already available. The fisheries scientist Jennifer Jacquet summed up the skeptics' position when she pointed out on her *Guilty Planet* blog that Wal-Mart was already failing to meet the aggressive sustainability deadlines it had set for itself for seafood. Why, then, she asked, should we fall head over heels for this latest announcement, which would be no more than talk for years? "We must really be on the lookout for extreme greenwashing," she warned.[9] Marc Gunther wondered on The Big Money Web site, "Who chose Wal-Mart to be America's regulator?"[10]

But for the most part, the media and those it quoted were favorably impressed. Professor Jay S. Golden, a researcher at Arizona State University's School of Sustainability who would be working to construct the database at the root of the new sustainability index, was fervent about the project. He likened its potential impact to that of NASA's moon mission, which not only inspired a generation of young people to become scientists and engineers but also mobilized whole industries to innovate new materials, new technologies, and new designs. "This event, from a scientific point of view, and for the consumers, has the potential to be just as seminal an event," Golden said.

Daniel Goleman, the author of *Ecological Intelligence: How Knowing the Hidden Impacts of What We Buy Can Change Everything* and a former *New York Times* science reporter, wrote that the Wal-Mart index was a "blockbuster for ecological transparency" that will "herald the death of 'greenwashing.'"[11] In a *Times* column, he was almost giddy over the impact he believed The Index would have on consumers: "We will no longer be impressed by an organic T-shirt if its cotton was grown by hogging water in an arid and impoverished land, or if its dye puts workers at heightened risk for leukemia, or if it was stitched together in a sweatshop where young women suffer from needless injuries."

The Web site Inhabitat upped the ante further when it editorialized, "Wal-Mart's sustainability index may be a game changer and could easily have as much impact as a cap and trade program." And Brian Merchant at TreeHugger.com wrote, "I hate to admit it, but it's true—it's getting harder and harder to hate Wal-Mart. . . . If it's successful, The Index could literally change the face of retail forever."

GIVEN THE FANTASTIC NUMBER of products sold in American stores, with their constantly changing ingredients and features, the

Sustainability Consortium's task of figuring out the footprint of the stuff we buy seemed all but impossible—as complex as the Manhattan Project and nearly as explosive (politically, not atomically). There were nervous companies that were unsure if they really wanted to be involved. There was a near insurrection among the food manufacturers, half of which were dying for The Index, while the other half, though eager to understand the path to greater sustainability, didn't want their scores aired publicly. The electronics companies said they wanted an Index within a year, or they'd go elsewhere. The codirector, Jon Johnson, found himself spending his first months on the job doing more peace talks than sustainability research, more placating than product evaluating—and even more time explaining what the consortium was *not*.

No, he'd tell manufacturers and news reporters, we're not creating a Wal-Mart Index. No, we're not picking winners and losers. We're not issuing scores. "We're not," he said at one point, "the umpires of sustainability."

Johnson was an old friend of Jib Ellison's, a fellow white-water paddler who had been involved with Project RAFT. Blu Skye never worked directly for the consortium—that would only have stoked concerns that The Index was too Wal-Mart–centric. But as part of their work for Wal-Mart, John Whalen and Blu Skye newcomer—management consultant Glen Low—were still able to help Johnson craft a launch strategy, develop a governance plan for what would inevitably be a fractious alliance of very diverse companies, and design the sort of cooperation-inducing meetings that Blu Skye was known for. All of that had to be resolved before the consortium could focus on its real job of building the precursor to a sustainability index: a database and software for measuring the life cycle of products. This task sounded simple in concept, but it was insanely complex in execution. The two dozen scientists and researchers at the consortium, assisted by crews of student volunteers, were tasked with explaining the birth, life, and death of a DVD player or a box of cornflakes—all the raw materials, the packaging, the pesticides; the good chemicals and the bad; the energy used and carbon emitted to make a product, ship it, package it, store it; the water use, the land use, the recyclability; the social impact, the implications for health and habitat. Every product could be a term report, a novel, an epic. One or two or ten or even a hundred such reports posed no problem for the kind of scientific fire-power the Sustainability Consortium had lined up. But multiply that by 500,000 products—then it became a problem. Impossible amounts of money and manpower would be needed, and even then the informa-tion would be obsolete before the work was close to finished. Figuring out a shortcut that could get the job done without taking decades and many millions of dollars, and then a way of presenting that informa-tion in a succinct and useful way, was the first order of business.

Once that work was complete, companies could then use the data-base internally to make better products—to figure out the best (and most profitable) opportunities for sustainability. Governments and en-vironmental groups could do the same; the information was supposed to be open and public. And yes, it could be used to build The Index or something like it, Johnson explained time and again. But that would be someone else's job. The consortium needed to stay out of the judging and scoring business, he insisted, and stick with science.

That division had not been the original plan, but Johnson realized the project would likely fail—it was the only way to mollify skittish member companies. But because most of the press coverage of the an-nouncement had blurred the line between the consortium's work and The Index, Johnson's clarification left the impression that the project had been scaled back from its ambitious initial pronouncements. What had sounded straightforward when Mike Duke outlined it now sounded more ambiguous and uncertain. Skepticism about Wal-Mart's motives and the project's likelihood of success began to mount. "There's both more and less going on here than meets the eye," commented Greener

World Media's executive editor, Joel Makower, whose publication had broken the sustainability index story in the first place. Now he wrote that the entire story might have been overhyped.

This skepticism was part of a larger, growing disillusionment among businesses, consumer advocates, and the public over the confusing array of green product labels and eco-ratings that seemed to be everywhere in the supermarket aisles these days. How could anyone keep track of them or tell which were credible and which were empty or misleading marketing? Products were being labeled sustainable, natural, responsible, organic, fair-trade, carbon-free, carbon-neutral, eco-efficient, certified vegan, certified naturally grown, certified wild-life friendly—and on and on. By 2010, there were at least 340 different environmental and health certifications available from private and nonprofit ratings organizations, plus thousands more company-created green labeling claims.

Few of the ratings practices or labeling claims were ever policed or verified, leading to rampant greenwashing. In the decade between 2000 and 2009, magazine ads that touted green product claims rose from 2 percent to 10.4 percent of total advertising. But during that same period, the government agency charged with policing greenwashing, the Federal Trade Commission, took only three enforcement actions against false environmental claims (with all three cases abruptly announced on the day of a congressional hearing on the problem).[12] Yet a study by TerraChoice Environmental Marketing, which certifies green product claims, found that 98 percent of eco-labels contained some false or misleading information.[13] "For a fee, [some of] these companies will certify *anything* as green, affording false comfort to purchasers that the products meet environmental and safety standards," warned U.S. Representative Bobby L. Rush of Chicago as he convened a June 2009 oversight hearing entitled "It's Too Easy Being Green."[14]

The problems with labeling and index projects were highlighted by an embarrassing scheme called "Smart Choice," launched by the nation's top food manufacturers shortly after Wal-Mart announced its index initiative. Smart Choice's bold, bright green label with a check mark was supposed to guide consumers to the most nutritious and healthful food choices. But the standards for being "smart" were so weak that they branded such dubious sugary choices as Froot Loops and Cocoa Puffs cereals as healthy and smart. Scathing press coverage led to the demise of the Smart Choice standard in just a few months, but not before it raised questions about corporate motives underlying the proliferation of such labels and certifications in general. Most of the companies involved, after all, sold more of their Smart Choice products at Wal-Mart than anywhere else on the planet. Would the sustainability index just be more of the same?

Even respected and reputable eco-labels, such as the familiar U.S. Department of Energy's "Energy Star" certification, which is supposed to guarantee energy efficiency in appliances and other electronic products, have let consumers down. One congressional witness at the 2009 hearing reported buying a $2,500 LG brand refrigerator at Sears, only to learn that the appliance used twice as much energy as advertised. It should never have qualified for an Energy Star label. It turned out that Energy Star was operated on the honor system, with manufacturers trusted to accurately report the power consumption of their own electronics (unlike the testing and verification conducted by similar programs in other countries).[15] And even the most rigorous labeling and certification programs cannot keep up with the deluge of new products, testified Berkeley researcher Dara O'Rourke, who would be rafting on the Tuolumne River later that month, lending his expertise to The Index. The creator of the Web-based GoodGuide to sustainable and healthy products, O'Rourke had found that, in just one year, 33 percent of newly introduced food products claimed to be "natural."[16] No one can keep up with that number of products and claims, he said. Nor is there any agreement on what the word "natural" means. Many highly toxic and environmentally harmful chemicals are derived from natural sources and are chemically identical to synthetic

compounds. So for many products, the word "natural" is either meaningless or misleading.

Some green ratings systems seek to avoid this confusion by using
an approach that focuses on product ingredients. If certain chemicals
linked to cancer, allergies, or hormone disorders are among a product's ingredients, it receives a negative score. This is how GoodGuide,
among others, creates a health or environmental score for a broad
array of products. A system built on this sort of rating is the most
straightforward to construct, in part because the publicly available
information on product ingredients and their effects on the body or
nature is extensive and reliable. But this "recipe" approach to evaluating cereal or cell phones is insufficient to measure sustainability or
social and ethical aspects of consumer goods. It reveals little about
energy use, carbon emissions, recyclability, water use, ethical sourcing,
or disposal. That requires a life-cycle analysis.

Unlike ingredients lists, companies do not often make public the
life-cycle data on their products. Few even have such information (90
percent of Wal-Mart suppliers did not when those fifteen questions
went out). GoodGuide tries to fill this vacuum by basing ratings data
culled from the annual corporate sustainability reports generated by
the companies themselves, as well as from government, academia,
media reports, and nonprofits. Scores based on such data can give
an idea of the sustainability of whole companies and the life cycle
of broad product categories but not individual products. (Corporate
sustainability reports can also create misleading scores: North Carolina–based utility giant Duke Energy scored high on the Global 100
list of sustainable companies by touting its solar and wind projects,
despite Duke's continuing reliance on carbon-rich coal for most of
its revenues.)

The Sustainability Consortium sought to overcome such obstacles
through its unusual access to member companies' private data and by
taking a hybrid approach that combined life-cycle studies with the
recipe method of analyzing a product's attributes. Johnson and his

colleagues realized at the outset that trying to perform a life-cycle analysis for every individual product would be too big and too futile an endeavor. Instead, the consortium began calculating the life-cycle impact of every *type* of product. So instead of hundreds of different analyses of big-screen televisions, there would be one. One for wheat cereal, another for oat cereal. One for lipstick, one for laundry detergent, one for socks, one for apple juice. Life-cycle studies would lead to a baseline score for the overall impact and sustainability of each type of product—not an average, but a starting point. Every big-screen TV or lipstick would start out with the same score.

Then the other "recipe" information could be factored in—the unique attributes of a product. Is it certified as nontoxic? Is it manufactured with renewable energy or recycled materials? Is it grown with low-carbon, no-till methods or water-saving measures? Adoption of certain sustainable practices or earning a verified certification for ethical sourcing or fair trade would also be considered. This is the part of the analysis that would credit the efforts of Wal-Mart and any other company that could document its reduced packaging or carbon emissions—assuming those measures could be tied to an individual product.

The consortium also had to figure out what weight to assign to these different attributes and to create software that could adjust them based on the degree of sustainability. Was that computer made with 30 percent recycled plastic or 60 percent? Does the manufacturer offer a one-year guarantee or three years (a reflection of durability)? Does that perfume have ten "chemicals of concern" on its ingredient list or only five? Or none? The consortium adopted an open-source, Web-based computer program called Earthster to merge all this information to create a final score. Just enter the product type, add the recipe information, press the button, and the sustainability score of a product appears.

For all his protests to the contrary, this work represents most of the science needed to create The Index that Mike Duke first described and that so excited the press and the environmental community. All that would be needed to finish the job is the creation of a simple format for public consumption and a subjective decision on a scoring algorithim that will draw the line of comparison—the threshold between "pass" and "fail." This is the dicey part, though. Given that this is an industry initiative, run by the people whose products will be scored, reaching consensus on this key algorithm will be a huge undertaking. It explains why Johnson has been so adamant that this last piece of the puzzle must be solved outside the consortium. And why skepticism about the project remains.

The original estimate for completing the project was five years, but it was moving very slowly as the disparate companies involved—some eager, some fearful, some only along for the ride because they didn't want to say no to Wal-Mart—found it hard to reach consensus. This is often the bane of projects run by committee, and the only reason the project kept moving forward at all was due to Wal-Mart's involvement and clout. Even so, plans were in place to roll out partial results much sooner, starting with laptops, desktop computers, and monitors in 2011. The electronics companies and retailers involved—Best Buy, Wal-Mart, HP, Dell, Toshiba, and Intel—wanted to jump-start the electronics portion of The Index right away to build on the more established but less complete electronics ratings such as Energy Star and EPEAT (Electronic Product Environmental Assessment Tool). According to Johnson, the electronics companies would be using the consortium's data to go public with the most detailed and farthest-reaching sustainability analysis yet available for this range of products.[17] The success or failure of this early rollout could easily determine the fate of the entire Index.

Yvon Chouinard of Patagonia once told an audience of Wal-Mart employees that if a company was going to make things, it had to acknowledge that it was going to damage the world. There's no way around it, he said, and the only question is, what do you do about it? This is one of the unpleasant realities that the consortium's data will inevitably reveal, sometimes painfully: no one is going to get the sustainability equivalent of a 4.0 grade point average. Just as Wal-Mart thought it was efficient before Jib Ellison came along, only to discover that it was riddled with waste and inefficiency, the consortium's rigorous, scientific, objective look at life cycles will be traumatic for most companies. That's the reason that consumer products' dirty secrets are *secret*, and have been for a long time. Opening that Pandora's box will be rife with risks. Whenever there is a score, there are winners and losers—and temptations to rig the rules.

On the plus side, there is little doubt that the data being gathered by the consortium will be used inside companies to become more sustainable—they'd be foolish not to seize those green opportunities. But the public face of the project—The Index—is another story, and the outcome will not be known for several more years. Depending on how far the participating companies are willing to go in making their products' secret lives transparent, The Index really could change the world. Or it could end up little more than a bigger, more expensive Smart Choice, where Froot Loops are health food and dirty is clean.

CHAPTER TEN

No Free Lunch at the Nature Market

As is customary, the keynote speaker at the Wal-Mart sustainability summit in Vancouver praised the retailer for its environmental initiatives, its efforts to lower its carbon footprint, its plans for The Index. "These are exciting developments," he enthused. Then David Suzuki, Canada's best-known environmentalist, a smiling seventy-three-year-old thinker and television celebrity with wild gray hair and a wispy beard, added, "I believe they are all doomed to fail."

Three hundred fifty corporate executives stared at the man behind the lectern. Some weren't sure they had heard him right. Others glanced uneasily at their neighbors. This was not what they expected to hear at a Wal-Mart-sponsored meeting entitled "The Green Business Summit." They had convened in February 2010 to bring Wal-Mart, its suppliers, and some of its competitors together to discuss and promote successful strategies for sustainability—not to hear how they were failing.

But Suzuki wanted to shake up these businessmen and businesswomen so proud of their new green credentials, and this, he said, was his chance. As the frequent critic of corporate and government environmental policy said at the beginning of his speech, "I am now being invited to meetings and boardrooms where only a few short years ago they would have barred the door and said, 'Don't let that bugger in!'"

Suzuki tempered his pronouncement of doom by assuring the
Wal-Mart brass in the room that there was nothing wrong with their
sustainability projects. He thought they were great, important, worth
replicating. But their positive effects were dwarfed by a larger problem
infecting the entire human economy: we pretend that nature has no
dollar value. And until that pretense is swept aside, our best efforts at
sustainability will always be too little, too late. No matter how much
we preach the virtues of sustainability as a force for profit and planet,
our world economy is still based on the assumption that nature and
everything it does for us is free—and that damaging and exhausting
natural resources therefore costs nothing.

"If that's not a fundamental flaw in our economic system, I don't
know what is," Suzuki said. "We have to understand that the economy
is something humans created, and that nature is the very source of our
economic well-being."

He then reviewed some of the "services" that nature performs for
humans (and all other creatures): It cleanses our water with root systems and aquifers no human engineer could outdesign. It purifies our
atmosphere, putting in oxygen and removing carbon dioxide. It ab-
sorbs and breaks down our waste. It protects us from cosmic radiation
and harmful ultraviolet rays. It puts nutrients into the soil and provides
birds and bees to pollinate our plants, without which we'd starve. It
moderates our climate, provides us energy, provides us a food chain.
Then Suzuki asked: What if we had to do all that ourselves? What
would it cost to build those services or buy them from someone else?

Turns out, he said, that someone did that complex calculation back
in 1997: those natural services we take for granted would cost a minimum of $33 trillion a year, and probably much more by now. That
amounted to twice the economic output of every nation in the world
at the time.

In other words, if people, businesses, and countries had to pay for
what nature provides, Suzuki said, no one could afford it. And at the
rate human activity is destroying nature now, he warned, civilization

will soon reach that budget-busting point. Before that happens, the economy must be adjusted somehow to acknowledge the value of those natural services so that businesses begin to operate in ways that protect and enhance them, rather than use up and destroy them. "That," he predicted, "is the next challenge."

In the conference room listening to Suzuki was Tom Miller, a recent arrival at Blu Skye who had spent much of his career advising financial institutions. Amid the executives from retailers and manufacturers in the audience, who rose to give Suzuki a polite round of applause, Miller was struck by the implications of these unfamiliar ideas, which, now that he had heard them spoken aloud, seemed undeniable. And he wondered: What if we did exactly what Suzuki suggested? What if we reset the stock market and the economy to acknowledge the value of nature and the costs of exhausting what's sometimes referred to as "ecosystem services," in the same way that interest rates, unemployment, and other forces are acknowledged? Not necessarily to make companies pay for nature's services but to value more accurately the businesses that are the most sustainable, the best stewards, the least damaging—and vice versa. What would that look like? What might it accomplish?

Miller wasn't sure yet, but he could not stop thinking about this "next challenge" of Suzuki's and the possibility that it could expand the business case for sustainability beyond anything previously imagined.

As MILLER BEGAN RESEARCHING what he began to think of as the ultimate business case for green, the very notion that corporations have a social responsibility to embrace public goods such as sustainability came under heavy fire.

The Wall Street Journal devoted a full-page section cover of the newspaper to "The Case Against Corporate Social Responsibility," authored by a University of Michigan business strategy professor who asserted, "the idea that companies have a responsibility to act in the public interest and will profit from doing so is fundamentally flawed."[1] *The Washington Post* published an op-ed piece that took the argument even farther, claiming that corporate efforts to be socially and environmentally responsible had become a dangerous and distracting "fetish" that had helped bring on a long list of recent business disasters, including the BP oil spill in the Gulf of Mexico.[2] Yet another *Wall Street Journal* opinion piece condemned as outright "theft" the practice of spending valuable capital on being good rather than passing it on to investors.[3] The leader of a group of Wal-Mart shareholders at the annual company meeting denounced corporate social responsibility at the retailer and elsewhere as a "socialist scheme" that was "betraying the legacy" of Sam Walton—remarks he was invited to repeat on Fox News.[4] And the *Harvard Business Review* questioned the wisdom of allowing companies such as Wal-Mart to impose corporate social responsibility measures on their suppliers by forcing all those businesses to reduce carbon emissions and participate in sustainability projects such as The Index. The article characterized what Wal-Mart was doing as a "blunt form of regulatory vigilantism."[5]

Without actually saying so, most of these attacks sought to resurrect the 1970s economic theories of the free-market icon Milton Friedman, particularly his stricture that corporations' only social responsibility was to make ever-increasing amounts of money.[6] "It is the relentless maximization of profits, not a commitment to social responsibility, that has proved to be a boon," Aneel Karnani wrote in his full-page *Journal* piece. This argument was used in the 1980s to justify deregulation and capital gains tax cuts that favored corporations and wealthy investors during the presidency of Ronald Reagan—the resulting wealth, the argument went, was supposed to "trickle down" to the rest of America.[7] In 2010, a new concern was being voiced: instead of taxes and regulation getting in the way, it was corporate spending on sustainability and other CSR causes that would impede recovery from the economic recession.

The sins of corporate social responsibility, of trying to "do well by doing good," were ceaseless, according to these critics. *Washington Post* guest writer Chrystia Freeland opined that "the cult of corporate social responsibility" had led BP to market itself as a green company researching renewable energy, instead of focusing on its core business of fossil fuels—and this "distraction" had somehow led to the worst oil spill in history. The author of the *Harvard Business Review* article, Bob Lurie, a corporate sustainability consultant with the Massachusetts-based Monitor Group, predicted that Wal-Mart's sustainability mandate to suppliers would raise prices for consumers. Karnani's primary example in the *Journal* article of why CSR is both irrelevant and a failure was the decision by fast-food chains to introduce salads and other healthier foods. They had done this only, Karnani asserted, after consumer demand made it profitable—something that a decade of activists' protests and appeals to corporate social responsibility had never accomplished. He summed up his case with a warning that any expectation that companies should or could act for the public good is "an illusion, and a potentially dangerous one." (*The New York Observer* pithily mocked Karnani's argument as amounting to a new commandment for corporations: "Be Evil.")[8]

The problem with these arguments—pointed out in many published replies from businesses, environmentalists, and even the Motley Fool investment advice Web site—is not the fact that they are dated (trickle-down economics was as flawed a theory in 1970 as it is today) but that they are based on false assumptions. First there is the assumption that CSR is an impediment to an otherwise free market where the pursuit of profits leads to social good. The problem is that no such free market exists. Corporate expenditures on CSR are dwarfed by corporate spending on lobbyists, loopholes, and junk science that masks the dangers of pesticides, the health risks of tobacco, the problem of climate change, and the true health costs of chemical additives and pollutants—to name just a few. This sort of spending serves to distort market forces and allow companies to evade social responsibility. Or consider the Wright County Egg factory in Clarion, Iowa, the source of 380 million of the

500 million salmonella-tainted eggs that were recalled nationwide in August 2010. Nearly 1,500 people suffered serious illness because of those eggs. The owner of the factory had been cited repeatedly for deplorable conditions and had been branded a "habitual violator" of state environment laws in 2000.[9] Yet the consequences were so slight for so many years that there was, in effect, an incentive to profit from behaving badly. Those actions continued right up to the point when a costly disaster occurred that harmed both consumers and company—a disaster that a corporation concerned with social responsibility could have averted.

Another false assumption implicit in these arguments is that corporate social responsibility is merely a cost rather than a source of value. Yet Wal-Mart's socially responsible pursuit of sustainability is grounded in profitability and a proven return on investment. Its charitable disaster relief after Hurricane Katrina, while certainly a cost without any direct source of revenue in return, nevertheless had enormous value for the company for the effect it had on Wal-Mart's previously battered brand image. That act of giving accomplished what millions of dollars of advertising expenditures could never have achieved. And contrary to Karnani's claims, fast-food restaurants' decision to add green salads and other lower-calorie fare to menus dominated by fat-laden burgers and fries wasn't based on a belief that those products would be profitable—indeed, many of them are loss leaders. Rather, the menu additions came in response to relentless activism and publicity linking fast food to poor health and rampant obesity. Expanding the menu with some healthier, less fattening items helped fast-food restaurants begin to restore their tattered reputations, as well as stave off the possibility of government scrutiny and regulation of the industry. CSR, then, often has value for companies independent of any direct profits. As for the bizarre argument that CSR contributed to the BP oil spill, the writer had it backward. It was the *lack* of corporate social responsibility coupled with perverse economic incentives to be irresponsible that led to disaster. Skimping on safety measures, taking advantage of lax regulatory oversight, and ignoring huge environmental risks may have saved the company some money in the short term, but BP cost its shareholders billions of dollars more in damages in the end, not to mention the damage to the corporate image. For that matter, the current economic recession, sparked by the financial industry's irresponsible lending and investing practices, showcases (by its absence) one of the most beneficial aspects of corporate social responsibility: the enormous value of *not* doing things that harm the public.

The question about Wal-Mart's role as self-appointed regulatory vigilante was more nuanced and seemingly reasonable, but the argument is still flawed. Wal-Mart's attempts to green its supply chain are indeed a kind of regulation, but they do not amount to a usurpation of government authority. Wal-Mart suppliers still have a choice. They can accept the sustainability mandate, or they can refuse and take their business elsewhere. With true regulatory authority, everyone has to obey. So the real question becomes: What exactly is wrong about a company seeking to voluntarily lower its carbon footprint and become more sustainable—and asking its business partners to do the same?

Where the *Harvard Business Review* saw abuse, Jib Ellison and Tom Miller see free enterprise in action. Or maybe just freedom. But this new climate of objections to socially responsible business plans did make one thing clear to both men: acting on David Suzuki's ecosystem services challenge, which would amount to the most radical corporate social responsibility project in history, would generate far greater outcry, opposition, and fear.

AROUND THE SAME TIME that these criticisms were being published and debated, the leaders of sixteen major global apparel makers and retailers were meeting, and, by action rather than argument, they repudiated the case against corporate social responsibility.

The CEOs of these sixteen leading global brands agreed to form an apparel industry coalition to promote sustainability. They promised to create open, publicly shared standards for measuring the sustainability, toxicity, and environmental footprint of the clothes, shoes, and athletic gear they made and sold. The goal was to create a sort of mini-index to share information, research, and technology within the industry, and to give consumers an accurate picture of the sustainability of apparel—for better and worse.

This effort was separate from Wal-Mart's big sustainability index project, though inspired by it. The two projects would likely mesh in the in the end, with the apparel coalition sustainability rankings remaining independent but incorporated into The Index scores once the research was complete.

Like the dairy initiative, the apparel project's mission was to turn an entire industry toward sustainability, though this time not with a single trade association at the helm. The apparel effort would be undertaken by a group of competitors in the world's most chemically intensive business, sharing what had previously been kept secret. According to a leader of the effort, Rick Ridgeway of Patagonia, these companies were doing it because they saw this sort of corporate responsibility project as a business opportunity rather than a liability. Indeed, after the project began, other companies asked to join, bringing the total to twenty-five. Together, these companies generate about 60 percent of global apparel sales.

The apparel companies, which include Nike, Gap, Levi Strauss, Patagonia, REI, JC Penney, Kohl's, and Wal-Mart in the United States, as well as the European retailers C&A, H&M, and Marks and Spencer, were just getting started in late 2010. But they expected to move quickly, as this coalition was more united in purpose and opinion than the much larger and more divided membership of the Sustainability Consortium. The project could also move more quickly because quite a few of the companies in the coalition—Patagonia and Nike in particular—had already done considerable research on sustainable apparel chemicals and materials and were willing to share. The Outdoor Industry Association also agreed to share its "Eco Index" data for outdoor gear.

The catalysts for this project had been Wal-Mart's chief apparel executive, Mary Fox, one of the first at the retailer to embrace sustainability, and Ridgeway, mountain climber, outdoor adventurer, author, Emmy-winning filmmaker, and member of a small group of environmentalist-outdoorsmen friends who include Ellison, Patagonia founder Chouinard, and former Esprit CEO turned eco-philanthropist Doug Tompkins. Ridgeway, who met Ellison while filming Project RAFT for ABC, had been part of the first American team to reach the summit of K2, the world's second tallest mountain, where he almost froze to death. At age fifty-five, Ridgeway had taken his first-ever office job when Chouinard hired him as Patagonia's vice president for environmental initiatives in 2004. It didn't take long for Ellison, who had just arrived at Wal-Mart that year, to begin begging Ridgeway to bring Chouinard to meet Lee Scott. Who could be a better sustainability teacher for Wal-Mart, Ellison asked, than the founder of Patagonia, one of the world's first green companies? Ridgeway agreed, but it took him two years to persuade the sometimes crusty Chouinard, who wanted nothing to do with Wal-Mart. The Patagonia chief finally agreed to let Ridgeway provide some assistance with Wal-Mart's efforts with organic cotton. Then he gave Ridgeway the okay to work with Wal-Mart on The Index, and in 2009, he finally agreed to fly to Bentonville to talk to Wal-Mart buyers about building sustainability into their buying decisions. In 2010, the new CEO of Wal-Mart, Mike Duke, and Chouinard cosigned a letter to apparel industry leaders proposing the formation of a coalition for sustainability with Ridgeway as organizer and Blu Skye's assistance. Fox and Ridgeway had hatched this plan, calling it "the marriage of David and Goliath." Neither company alone could have persuaded the other corporate leaders in apparel to agree to this coalition, Ridgeway says. But when they did so together—with Wal-Mart's market clout and Patagonia's stellar environmental credentials—no one said no.

The selling point for the two-year project was one that Ridgeway had discussed with his colleagues years before on that rafting trip on the Tuolumne, where part of the groundwork for the coalition was laid. They would use transparency to give their companies a competitive edge across the board: with consumers who want greener options; with companies such as Wal-Mart that want a greener supply chain; and with investors who are leery of the next BP and are seeking profitable businesses that are also good stewards of the environment. That's why this coalition of apparel competitors is willing to spend the next two years trying to expose where their products and companies are sustainable and where they are not. In this new reality, Ridgeway says, the socially responsible business should wind up being the most sought after and successful.

At the same time, none of these companies want to be in the index business. It's complex, time-consuming, and costly, and if every company tried to invent its own standard, suppliers would be thrown into chaos. Several of the coalition members learned this the hard way years ago when they instituted programs of audits and inspections to safeguard against sweatshops and other objectionable labor and social practices in the supply chain. Each company—Gap, Nike, and Wal-Mart, to name a few—instituted different standards and expectations, inadvertently forcing manufacturers to move everything from lighting to fire extinguishers around their factories depending on whose inspector was coming that day. It was counterproductive and costly. For sustainability, the coalition members wanted a single standard for apparel, and they were willing to share and cooperate with competitors to get it, because the alternative made no sense.

"It's a hugely daunting task," Ridegway says. "But when we're done, the apparel business could be transformed."

THE FORMATION OF THE apparel coalition decided matters for Tom Miller. He saw it as the latest piece of evidence that corporations were increasingly eager to measure and minimize their impact on nature. There was the Wal-Mart index project. There was the announcement in

July 2010 that the 116-year-old Underwriters Laboratories (the makers of the familiar UL Listed label on every lamp, toaster, and electrical gadget) would construct its own rating system of corporate sustainability. There was the decision by Goldman Sachs (with General Electric and the World Resources Institute) to create a Water Index, designed to measure the risks to businesses associated with water shortages, regulation, and quality issues. Dow Chemical, long criticized by environmentalists for toxic emissions, announced a $10 million collaboration with The Nature Conservancy to figure out how to "recognize, value, and incorporate nature into global business goals." A small, London-based environmental analytics company, Trucost, used decades of ecosystems academic research combined with publicly available corporate data to help calculate *Newsweek* magazine's annual ranking of green businesses. Trucost was then hired by the Northern Trust financial holding company of Chicago (which manages $3.6 trillion of assets) to calculate the carbon footprint of potential investments. Bit by bit, the sorts of impacts on the natural world that David Suzuki had said businesses habitually ignored were now being acknowledged. Wouldn't the next logical step be to try to assign values to those natural services—and the business world's attempts to preserve them? Then the values could be tracked and counted by the banks and stock analysts as new types of assets and liabilities—natural capital. That's what it would take, Miller figured, to create a full-blown market for sustainability. He wanted this to be Blu Skye's next big thing.

Miller, a wiry and intense man who had worked for financial institutions the world over, had come to Blu Skye a little more than a year earlier. He and Ellison were old friends: Miller had hired the river guide at Human Factors, the Marin County consultancy that specialized in leadership training. They had been cofounders of and partners at The Trium Group, where Miller had said no to Jib's idea of adopting sustainability as the company's mission. Then Miller had watched Ellison go it alone and land Wal-Mart as his client, and he could only marvel at his friend's knack for timing. Miller had continued his lucrative career at Trium but had departed five years later with several new business ventures in mind, though he had settled on none. None had seemed right. And then Ellison called unexpectedly and announced he was taking a yearlong leave of absence from Blu Skye to travel the world with his wife and twelve-year-old daughter. He needed someone to take over the company for a year, someone he could trust. Was Miller interested? Once again, Miller had to shake his head in wonder at Ellison's timing. A month or two earlier or a month later, and he would have said no. But that day Miller said yes, it was just the opportunity he had been looking for.

The two men came to sustainability from opposite directions, the river guide at one end, the strategy and organizational guru at the other. Miller brought some new management strengths to Blu Skye, and some new clients, too, and the year sped by. Ellison was hoping to return with some amazing new insights into sustainability from his world trip, but it was Miller who was waiting for him with a big idea. They agreed he should stay on beyond the one-year commitment to pursue this ecosystems services project.

The leviathan task of putting a value on the complex web of nature's "assets" had been pioneered in the 1990s by Robert Costanza, a professor of ecological economics then at the University of Maryland (now director of Portland State University's Institute for Sustainable Solutions). Costanza developed a mathematical framework for valuing seventeen different categories of ecosystem services and, in a 1997 paper, came up with the $33 trillion estimate, which he considered to be very conservative and likely too low. The world economy that year had a combined value of $18 trillion.[10] To this day, Costanza is one of a handful of researchers in the world who specialize in this sort of complex calculation of the value that natural systems provide to countries, companies, and individuals.

Two years after Costanza came up with his $33 trillion figure, the book *Natural Capitalism* was published, in which the authors, Paul Hawken, Amory Lovins, and L. Hunter Lovins, argued that the human economy had to begin accounting for this immense value within nature in order to prevent the complete exhaustion of all resources. The authors argued that proper accounting would place the human economy inside the larger natural economy—in diagram form, a small circle inside a much larger one—rather than pretending, as is currently the case, that the two are separate or barely overlapping. Businesses would have to become much more sustainable in this scenario, and the authors suggested that one of the primary mechanisms for driving this transition should be a restructuring of tax codes to discourage consumption and encourage conservation. Growth would no longer be the key to financial success, then—stewardship would.

This idea, however theoretically sound it might be, would have been a nonstarter in any American era or political reality. But it was an especially difficult sell in the prosperous and profligate America of 1999, when unemployment dropped to 4.2 percent, the ten-mile-per-gallon Hummer SUV was a high-status symbol, the book *Dow 36,000* became an instant best seller, and the idea that future generations might lose everything by using up nature gained no traction.

But by 2010 the picture had become very different, and it terrified Miller. He and his team did some rough estimates to update Costanza's work. For one thing, they found out the value of the world's natural capital—due to inflation and increasing scarcity—had climbed to a minimum of $72 trillion (compared to a global human economy of about $60 trillion). And ecosystem services were being used up or destroyed at a rate of $2 to $5 trillion a year.[11] At that rate, factoring in the current growth in population and manufacturing set against nature's innate ability to replenish itself, the world's natural capital—fresh air, fresh water, all the other things we depend upon—will be depleted by the year 2046. Unless there is a profound change in the way we do business, Miller says, the natural economy will collapse around the time today's infants reach the prime of life, and the human economy will collapse with it.

The other big difference between 1999 and 2010 was more

encouraging: the growing acceptance by mainstream businesses of sustainability as a profitable strategy. Driven by Wal-Mart and a handful of other companies, this acceptance was spawning such new market forces as The Index and the apparel coalition.

The final difference was new data sources and technology: Miller learned from Costanza and others in the field that recent research had led to methods of combining calculations of ecosystem service values with data from companies and their supply chains. The result was a reasonably precise measurement in dollars of a business's total environmental footprint, with which companies could craft strategies to improve that footprint.

A beer company with breweries spread around the globe, to cite one real-world example, knew that it used a total of 150 liters of water for every liter of beer it produced. But that sort of broad overview information did not provide the company's leaders enough insight into exactly where and how the company could most effectively conserve water. This posed a major investment risk in areas of the world where beer is popular but water scarcity is an issue. This new ecosystems services science, however, informed the beer company where it could most productively spend money on water conservation and sustainability, then placed a precise dollar value on the natural capital that was saved as a result. That information, in turn, was then shared with government regulators, stock analysts, and investors to show how the beer company's sustainability efforts had helped the environment while also lowering its financial risks and improving its prospects in the world market.

What could that sort of information do for a Wal-Mart, Miller wondered, which consumes billions of dollars' worth of water across its immense supply chain every year? Could this deep analysis be applied to its supply chain to manage carbon emissions, fuel consumption, or packaging reductions that could save whole forests worth billions in natural capital?

Instead of *Natural Capitalism*'s suggestion for a new tax system,

Miller proposed three possible ways to use this sort of information to bring ecosystem services into the human economy's balance sheet. One tactic would be to create a new competitor for the S&P 500 or Dow 30, a new market index that would include natural-capital "savings" and "expenditures" when it evaluated company performance. Another approach would be to have a large bank or other financial institution develop a trading market for ecosystem services credits—something similar to the current carbon trading markets around the world. Or a financial institution could set itself up as a "Bloomberg for the sustainability age"—a new business that would distribute the most complete and reliable information in the financial world for evaluating sustainability investment risks and opportunities, using ecosystems services science as its foundation.

The goal, according to Miller, would be to put an end to "externalities"—the pretense Suzuki spoke of that natural capital lies outside the human economy. Only by ending that faulty worldview, which Miller likens to an accountant cooking the books, can those vital natural services be preserved for future generations and that doomsday prediction for 2046 averted.

The problem, of course, as Jib Ellison pointed out during early discussions, is that it will be difficult to persuade banks and businesses to internalize those external costs voluntarily because then some government somewhere is going to try to get them to pay for it all. The year 2046 was a long way away. Why would they agree to open such a can of worms now?

But Miller has an answer for that: it's already happening. Investment analysts and government bodies have begun to use ecosystem services calculations to measure the negative impact of corporations. The United Nations released in October 2010 a report that slammed global corporations for their disregard for the environmental harm they were causing. Preliminary estimates for that report attributed more than $2 trillion a year in damages to ecosystems services around the world, caused by the activities of the three thousand largest global

corporations.[12] This calculation was made largely without the cooperation of the business world, using public corporate disclosures and
rough estimates rather than the more exacting proprietary data that
corporations generally decline to make public. Miller predicted that
the UN report would increase worldwide pressure for greater regulation of business activities that harm the environment. That demand
for regulation will likely build in the coming years as environmental damage worsens and becomes more obvious to ordinary citizens,
making government intervention inevitable sooner or later. Europe is
likely to act first, Miller suggests, as voters there are more approving
of environmental regulation. Or there might be a crackdown in Africa
or China, where accelerating environmental damage from industry is
so sweeping and obvious. It's years off, but it's coming, and in the end
American companies will be forced to act as well.

In Miller's view, this dynamic left an opportunity for major financial institutions to take the lead now. Unlike the United Nations,
they could gain access to the more precise company data as part of the
stock rating and analysis process. Their picture would be more accurate. Then, instead of waiting for government regulation to punish
environmental offenders, a market could be created that would reward
environmental stewardship and sustainability, creating financial incentives for the preservation of the ecosystems the world needs. The
regulation might still come, but the business world—at least the part
of it that acts soon—would be ready for it, could even welcome it, as
Miller sees it.

The idea attracted the interest of Conservation International for its
environmental appeal and of the investment guru Lee Kranefuss for its
financial possibilities. In 2000, Kranefuss helped create the market for
a new investment vehicle, exchange-traded funds, that became a $500
billion business he ran for Barclays Global Investors. Now he wanted
to partner with Blu Skye and Conservation International on this project, and several major banks were interested in plotting a strategy for
making ecosystem services a market force. Or a market in itself.

There are no guarantees. Miller knows this. Even if the idea catches on, it could take a decade for anything tangible to come of it. But he has become obsessed with the possibility, however remote, that this idea of his could move the world in a better, safer, cleaner, and more prosperous direction—using the very same forces of capitalism that got the world into this fix in the first place. In an era of political grid-lock, when even the most modest proposals on climate and energy go down in flames in Washington, this crazy idea about the dollar value of nature, Miller says, might be the world's best shot. When even such diverse entities as Dow Chemical and the World Economic Forum in Geneva are expressing excitement about Miller's white paper on the subject, he feels certain he's on to something.

If he's right, the sustainability quest that began with just a few prod-ucts at Wal-Mart and a river guide's vision, will have taken a remark-able turn. First it spread throughout a whole company not previously known for its green tendencies. Next it moved into that company's 100,000-manufacturer supply chain—a work in progress. Finally it infected whole industries with the quest for sustainability. And now, if Miller succeeds, the entire economy could at last become a force of nature.

Epilogue: Generation Green

*It's cheaper to take care of something—a roof, a car, a planet—
than to let it decay and try to fix it later.*

—PAUL HAWKEN[1]

The question is the same today as it was in 2004, when Jib Ellison first pitched Lee Scott the idea that sustainability is the biggest business opportunity of the twenty-first century: Can Wal-Mart be sustainable? Can the biggest retailer in the world—can any large, mainstream business in this outsourced consumer economy—be green?

The simple, accurate answer is no. Despite all the good works that Wal-Mart (and Nike and Procter & Gamble and others) have done on the environmental front, such corporations as we know them cannot be sustainable. Yet, paradoxically, the answer to another important question—Has Wal-Mart led the business world toward a new age of sustainability?—is yes.

Wal-Mart is an imperfect vehicle to carry this banner. The company has a long history of poor policy and behavior on labor issues, gender equality, health care, land use, and, through its supply chain, human rights. It has destroyed local businesses, lowered wages in communities where it opened stores, and added children to the medical-welfare rolls because so many Wal-Mart employees could not afford Wal-Mart's insurance plan. The company earned its bad reputation over a period of decades. In the last few years, it has made progress on many of these shortcomings, sometimes significantly so, but it still has far to go. Even as it has championed sustainability, its signature effort to be good, Wal-Mart had to be sued by environmentalists to compel installation of solar panels on some of its California stores (where state law requires greenhouse gas mitigation for new construction). In 2010, the company agreed to pay $28 million to settle state charges that it had mishandled and illegally dumped hazardous and toxic wastes at stores and distribution centers throughout California for years.

Beyond such specific flaws in Wal-Mart's behavior and impact is something much more basic that is fundamentally unsustainable: the retail chain epitomizes the entire modern American economy of global, outsourced, big-box consumerism, which displaced a more local and infinitely more sustainable Main Street economy. As American shoppers said hello to Wal-Mart a half century ago, they said farewell to a society of less stuff, of products built in America and built to last, of saving instead of spending, of postponing purchases rather than borrowing for them, of knowing your customers personally rather than surveying their demographics. Durability, repairability, and quality were supplanted by low price. If that $39 DVD player from Wal-Mart breaks after a year, so what? Just get a new one. The same is true of the $99 power mower and the half-price Levi's blue jeans exclusive to Wal-Mart, which displayed the famous brand's distinctive label but otherwise bore little resemblance to the classic denims known worldwide for their durability. The drop in product quality led to a nearly constant stream of recalls, from flip-flops that left chemical burns on bare feet to coffeemakers that made flames instead of brew.[2] Meanwhile, American brands from Huffy bikes to Master Lock, under pressure to lower prices for Wal-Mart, moved production offshore.

This sort of outsourcing brought lower prices, but it also eliminated whole sectors of good-paying blue-collar domestic manufacturing jobs that once provided a viable path to the middle class for millions of U.S. workers, whole generations of them. The irony is that the effort to provide consumers a bargain cut off millions of them from once-prosperous livelihoods. The entire economy became less sustainable.

Yet Wal-Mart's core business strategy calls for still more such growth—more stores, more customers, more shelf space year by year, and more consumption of natural capital. There is an expanding middle class out there in the world, in China and India and elsewhere, and those emerging consumers are Wal-Mart's sweet spot. Which is why Wal-Mart, as long as it looks anything like the Wal-Mart we know today, is never going to be truly green or wholly sustainable. Because any gains it makes in efficiency, conservation, and clean energy will be matched by the continued growth of a company that, since the day Jib Ellison arrived in Bentonville in 2004, has grown 43 percent to $408 billion in annual revenue as of 2010. In that same space of time, Wal-Mart added more than 1,200 stores to its global legion of Sam's Clubs, supercenters, and other outlets, which by early 2010 numbered 8,416. More than 200 million people worldwide visit those stores every week.

This is why the company's toughest critics remain unimpressed by Wal-Mart's sustainability moves. As they see it, no matter how genuine the effort and positive the result, sustainability only distracts the press and public from the fact that the real problem is the big-box economy itself. To them, the only truly sustainable Wal-Mart is a shuttered Wal-Mart.

Still, the critics' fondest wish—making Wal-Mart and the other big boxes disappear—is no solution. Yes, it could lead to the resurgence of small businesses and local economies, but good luck finding a pair of sneakers, a computer, a cell phone, a T-shirt, or flashlight batteries in that alternate reality at anything close to current prices. Or perhaps the big-box critics would settle for something a little less draconian than a total big-box shutdown, say a new federal regulation requiring all imported goods to originate from farms and factories that meet the most stringent U.S. environmental, health, labor, and welfare standards. A company could import all it wanted, as long as the factory would be as legal in Poughkeepsie as it is in Punjab. Such a policy sounds fair and reasonable, a way to discourage sweatshops and toxic landscapes by withholding our dollars from products with a dirty, deadly provenance. Such a policy could effectively end the era of supercheap imports and Wal-Mart's main advantage over what's left of the U.S. Main Street economy.

Perhaps if the United States had adopted such a moral stand a half century ago, before big business outsourced the best parts of American industrial capacity, it could have accomplished something positive. But try it today, and there would be economic collapse, shortages of every-thing, protectionism gone wild, trade wars, maybe real wars. America is more dependent on foreign-made products today than at any time since the Revolutionary War. It's not just Wal-Mart underwear, dog food, and toothpaste. Even the manufacturing of the computer chips in our military hardware is outsourced to factories in China. In any case, history suggests that such a regulatory fix wouldn't work anyway. The regulatory approach to environment that began in the 1960s has saved important parts of the natural world: the Cuyahoga River no longer bursts into flames, our cities are no longer shrouded in smog, and the bald eagle and thousands of other species aren't extinct. But regulation hasn't made America green and sustainable in nearly fifty years of trying, because regulation is about establishing a floor, a lowest common denominator. Regulation begets, at best, grudging com-pliance—and depending on who's in the White House at any given moment, it often fails to deliver even that much. The regulatory model is rarely about raising the ceiling; merely forcing compliance is not the same as inspiring a race to the top. Sustainability requires both.

Therein lies the true value of Wal-Mart's sustainability efforts and why they matter—and why asking if Wal-Mart will ever be truly green misses the point. For the first time, Wal-Mart's size and domi-nance are being put to use as positive forces for something other than (and arguably greater than) lower prices. Wal-Mart has jump-started a transition. It has put market forces into motion to green not just itself, but its partners, its suppliers, and even its competitors.

Beyond its direct influence on the 100,000 companies it does business with, Wal-Mart has made it impossible for any corporation to claim plausibly that sustainability is a risky choice. It has proven that ignoring sustainability is the riskier course. The evidence—from the dairy industry to the electronics sector to the fashion business to, possibly, the banking and financial community—suggests that big business is heeding that message.

THE OPPORTUNITY HAD BEEN there all along, of course. The alignment of profit and planet was just as possible in the nineteenth and twentieth centuries as it is now. The touchstones of sustainability—conservation, recycling, using energy wisely, cutting waste, husbanding natural resources, using fewer dangerous materials, burning less fuel—have always been waiting there. Some businesses have pioneered sustainability long before Wal-Mart, and others are taking it far beyond. Patagonia, for one, announced in 2010 its plan to accept responsibility for the complete life of its products, from manufacture to disposal. When you finish with a Patagonia product, if it's worn out or you no longer want it, company founder Yvon Chouinard wants you to send it back. The company will recycle or repurpose it, closing the loop on the life of the product. This sort of product stewardship is the only sure strategy for preserving the services nature provides. It is the only way to make consumption sustainable—and it shows how far Wal-Mart has to go in its sustainability quest.

"Even Wal-Mart, which really gets it, could move five times faster, safely, without destroying shareholder value," Jib Ellison says. "But I'm just impatient."

The company has continued to set some impressive goals, however. In 2010, it announced a project to remove 20 million metric tons of greenhouse gas emissions from its supply chain—the equivalent of taking 3.8 million cars off the road for a year. It also equals one and a half times the emissions that will be caused by the projected growth in Wal-Mart stores and sales for the next five years—which means that the project is supposed to more than compensate for the chain's growth through 2015. The project is being run with the Environmental Defense Fund, the University of Arkansas sustainability scientists already at work on The Index project, and the auditing giant PricewaterhouseCoopers, which is charged with verifying the carbon emission reductions. The effort will focus on products known to generate large amounts of carbon and on high-volume items, such as bread, pork, and clothing, that may not be the worst greenhouse gas offenders but still have a large footprint because of the large quantities sold.

At the same time, Wal-Mart has sent energy experts from the Environmental Defense Fund to China to start working on energy efficiency projects for the 30,000 factories there that supply Wal-Mart. The goal is to cut energy use by 20 percent in those plants by 2012, but EDF's initial findings after visiting three hundred factories suggests that double those reductions could be achieved with simple efficiency fixes (replacing old motors is a big one). The retooling would pay for itself in six to eighteen months at most Chinese factories.

Wal-Mart's 2010 progress report on sustainability shows:

- Carbon emissions from Wal-Mart's stores, trucks, and other operations declined from 60 metric tons per $1 million in sales in 2005 to just over 50 metric tons in 2008, a 16 percent reduction (though because sales increased in that same period, total carbon emissions still went up from 18 million to 21 million metric tons).
- The efficiency of the Wal-Mart U.S. truck fleet increased by 60 percent compared to 2005, delivering 77 million more cases yet driving 100 million fewer miles, resulting in 145,000 fewer metric tons of CO_2 emissions.
- 127 million pounds of food that previously would have been thrown away was donated to food banks.

- Wal-Mart stores recycled or reused 64 percent of its garbage, recycling more than 13 million pounds of aluminum, 120 million pounds of plastic, 11.6 million pounds of paper, and 4.6 billion pounds of cardboard.
- Wal-Mart reduced the number of store reports automatically printed out (and frequently simply thrown out) at stores, eliminating the annual use of 350 million pieces of paper for a $20 million savings.
- Plastic bag waste was cut by 4.8 billion bags weighing 66.5 million pounds—a 16 percent reduction since 2007. Wal-Mart's goal is to reduce plastic bag use by 33 percent by getting U.S. customers to use reusable bags.
- Twenty-five percent of the wood furniture and 35 percent of picture frames sold by Wal-Mart were certified as coming from responsibly sourced resources. (This is a major improvement compared to 2005, but it's winning few praises from environmentalists, as Wal-Mart is still selling many more items worldwide sourced from companies linked to massive deforestation in Indonesia. Wal-Mart's stated goal is to stop selling any wood products from "unwanted sources" by 2013.)
- Phosphates in dish and laundry detergents on Wal-Mart shelves were cut by 29 percent in Canada, Mexico, Central America, and South America, with reductions scheduled to hit 70 percent by 2011. Phosphates have been removed entirely from products sold in the United States.
- Energy-saving light-emitting diodes were installed in refrigerated display cases in 1,000 stores, saving $5.2 million per year in energy costs and carbon emissions.
- All personal computers sold in U.S. stores met Europe's stringent hazardous substances rules.
- Wal-Mart has sold 350 million compact fluorescent lightbulbs since 2007.
- All TVs sold by Wal-Mart in the United States and Japan are now 67 percent more energy-efficient than in 2008 (surpassing

Wal-Mart's original goal of a 30 percent increase in efficiency).

- Fifty-five percent of wild-caught seafood was certified as sustainable.
- One hundred percent of farmed shrimp was certified as sustainable, but Wal-Mart has not yet sought certification for other farmed fish, such as salmon, though the company promises that will happen.
- All Wal-Mart-branded children's and baby clothes were to be made of organic cotton by spring 2011.

Two of Wal-Mart's newest and splashiest green initiatives revolve around food, where America's leading grocer can choose to tackle (or ignore) a whole universe of sustainability, health, and social problems in every grocery sack and farmer's field.

The first of these new food-related efforts is a sustainable agriculture initiative, announced in October 2010, in which the retailer laid out its five-year plan to buy less food from factory farms and more food—$1 billion worth—from a million small and midsize farmers around the world. Also, by 2015 Wal-Mart vowed to reduce food waste (and associated greenhouse gas emissions) by 10 to 15 percent, depending upon the region of the world. Local produce sold in Wal-Marts would double under the plan as well. Finally, the company said it was phasing out two environmentally destructive products by 2015—palm oil and beef produced in deforested regions of the Amazon—and replacing them worldwide with sustainable alternatives. Palm oil is used in hundreds of processed foods, and demand for new palm oil plantations had contributed to worldwide deforestation. The palm oil switch in Britain and America alone is expected to reduce greenhouse gas emissions by an estimated 5 million metric tons. And lowering incentives for cattlemen to cut down Amazonian rain forest is considered imperative by environmentalists, who have estimated that 60 percent of deforestation in Brazil is due to cattle ranch expansion.

The second food announcement, this one in January 2011, brought First Lady Michelle Obama together with Wal-Mart executives at a

Washington, DC, community center, where they jointly announced a five-year Nutrition Charter, in which the retailer committed to sell healthier foods and to cut prices on that food. The stated goal is to make healthier low-sugar, low-fat, low-sodium food the most affordable alternatives for the half of all Americans who buy their groceries at Wal-Mart. The new mantra Wal-Mart officials kept repeating: No family should have to choose between healthy food and food they can afford.

Mrs. Obama, who has made nutrition and childhood obesity her signature issue, lavishly praised Wal-Mart, calling the company's collaboration with her Let's Move! campaign for better nutrition a victory for parents and children.

Only a few months before the announcement, a study released by a University of North Carolina researcher found a correlation between the growth of Wal-Mart supercenters and America's propensity for getting fat, with about 10.5 percent of the nation's rise in obesity since the 1980s linked in the study to Wal-Mart proliferation.[3] The new Nutrition Charter, while not acknowledging the study's claims, in effect would seek to undo any harm that selling salty, sweet, and fatty processed foods cheap for so many years may have wrought on America.

Among other promises, Wal-Mart officials said they would cut a fourth of the salt in the retailer's house brand foods, cut 10 percent of added sugar, and entirely eliminate trans fats, all of which contribute to obesity, high blood pressure, and heart disease. The company said it would develop front-of-the-package nutrition labeling so consumers would be informed that some processed foods are healthier than others. Wal-Mart also promised to use its market clout to persuade national brand food makers to match their more healthful formulations of processed foods. Finally, Wal-Mart vowed to build small-scale stores in underserved "food deserts" in urban and poor areas so these healthier, affordable foods would be available where they were needed most.

These announcements, and particularly the star presence of Michelle Obama at a Wal-Mart event, reflected the growing influence of Leslie Dach, the company executive vice president who oversees sustainability. He has often kept a low public profile, but Dach has worked closely with Blu Skye for years; supervised sustainability point man Matt Kistler and his recent replacement, Andrea Thomas; and brings to Wal-Mart credentials as a former Democratic strategist that make him nearly unique in Bentonville's conservative upper echelons. His evolution from public relations consultant brought in to rehab the retailer's battered image into a senior executive and a leading proponent of sustainability in the world of global big business is unprecedented at Wal-Mart. No one at the company but Dach could have brokered the deal that put Wal-Mart representatives in the White House to work for more than a year with First Lady Obama's staff, crafting the new healthy foods initiative. Such collaboration just a few years earlier would have been unthinkable. Now it's common for Wal-Mart's sustainability and energy experts to show up on Capitol Hill to brief congressmen, senators, and other policymakers, regardless of party or administration.

As with all of Wal-Mart's sustainability efforts, these latest announcements were greeted with a mixture of enthusiasm, surprise, and skepticism among environmentalists and food activists. Some agreed with the First Lady, who said Wal-Mart's commitment had "the potential to transform the marketplace and help Americans put healthier foods on their tables every single day." Others suggested that Wal-Mart was trying to defuse more stringent labeling and regulatory requirements by the federal government, and that the new food formulations and other commitments did not go nearly far enough. Some speculated that the offer to build in urban food deserts might represent a convenient way into cities that had previously been resistant to Wal-Mart expansion. But in the end, it was hard for even the company's toughest critics to argue against a move that would use Wal-Mart's size and clout to transform the packaged foods so many Americans eat so regularly into something healthier and less fattening. "Wal-Mart has graphically demonstrated the damaging aspects of severe market consolidation in the food industry," wrote Tom Philpott, Grist.org's senior food and agriculture writer. "If it can now demonstrate a benevolent side to market domination, then I salute it."[4]

THERE'S NO HANDBOOK FOR how Wal-Mart and Blu Skye set this sustainability quest into motion, but if there were, there would be a few simple rules:

1. Start with the hire-fire guy: A company has to become sustainable from the top down (no Lee Scott, no greener Wal-Mart).
2. Bake it in: Sustainability must be part of every employee's mission; relegate it to its own department, and it will fail.
3. Waste = money (with the real question being whether it's lost or found money).
4. Carbon = energy = money. (That's right, cutting carbon emissions can make money. U.S. Congress, are you listening to Wal-Mart on this one?)
5. Burst the bubble: Talk to environmentalists and activists, consider their criticism and advice—it's free. (Or, to use a bit of corporate-speak: network.)
6. Green is what the next generation of customers cares about.

This last one is key. Wal-Mart's leaders say they see a true business opportunity in sustainability, and they have the results to prove it. But they are also motivated by fear—of the next generation. Wal-Mart is afraid of teenage girls.

Here are some simple facts: Moms shop at Wal-Mart; their daughters shop at Target. Target is cool; Wal-Mart is not. This won't matter too much to the Wal-Mart bottom line for another fifteen years or so, but it will some day. Wal-Mart is afraid of that day. And it is the daughters, not the sons, that it worries about. When a Wal-Mart executive talks about a Wal-Mart customer, the pronoun used is "she." That's just reality, not gender bias. The vast majority of spending in Wal-Mart stores is done by women. Wal-Mart has won "her" loyalty—for now. But Wal-Mart is worried about her daughter.

In a rare moment of candor about what gives Wal-Mart executives nightmares, John Fleming, then the company's chief of merchandising, explained it at the launch of the sustainability index: "Since the beginning of modern retailing in the United States, there has never been a retail brand that has transitioned from one generation to the next. This is our opportunity to connect with the next generation. . . . We may never be cool. But we care. And we can make a difference."

Wal-Mart, in short, has seen that the generation now approaching adulthood is deeply concerned about the environment. It's one of the main topics Wal-Mart recruiters and speakers are asked about on college campuses, according to Fleming. "They know it's their future."

So many of the towering retailers of past generations are now gone or diminished: A&P, Gimbels, Montgomery Ward, Woolworth's, Sears, May, and endless other, older competitors no one even remembers now. All once seemed eternal, invincible, too big to fail. But one by one, the next generation abandoned them.

Wal-Mart vows that it will not let history repeat without a fight. It wants the daughters, it wants generation green. And it is willing to turn itself inside out to be sustainable for them, its best hope for breaking the age-old pattern and holding on to the next generation of consumers. On the one hand, it sounds like a selfish motive for committing to sustainability, yet it also strikes a strangely hopeful note for such a profit-driven company. If Wal-Mart's legion of marketers, sales analysts, merchandisers, and risk managers is right, the coming generation of customers they are predicting won't just use a sustainability index, they'll demand it, as they—not Wal-Mart, not Blu Skye, not coalitions or consortiums or stock indices—become the true force of nature.

Acknowledgments

I am deeply grateful to all the men and women of Blu Skye Sustainability for their help and patience, in particular: Jib Ellison, Tom Miller, John Whalen, Dave Sherman, Nicole Conroy, Glen Low, Tripp Borstel, Carrie Hendrickson, Adam Hyde, Diana Rothschild, Ryan Young, and John Nixon. I also wish to thank Matt Kistler and Jim Stanway of Wal-Mart; Mike Grant, formerly of Project RAFT and now the Marin County Schools; Erin Fitzgerald of Dairy Management, Inc.; Rick Ridgeway of Patagonia; and Bill McDonough, architect and coauthor of *Cradle to Cradle*. Thanks also to river guide extraordinaire Beth Rypins, who made the Tuolumne look easy (and kept the rest of us soaked but safe).

Notes

PART 1: THE NUDGE
1. Alfred J. Kolatch, *Great Jewish Quotations* (1996), p. 115.

CHAPTER 1: EXPOSURE
1. Source: Wal-Mart and Blu Skye Sustainability. Unless otherwise noted, statistics in this book documenting the value and effect of Wal-Mart's sustainability efforts originated with one of these sources.

CHAPTER 2: THE SOUL OF A DISCOUNTER
1. Wendy Zellner, "Retailers: Someday, Lee, Wal-Mart May All Be Yours," *Business-Week*, November 15, 1999; Richard Fletcher, "The Big Boss from Bentonville," interview with H. Lee Scott, *The Telegraph* (U.K.), August 10, 2003. Changes per www.businessweek.com/datedtoc/1999/9946.htm.
2. "Reviewing and Revising Wal-Mart's Benefits Strategy," fiscal year 2006 memo to the Wal-Mart board of directors from Susan Chambers, Wal-Mart executive vice president for benefits.
3. Steven Greenhouse and Stephanie Rosenbloom, "Wal-Mart Settles 63 Lawsuits over Wages," *The New York Times*, December 23, 2008.
4. Steven Greenhouse, "Wal-Mart to Pay $54 Million to Settle Suit over Wages," *The New York Times*, December 9, 2008.
5. Steven Greenhouse, "Workers Assail Night Lock-ins by Wal-Mart," *The New York Times*, January 18, 2004.
6. "Wal-Mart Wage and Hour Settlement," fact sheet, http://action.walmartwatch .com/page/-/Wal-Mart%20Wage%20and%20Hour%20Settlement.pdf.
7. *Braun v. Wal-Mart, Inc.*, First Judicial District, Dakota County, Minnesota, File No. 19-CO-01-9790, findings of fact, conclusions of law, and order by Judge Robert R. King.

8. Ibid.

9. Orson Mason, "Labor Relations and You," a September 1991 manual by a Wal-Mart employee first made public in by *Harper's* magazine in October 2004; Bob Ortega, *In Sam We Trust* (New York: Crown Business, 1998).

10. John Huey, Sarah Smith, and David J. Morrow, "Will Wal-Mart Take Over the World?" *Fortune*, January 30, 1989.

11. Ortega, *In Sam We Trust*.

12. *Dukes v. Wal-Mart, Inc.*, U.S. Ninth Circuit Court of Appeals, Case No. 04-1668. In affirming a lower court ruling that the original lawsuit by six women should be expanded to represent an entire class of plaintiffs—which could eventually reach 2 million women and cost Wal-Mart billions of dollars in damages—the Ninth Circuit opinion concluded, "Plaintiffs' factual evidence, expert opinions, statistical evidence, and anecdotal evidence demonstrate that Wal-Mart's female employees nationwide were subjected to a single set of corporate policies (not merely a number of independent discriminatory acts) that may have worked to unlawfully discriminate against them."

    As of late 2010, Wal-Mart had appealed the expansion of the case to class-action status to the U.S. Supreme Court, arguing that each woman alleging gender discrimination should file suit individually.

13. *Dateline NBC*, December 22, 1992; Eric Barton, "Life Without Wal-Mart," December 7, 2006, www.pitch.com/2006-12-07/news/life-without-wal-mart/.

14. *Dateline NBC*, December 22, 1992.

15. Ibid.

16. "Children Exploited by Kathie Lee/Wal-Mart," testimony of Charles Kernaghan, National Labor Committee, before the Democratic Policy Committee hearing chaired by U.S. Representative George Miller, April 29, 1996; Lynne Duke, "The Man Who Made Kathie Lee Cry," *The Washington Post*, July 31, 2005; "Gifford Takes Case to Workers," Associated Press, June 8, 1996.

17. "Wal-Mart: Why an Apology Made Sense," *BusinessWeek*, July 3, 2000.

18. Ibid.

19. "250 Arrested at Wal-Mart," October 23, 2003, http://money.cnn.com/2003/10/23/news/companies/walmart_worker_arrests/; Steven Greenhouse, "Wal-Mart Is Said to Be in Talks to Settle Illegal-Immigrant Case," *The New York Times*, August 5, 2004.

20. Steven Greenhouse, "Wal-Mart to Pay U.S. $11 Million in Lawsuit on Immigrant Workers," *The New York Times*, March 19, 2005.

21. "The Costco Way," *BusinessWeek*, April 12, 2004.

22. Chambers, "Reviewing and Revising Wal-Mart's Benefits Strategy."

23. David Neumark, Junfu Zhang, and Stephen Ciccarella, "The Effects of Wal-Mart on Local Labor Markets," California Public Policy Institute and National Bureau of Economic Research, November 2005.

24. H. Lee Scott, speech at Town Hall, Los Angeles, February 23, 2005.

25. Richard Fletcher, "The Big Boss from Bentonville," interview with H. Lee Scott, *The Telegraph* (U.K.), August 10, 2003.

26. Michael Barbaro, "Wal-Mart Chief Defends Closing Unionized Store," *The Washington Post*, February 11, 2005.

27. Amy Joyce and Ben White, "Wal-Mart Pushes to Soften Its Image," *The Washington Post*, October 29, 2005; "Another Internal Document Reveals Wal-Mart's Road to Reputation Rehabilitation," October 31, 2005, walmartwatch.com; "Is Wal-Mart Really a 'Green' Company?" September 2007, http://walmartwatch .com/img/blog/environmental_fact_sheet.pdf.

CHAPTER 3: THE CEO WHISPERER

1. Angus Phillips, "Shooting the Siberian Rapids to Promote Peace," *Los Angeles Times*, November 10, 1989.

2. "Paddlers of the Century," *Paddler*, January 1, 2000.

3. Ellison's relationship with Ridgeway would play an important role in his future work with Wal-Mart.

4. The Nature Conservancy, "Facts About Rainforests," 2010.

5. "Portfolio's Worst American CEOs of All Time," February 24, 2010, www.cnbc .com/id/30502091/Portfolio_s_Worst_American_CEOs_of_All_Time.

6. David Cho, Peter Whoriskey, and Amit R. Paley, "Pay Rule Led Chrysler to Spurn Loan, Agency Says," *The Washington Post*, April 21, 2009.

7. The Natural Step (www.naturalstep.org/the-system-conditions).

8. Michael E. Porter, "America's Green Strategy," *Scientific American*, April 1991.

PART 2: BURSTING THE BUBBLE

1. University of Arkansas Applied Sustainability Center Speaker Series, March 14, 2007. Transcribed by the author.

CHAPTER 4: DOING THE MATH

1. Lawrence Jackson, "Environmental Sustainability for Cheap," Social Innovation Conversations, Stanford University, April 3, 2007, http://sic.conversationsnet work.org/shows/detail3249.html.

2. Lyn Denend, "Wal-Mart's Sustainability Strategy," case study, Stanford Graduate School of Business, April 17, 2007; "Sustainable Textiles Fact Sheet," Wal-Mart, Inc.; Vijay Sathe and Michael Crooke, "Sustainable Industry Creation," *Journal of Corporate Citizenship*, Spring 2010.

3. Jackson, "Environmental Sustainability for Cheap."

4. Ibid.

5. From the author's interview with Adam Werbach.

CHAPTER 5: KATRINA IN SLOW MOTION

1. The Federal Emergency Management Agency's flat-footed response to Hurricane Katrina provided an opportunity for Wal-Mart to shine; FEMA was widely condemned by both major political parties and officials throughout the Gulf Coast. This surprised many, as the head of FEMA under the Clinton administration, James Lee Witt, who had extensive experience in disaster relief work, had

been widely credited with making FEMA an effective agency, in part by ending long-standing political patronage in hiring. President George W. Bush's hiring of Michael D. Brown, however, marked a return to political appointments—the failed Republican congressional candidate had little experience relevant to FEMA, and his last position had been as judges and stewards commissioner for the International Arabian Horse Association. Shortly after Katrina hit, Bush publicly praised FEMA by saying, "Brownie, you're doing a heck of a job." The phrase "Heckuva job, Brownie" soon entered popular culture as sarcastic slang for cronyism and incompetence.

2. Stacy Mitchell, "The Impossibility of a Green Wal-Mart," March 28, 2007, www .grist.org/article/mitchell.

3. Wal-Mart's counterargument is that its suppliers get a return on investment from the sustainability imperative: if they become more efficient and lower their waste and energy use, their profitability and competitiveness will improve as well.

4. John Carlisle, "The Greening of Wal-Mart America," *The American Spectator*, November 14, 2007.

CHAPTER 6: BECAUSE EVERYONE LOVES A GOOD DEAL

1. The fourteen Sustainable Value Networks were divided into three categories:

   Sustainable Products
   Textiles
   Electronics
   Food & Agriculture
   Forest & Paper
   Chemical Intensive Products
   Jewelry
   Seafood
   China

   Zero Waste
   Operations & Internal Procurement
   Packaging

   Renewable Energy
   Global Greenhouse Gas Strategy
   Alternative Fuels
   Energy, Design, Construction & Maintenance
   Global Logistics

2. David L. Cooperrider and Diana Whitney, "A Positive Revolution in Change: Appreciative Inquiry," undated draft report, http://appreciativeinquiry.case.edu/ uploads/whatisai.pdf.

3. "Fooling with Nature," *Frontline* special report, PBS, June 2, 1998, www.pbs.org/ wgbh/pages/frontline/shows/nature/disrupt/sspring.html.

4. The three chemicals were propoxur and permethrin, both used in household

insect control products, and nonylphenol ethoxylates (NPE), an ingredient in some cleaning products, usually used as a surfactant in detergents. In the environment NPE breaks down into its constitutuent nonylphenol (NP), which is toxic to aquatic life. Permethrin is a common insecticide used in pet flea treatments and other household insect repellants, as well as commercial and agricultural applications. It is highly toxic to aquatic life and is classified as a likely human carcinogen. Propoxur is a carbamate insecticide for outdoor use known to be highly toxic to birds and honeybees. It is not approved for indoor use because it is toxic to children who are chronically exposed. (Source: Environmental Protection Agency.)

5. Denend, "Wal-Mart's Sustainability Strategy."
6. From Wal-Mart's "Climate Policy," 2011, http://walmartstores.com/Sustainabil ity/9555.aspx.

CHAPTER 7: COTTON, FISH, COFFEE, AND AL

1. Environmental Justice Foundation in collaboration with Pesticide Action Network UK, "The Deadly Chemicals in Cotton," 2007, www.ejfoundation.org/pdf/ the_deadly_chemicals_in_cotton.pdf.
2. Denend, "Wal-Mart's Sustainability Strategy."
3. Yale Project on Climate Change and the George Mason University for Climate Change Communication, "Americans' Actions to Conserve Energy, Reduce Waste and Limit Global Warming," January 2010; "Seventh Generation Laundry Survey," conducted by Kelton Research between May 31 and June 4, 2010.

   While cold-water washing is the environmentally preferred choice, there may be valid reasons for using hot water in many households. Between 18 and 30 percent of Americans have sensitivity or allergic reactions to dust mites. The microscopic organisms are everywhere, and a principle source of exposure is bedding. Washing sheets and pillowcases in very hot water is the only nonchemical means of controlling the pests.
4. "*Science* Study Predicts Collapse of All Seafood Fisheries by 2050," *Stanford Report*, November 2, 2006.
5. The Marine Stewardship Council is an independent nonprofit organization founded in 1997 by the World Wildlife Fund and Unilever. It certifies wild seafood practices as sustainable and supports itself by charging fees for its certification process. It also receives grants and donations, including $3.3 million in grants in 2007–2008 from the Walton Family Foundation, the philanthropic organization set up on behalf of the family of Wal-Mart founder Sam Walton. The council has been both praised for its science-based work and criticized for too readily certifying types of fish that are under environmental stress. The Global Aquaculture Alliance is a nonprofit organization but is not independent; it is governed by the seafood industry. It certifies fish farms and related operations as using "responsible" rather than sustainable practices by examining environmental and social responsiblity, animal welfare, food safety, and traceability. It currently provides certification for seafood-processing plants and feed mills, and

farms that raise shrimp, tilapia, channel catfish, and *Pangasius* (a type of catfish). It does not certify salmon farms.

6. Beth A. Polidoro, Kent E. Carpenter, Lorna Collins, Norman C. Duke, Aaron M. Ellison, et al., "The Loss of Species: Mangrove Extinction Risk and Geographic Areas of Global Concern," PLoS ONE, April 8, 2010, www.plosone.org/article/info%3Adoi%2F10.1371%2Fjournal.pone.0010095.

7. *State of the World: 2004* (Washington, D.C.: Worldwatch Institute, 2004).

8. Denend, "Wal-Mart's Sustainability Strategy."

9. "Wal-Mart Sustainability Report," 2010.

10. "Carting Away the Oceans," Greenpeace, 2010 update.

11. Mining and other "extractive" industries are often at odds with environmental groups and regulatory agencies because of their inevitable and often dramatic impacts on terrain and watersheds. Rio Tinto, one of the largest global mining concerns in the world, a British-Australian multinational company operating on every contintent except Antarctica, has been a frequent target of criticism. The government of Norway divested all investment in Rio Tinto because of concerns about the environmental impact of its operations at the Grasberg Mine in Indonesia, the world's largest gold mine and third largest copper mine. Newmont Mining Corporation, one of the world's largest gold-mining companies, has been similarly criticized for its operations in Peru, Ghana, and Nevada; the Great Basin Resource Watch environmental group estimates that 100 to 200 tons of earth have to be moved for every ounce of gold produced by its Nevada mines.

12. "Fleet efficiency," as calculated by Wal-Mart, is a measure of fuel economy combined with the amount of freight delivered; as the fleet efficiency number rises, it indicates more freight delivered and less fuel used. Wal-Mart calculates fleet efficiency by taking the total number of miles driven in a year and dividing that number by the average miles per gallon achieved by Wal-Mart trucks. The result reveals the amount of fuel used by the fleet for deliveries in a year. That figure is then divided into the number of cases delivered to produce the fleet efficiency:

$$\text{NUMBER OF CASES DELIVERED} \div \frac{\text{NUMBER OF MILES TRAVELED}}{\text{MILES PER GALLON}}$$

13. Amanda D. Cuéllar and Michael E. Webber, "Wasted Food, Wasted Energy: The Embedded Energy in Food Waste in the United States," *Environmental Science & Technology*, July 21, 2010; "Half of US Food Goes to Waste," November 25, 2004, www.foodproductiondaily.com/Supply-Chain/Half-of-US-food-goes-to-waste; Kevin D. Hall, Juen Guo, Michael Dore, and Carson C. Chow, "The Progressive Increase of of Food Waste in America and Its Environmental Impact," PLoS ONE, November 25, 2009, www.plosone.org/article/info:doi%2F10.1371%2Fjournal.pone.0007940; "US Food Waste Worth More than Offshore Drilling," *New Scientist*, July 30, 2010.

14. John Vidal, "Rainforest Loss Shocks Brazil," *The Guardian* (U.K.), May 20, 2005,

and "Forces Behind Forest Loss," Mongabay.com. The rate of deforestation has slowed in Brazil since it peaked in 2004, but as of 2008 (the last year for which complete data were available), 4,600 square miles of rain forest were still being cleared annually for agriculture and grazing. At that rate, the existing rain forest will be reduced by 40 percent by 2030. Since 1970, 232,000 square miles of rain forest have been destroyed—an area nearly as large as the entire nation of France.

15. Stephanie Rosenbloom and Michael Barbaro, "Green-Light Specials, Now at Wal-Mart," *The New York Times*, January 24, 2009.

16. The impact of the energy saving tied to a switch to CFL bulbs can't be underestimated: If every home in America replaced just one incandescent bulb with a CFL, it would save enough electricity to light 3 million homes and reduce greenhouse gas emissions equivalent to 800,000 cars. If every bulb in every home in America were a CFL, it would save enough energy to power 60 million homes and would be like taking a third of registered cars off the road—or shutting down 1,800 electric power plants.

PART 3: BEYOND THE BOX

1. Speech at Walmart Canada Green Business Summit, February 10, 2010.

CHAPTER 8: THE COW OF THE FUTURE

1. "50% of Consumers Consider Sustainability When Picking Brands," *Environmental Leader*, January 8, 2008, www.environmentalleader.com/2008/01/08/50-of-consumers-consider-sustainability-when-shopping/.

2. There's nothing exotic about the UV process. It's sometimes called "irradiation," although there are no radioactive materials involved. The use of the germicidal properties of UV light dates back more than a century, to when the Danish physician Niels Ryberg Finsen won the Nobel Prize for using ultraviolet rays to sterilize skin lesions caused by the tuberculosis bacillus. At Dairy Management's request, the U.S. Food and Drug Administration approved plans to test a prototype UV sterilizer starting in 2007 and to conduct human taste tests through a research program at the University of California, Davis. The UV treatment can alter the taste of raw milk, but even if it did not, one of the first steps in bringing the new energy-saving technique to market would be to gauge consumer acceptance. Conventional heat pasteurization alters the taste of raw milk differently from UV treatment, but Americans used to the flavor of old-school pasteurization could be slow to accept a change. Anything that alters the taste of milk is controversial with farmers, who fear losing more sales to soft drinks or other beverages. The taste testing, as well as experimentation with different frequencies and duration of the UV exposure that may minimize the difference in taste, may determine the future of this technology in America.

3. United Nations Food and Agriculture Organization, "Greenhouse Gas Emissions from the Dairy Sector: A Life Cycle Assessment," 2010, www.fao.org/docrep/012/k7930e/k7930e00.pdf.

CHAPTER 9: ONE INDEX TO RULE THEM ALL

1. U.S. Food and Drug Administration, "Update on Bisphenol A for Use in Food Contact Applications: January 2010." The chemical, commonly referred to as BPA, is used in many plastic bottles and plastic baby toys, as well as the linings in food and beverage cans. The FDA says:

> Studies employing standardized toxicity tests have thus far supported the safety of current low levels of human exposure to BPA. However, on the basis of results from recent studies using novel approaches to test for subtle effects, both the National Toxicology Program at the National Institutes of Health and FDA have some concern about the potential effects of BPA on the brain, behavior, and prostate gland in fetuses, infants, and young children. In cooperation with the National Toxicology Program, FDA's National Center for Toxicological Research is carrying out in-depth studies to answer key questions and clarify uncertainties about the risks of BPA.
>
> In the interim, FDA is taking reasonable steps to reduce human exposure to BPA in the food supply. These steps include:
> - supporting the industry's actions to stop producing BPA-containing baby bottles and infant feeding cups for the U.S. market;
> - facilitating the development of alternatives to BPA for the linings of infant formula cans;
> - supporting efforts to replace BPA or minimize BPA levels in other food can linings.

2. Roger Entner, "Smartphones to Overtake Feature Phones in U.S. by 2011," March 26, 2010, http://blog.nielsen.com/nielsenwire/consumer/smartphones-to-overtake-feature-phones-in-u-s-by-2011/.
3. James R. Healey, "Surprise: Sales of Big SUVs Surging Faster than Small Cars," *USA Today*, July 30, 2010.
4. U.S. Department of Energy, "Big Results, Bigger Potential: CFL Market Profile," March 2009, www.energystar.gov/ia/products/downloads/CFL_Market_Profile.pdf; Network for New Energy Choices, "A Compact Fluorescent Truth," 2009, www.newenergychoices.org/uploads/CFL%20article.pdf.
5. The full questionnaire sent to Wal-Mart suppliers:

Energy and Climate: Reducing Energy Costs and Greenhouse Gas Emissions
1. Have you measured your corporate greenhouse gas emissions?
2. Have you opted to report your greenhouse gas emissions to the Carbon Disclosure Project (CDP)?
3. What is [*sic*] your total annual greenhouse gas emissions reported in the most recent year measured?
4. Have you set publicly available greenhouse gas reduction targets? If yes, what are those targets?

Material Efficiency: Reducing Waste and Enhancing Quality

1. If measured, please report the total amount of solid waste generated from the facilities that produce your product(s) for Walmart for the most recent year measured.
2. Have you set publicly available solid waste reduction targets? If yes, what are those targets?
3. If measured, please report total water use from facilities that produce your product(s) for Walmart for the most recent year measured.
4. Have you set publicly available water use reduction targets? If yes, what are those targets?

Natural Resources: Producing High Quality, Responsibly Sourced Raw Materials

1. Have you established publicly available sustainability purchasing guidelines for your direct suppliers that address issues such as environmental compliance, employment practices and product/ingredient safety?
2. Have you obtained 3rd party certifications for any of the products that you sell to Walmart?

People and Community: Ensuring Responsible and Ethical Production

1. Do you know the location of 100 percent of the facilities that produce your product(s)?
2. Before beginning a business relationship with a manufacturing facility, do you evaluate the quality of, and capacity for, production?
3. Do you have a process for managing social compliance at the manufacturing level?
4. Do you work with your supply base to resolve issues found during social compliance evaluations and also document specific corrections and improvements?
5. Do you invest in community development activities in the markets you source from and/or operate within?

6. BP heavily marketed its move to become a major producer of solar panels and its promise in 2007 to launch a major research effort into renewable energy, a commitment that has since faded with the closure of the company's London alternative energy offices. In 2001, British Petroleum shortened its official name to BP and created a marketing campaign, "Beyond Petroleum," to accentuate its commitment to sustainability. That same year, consumer surveys showed that BP had the most environmentally friendly image of any oil company. It was named as one of ten large companies that "put profits second" in favor of social good in a 2004 book by Christine Arena entitled *Cause for Success: 10 Companies That Put Profit Second and Came in First.* But BP's commitment to green technology never exceeded 4 percent of its exploratory budget and has since declined, according to "BP Funnels Millions into Lobbying to Influence Regulation and Rebrand Image," an interview with Antonia Juhasz, the author of *The Tyranny of Oil: The*

World's Most Powerful Industry—And What We Must Do to Stop It, May 5, 2010, www.democracynow.org/2010/5/5/bp_funnels_millions_into_lobbying_to.

 7. Members of the Sustainability Consortium are divided into three categories by tier:

Corporate Tier 1 Members ($25,000–$100,000 annual membership fee depending on size of company, with a seat on the consortium's steering committee): ASDA, BASF, Best Buy, Cargill, Church & Dwight (Arm & Hammer), Clorox, Colgate-Palmolive, Dairy Management, Inc., Darden, Dell, Disney, Earth Friendly Products, General Mills, Georgia-Pacific, Henkel, Hewlett-Packard, Kellogg's, Kimberly-Clark, KPMG, L'Oréal, Miller-Coors, PepsiCo, Procter & Gamble, SAP, Safeway, SC Johnson, Scientific Certification Systems, Seventh Generation, Stonyfield Farm, Sygenta, TetraPak, Tyson, UL Environment, Uniliver, Wal-Mart, Waste Management.

Government Tier 1 Members ($10,000 annual fee, seat on steering committee): U.S. Environmental Protection Agency, DEFRA (UK).

Tier 2 ($10,000–$50,000 annual membership depending on size of company): 3M, Ahold, Alberto Culver, Campbell Soup Company, Danisco, Ecolab, Forest Products Association of Canada, Intel, Johnson & Johnson, KIK Custom Products, Marks & Spencer, Sun Products Corporation, Toshiba.

Nongovernmental Organizations (no fee): World Wildlife Fund, BSR.

 8. Tilde Herrera, "Wal-Mart Sustainability Index Means Big Business," September 24, 2009, www.greenbiz.com/blog/2009/09/24/walmart-sustainability-index-means-big-business.

 9. Jennifer Jacquet, "Should We Believe Wal-Mart?," August 9, 2009, http://scienceblogs.com/guiltyplanet/2009/08/should_we_believe_wal-mart.php.

10. Marc Gunther, "Wal-Mart to Become Green Umpire," July 12, 2009, www.thebigmoney.com/articles/judgments/2009/07/13/wal-mart-become-green-umpire.

11. Daniel Goleman, "The Age of Eco-Angst," *The New York Times*, September 27, 2009.

12. Traci Watson, "Green Claims by Marketers Go Unchecked," *USA Today*, June 24, 2009; testimony of James Kohm, director of enforcement, Federal Trade Commission, before the U.S. House Committee on Energy and Commerce, Subcommittee on Commerce, Trade, and Consumer Protection, June 9, 2009.

13. Testimony of M. Scot Case, executive director of TerraChoice's EcoLogo certification program, before the U.S. House Committee on Energy and Commerce, Subcommittee on Commerce, Trade, and Consumer Protection, June 9, 2009.

14. Opening statement of chairman Bobby L. Rush, U.S. House Committee on Energy and Commerce, Subcommittee on Commerce, Trade, and Consumer Protection, June 9, 2009.

15. Testimony of M. Scot Case, executive director of TerraChoice's EcoLogo certification program, before the U.S. House Committee on Energy and Commerce, Subcommittee on Commerce, Trade, and Consumer Protection, June 9, 2009.

16. Testimony of Dara O'Rourke, cofounder, GoodGuide, Inc., before the U.S. House Committee on Energy and Commerce, Subcommittee on Commerce, Trade, and Consumer Protection, June 9, 2009.

17. Energy Star is an international rating system for energy efficiency launched by

the EPA in 1992 and later adopted by numerous other countries. It has been criticized in recent years by the EPA inspector general and several outside organizations in the United States for trusting private businesses to supply efficiency data without oversight and verification. In March 2010, the General Accountability Office reported that Energy Star had accepted for rating fifteen out of twenty bogus products submitted by undercover GAO operatives and approved four fake businesses as Energy Star partners. EPEAT, administered by an industry group, the Green Electronics Council, measures the environmental impact and sustainability of computers and monitors using twenty-eight mandatory criteria (Energy Star rating being one of them) and twenty-three optional criteria. Devices either fail or receive a bronze, silver, or gold rating. By a 2007 presidential order, all computers purchased by the federal government must be EPEAT-rated. The system has been used mostly for bulk purchasing by corporations and government agencies, although in 2010 consumer products began to promote their EPEAT qualifications, notably in Amazon.com's Green Electronics category.

CHAPTER 10: NO FREE LUNCH AT THE NATURE MARKET

1. Aneel Karnani, "The Case Against Corporate Social Responsibility," *The Wall Street Journal*, August 23, 2010.
2. Chrystia Freeland, "What's BP's Social Responsibility?," *The Washington Post*, July 18, 2010.
3. Jamie Whyte, "When Corporate Theft Is Good," *The Wall Street Journal*, July 21, 2010.
4. Fox News Channel interview with Peter Flaherty, president of the National Legal and Policy Center, June 6, 2010, www.nlpc.org/stories/2010/06/06/flaherty-blasts-wal-mart-fox-news-channel-0; video of remarks by Peter Flaherty at the Wal-Mart annual shareholders meeting in Bentonville, Arkansas, June 4, 2010, posted online by the National Legal and Policy Center, www.nlpc.org/stories/2010/06/04/wal-mart-support-obamacare-cap-and-trade-ripped-annual-meeting.
5. Bob Lurie, "Wal-Mart's Green Strategy Raises Serious Issues," *Harvard Business Review*, June 30, 2010.
6. Milton Friedman, "The Social Responsibility of Business Is to Increase its Profits," *The New York Times Sunday Magazine*, September 13, 1970.
7. The term "trickle-down economics" was popularized during the Reagan administration (primarily by Reagan critics); the administration preferred the term "supply-side economics." The first use of the term is attributed to the humorist Will Rogers during the Great Depression.
8. Mike Taylor, "WSJ: Be Evil," *The New York Observer*, August 23, 2010.
9. Tom Philpott, "A 'Habitual Offender' Unleashes Nearly Half a Billion Salmonella-Tainted Eggs," August 19, 2010, www.grist.org/article/food-a-habitual-offender-unleashes-nearly-half-a-billion-salmonella-t/; Liz Szabo, "CDC: Salmonella from Eggs May Have Sickened 1,300," *USA Today*, August 19, 2010; Verlyn Klinkenborg, "Egg Factory," *The New York Times*, August 28, 2010.
10. Robert Costanza et al., "The Value of the World's Ecosystem Services and

Natural Capital," *Nature*, May 1997. A condensed breakdown of ecosystem services and their values, in 1994 dollars, as calculated by Costanza, looks like this:

ECOSYSTEM SERVICE	ANNUAL VALUE (TRILLION $US)
Soil Formations and Net Primary Production	17.1
Nutrient cycling and pollutant detoxification	2.3
Water purification, regulation, and supply	2.3
Climate regulation (temperature and precipitation)	1.8
Habitat, erosion, and disease control	1.4
Flood and storm protection	1.1
Food and raw materials production	0.8
Genetic resources	0.8
Atmospheric gas balance (cleansing air)	0.7
Pollination	0.4
All other services	4.6
TOTAL VALUE OF ECOSYSTEM SERVICES	33.3

11. Tom Miller and Jib Ellison of Blu Skye Sustainability, Lee Kranefuss of Kranefuss Investments, and Peter Seligmann of Conservation International, "When Nature Gets Valued," unpublished white paper.
12. United Nations Environmental Programme, "The Economics of Ecosystems and Biodiversity: Mainstreaming the Economics of Nature," released October 2010.

EPILOGUE: GENERATION GREEN

1. Paul Hawken, "Natural Capitalism," *Mother Jones*, March 1997.
2. In recent years, Wal-Mart had to recall 16,000 Chinese-made air compressors because the $250 machines got dangerously hot and posed a fire risk; a half-million insulin syringes that contained more than twice the appropriate dose (potentially fatal); 210,000 General Electric brand Chinese-made toasters after 140 reports of the appliances catching fire or sparking and tripping circuit breakers; 200,000 George brand Chinese-made women's shoes ($13 a pair) with defective heels that fell off, causing falls; 1.5 million Durabrand Chinese-made DVD players ($29) that burst into flames; 900,000 GE brand coffee makers, another fire hazard; 50,000 packages of Great Value chicken nuggets (made by Perdue Farms for Wal-Mart) that had bits of plastic mixed in with the processed chicken; 900,000 bassinets and 600,000 cribs bearing the Simplicity brand, which posed suffocation and strangulation hazards linked to several infant deaths.

   Though they were not officially recalled, Wal-Mart also had to pull from its shelves Miley Cyrus celebrity-branded jewelry that contained toxic cadmium and Chinese-made flip-flops that caused chemical burns on bare feet.

3. Charles Courtemanche and Art Carden, "Supersizing Supercenters? The Impact of Wal-Mart Supercenters on Body Mass Index and Obesity," Social Science Research Network, September 10, 2010, available at http://papers.ssrn.com/sol3/papers.cfm?abstract_id=1263316.
4. Tom Philpott, "Walmart Vows to Use Its Power for Good Food, Not Evil," January 20, 2011, http://www.grist.org/article/food-2011-01-20-walmart-vows-to-become-the-benign-food-system-superpower.

Index